~ THE BEGINNING OF THE END ~

Walter Ellis, married, with one son, writes a column from New York for the *Belfast Telegraph*. He contributes to the *Sunday Times*, the *Times Higher Education Supplement* and *The Spectator*, as well as a variety of US papers.

THE BEGINNING OF THE END

The Crippling Disadvantage of a Happy Irish Childhood

WALTER ELLIS

MAINSTREAM
PUBLISHING
EDINBURGH AND LONDON

First published in Great Britain in 2006 by
MAINSTREAM PUBLISHING COMPANY (EDINBURGH) LTD
7 Albany Street
Edinburgh EH1 3UG

ISBN 1 84596 056 4

A catalogue record for this book is available from the British Library

Typeset in Bembo
Printed in Great Britain by
Clays Ltd, St Ives plc

This book is dedicated to my mother,
Molly (1916–2005),
who prayed for me every day,
knowing that I couldn't pray for myself

Acknowledgements

The author wishes to thank various people for the help given to him while researching and writing this memoir. David McKittrick was, as ever, generous with his time and provided me with the necessary shot in the arm (now wearing off) that kept me going when I started to lose the plot. Ace football writer Simon Freeman and Peter Millar, my Best Man, though heavily engaged in various literary projects of their own, were also believers, as were Graham Paterson and his wife, Sue, (my perennial London hosts) and Ronnie Payne, the sage of Minster Lovell. Alan Cochrane, Scotland's pre-eminent Unionist, and Iain Martin, editor of *Scotland on Sunday*, introduced me to Bill Campbell of Mainstream, who bravely took the decision to publish. Deborah Warner, my editor, polished up the text and pointed out to me the errors of my way.

My sister, Elaine, for whom the year 2005 was marked by the death of our mother and the marriage of her daughter, Christina, to Paddy, corrected various faulty recollections of our childhood. She was also responsible for sending me down several of memory lane's back alleys, both bright and dark.

Most of all, it was the support provided by my wife, Louisa, that sustained me – not least because she went out to work each day to secure our future while I sat down in front of my computer, with tea and toast, to contemplate the past. As we look ahead to a new chapter in our lives, she knows how much I owe her.

Finally, I have not seen her since 1975 – indeed, I don't know where she's living – but I would like to extend my sympathy across the years to Suzanne Bunting, wife of Ronnie. He was a desperately hard man to take on, but she bent herself heroically to the task. I hope that her life today, and the lives of her children, are in harmony with the new spirit of Ireland.

In print, and online, I had various unpaid associates. My basic references were these: *Lost Lives: The Stories of the Men, Women and Children who Died as a Result of the Northern Ireland Troubles* by David McKittrick, Seamus Kelters, Brian Feeney, Chris Thornton and David McVea (Mainstream Publishing, 2004); *Northern Ireland: A Political Directory, 1963–93* by Sydney Elliott and W.D. Flackes (Blackstaff Press, 1999); *Northern Ireland: A Chronology of the Troubles, 1968–1993* by Paul Bew and Gordon Gillespie (Gill & Macmillan, 1999); *INLA: Deadly Divisions – The Story of One of Ireland's Most Ruthless Terrorist Organisations* by Jack Holland and Henry McDonald (Torc Books, 1994); the CAIN Web Service (Conflict Archive on the Internet); and, of course, Mr Ephriam Google.

I also acknowledge, with thanks, the following for allowing me to quote various lines of poetry and song: Faber & Faber ('McCavity the Mystery Cat' by T.S. Eliot; 'Scaffolding' by Seamus Heaney; 'Aubade' by Philip Larkin); David Higham Associates ('Prayer Before Birth' by Louis MacNeice); Michael Sigman, son of the composer (*Robin Hood*); James Fenton ('A German Requiem').

I must also mention my smashing son, Jamie, who, while I was busy looking back, took time off from gigging and recording to educate me in the mysteries of indie rock. This will be the Year of Battle.

To anyone I left out, including Youngish Tom and Seaton, I apologise. Their part in my drama is assured.

Contents

Preface: Before the Beginning 11

I A Death in the Night 15

II Starting as He Meant to Go On 21

III The Butcher's Apron 73

IV Saint Cuthbert's Way 127

V On the Run 187

Epilogue: Chronicle of a Death Foretold 245

Before the Beginning

New York, March 2005

When I first came up with the idea for this memoir, my agent at the time warned me not to bother. The only memoirs that succeeded, he said, were those featuring celebrities or else those written in their own blood by grim individuals whose lives had plumbed new depths of depravity.

I don't believe this.

So far as depravity is concerned, I should confess straight away that I wasn't buggered as a boy, or flogged or starved. No one ever locked me in a cellar or forced me to dress up as a girl. The worst that happened to me as a child is that I was sometimes ignored and, once, I was forced to wear shorts *after* I had secured my first pair of long trousers. *The horror, the horror!*

Against that, I am, among all of my friends, the acknowledged master of the missed opportunity who invariably made the worst of everything on offer. If it is through failure, humiliation and bad judgement that we obtain wisdom and grace, then I must be among the wisest and most graceful people I know.

It is equally true, alas, that my life has not been marked by its celebrity. I know this not just because of the state of my bank account but because when I told Janet Street-Porter once that I had never eaten at The Ivy – in fact, I didn't even know where it was – she said I was a loser who had obviously lived a 'sad' life. But the sort of celebrity enjoyed by the likes of Street-Porter and David Beckham is not, I am glad to say, society's final word on a life well lived. If it was, situation comedy would replace grand opera as the high culture of the Establishment. Real life, in all its mess and clutter, is the inescapable raw material of fiction, honed to the condition of art. What is odd is that so many authors acknowledge this implicitly in their writing but not in their lives – so that book signings are for many a penance, to be indulged in while wearing surgical gloves. The situation is rich in irony. Snooty novelists and puffed-up 'personalities' are like the Marxist who insists on travelling first class and relies on the head waiter of a restaurant to give him a table removed as far as possible from the hoi polloi. Authors, and actors too, need to remember that while they may enjoy the plaudits of the crowd, it is their fictional creations, or the characters they play, rooted in the routines and trials of everyday life, that have the potential for immortality. My view, echoing Pirandello, is that we are all characters in search of an author, and if, at the end of the day, we can give ourselves a decent write-up, why not?

Yes, but who am I? Why me? For a start, I'm an east Belfast Protestant – and when did we last get a fair crack of the whip? Oh, it's fine if you're an Irish Catholic. Then the whole world loves you, or at least feels your pain. Publishers queue up to listen to you unburden yourself about the terrible time of it you had as a child. But Prods! We are like Afrikaners – down there with concentration camp guards and the Millwall Supporters' Club. To empathise with us is to stain your soul. Yet we, too, have known tragedy.

Take me! I was born into conditions of intolerable normality and forced to grow up in a household in which my father worked for a living and my mother was a full-time housewife. My childhood, as I will show, was interesting but, to my eternal regret, not miserable. All I can say is that I later made up for the deficiency: I was expelled from school and dropped out of not one but *two* universities, my first marriage ended in ignominy and I was either sacked from or lost a number of highly prized jobs. There were, of course, reasons for my downwards spiral, poignantly disclosed in these pages. Suffice it here to say that I feel lucky to have got out alive.

The tale you are, I hope, about to read deals with my childhood, adolescence and growing up to a kind of manhood. At the story's heart lies my best friend and distant cousin, Ronnie Bunting, a leader of the Irish National Liberation Army, who made my life a misery before going on to blow up Airey Neave, a close ally of Margaret Thatcher and one-time resident of Colditz, in the car park of the House of Commons. The present narrative does not cover my later life and career. For details of my more mature trajectory, you must wait for a future volume.

Suffice to say, I worked as a journalist in Dublin, London, Brussels, Amsterdam, Bonn, Strasbourg, South Asia and Jerusalem. The pace of my personal mayhem never slackened. Nor did I ever manage to shake off the virus of hope. I got married and had a son (now lead guitarist of Battle, one of the most successful indie bands in Britain, with a following around the world). Separation and divorce duly followed. My promising career as a Fleet Street 'heavy' came to an end after I was sued, disastrously, in the High Court by Andrew Neil, my own editor at the *Sunday Times*, who claimed I had traduced him in a previous life. Finally, before reinventing myself as a freelance, I was hired and sacked on a whim by media tycoon Robert Maxwell, who earlier warned me most solemnly not to rob him blind.

Different women came and went, including the novelists

Philippa Gregory and Allison Pearson, Kate Hogg, delicious youngest daughter of Lord Hailsham, and, most memorably, Jan Relly, whose father, Gavin, chairman of the Anglo-American Corporation, helped secure the release from prison of Nelson Mandela. Kate Hogg's explanation for dumping me was straight and to the point: 'Too old, not enough money,' she told me. But I wasn't done yet.

Out of the blue, direct from the Lonely Hearts column of the *Sunday Times' Style* magazine, came the love of my life, my second wife Louisa, descended, on her mother's side, from one of the most distinguished political families in nineteenth-century America, yet the most honest, down-to-earth woman I know. First, we bought a house in London. Next, we moved to Brittany. Today, while summering in France, we live in New York, where we struggle to make a living and pass our evenings wondering why there is nothing good on the television.

Does it all add up to a hill of beans? And what's a hill of beans worth anyway? I can't say. But if you'd care to discover how someone from a perfectly normal background, just like yours, went on to achieve nothing in particular, yet had an extraordinary time doing it, I invite you to continue reading. As they say in America, you're welcome.

I

A Death in the Night

IT WAS LATE afternoon, 5 November 1977, when the phone rang in my dreary second-floor flat in Bonn. I groaned. Probably the news desk in London pointing out some tiny discrepancy between my version of a story and one that had just landed over the wires from Reuters. As I reached reluctantly for the receiver, I noticed that it was still raining, which was hardly a surprise.

'Hello.'

'Walter, is that you?'

It wasn't *The Observer*. It was my sister, Elaine. She was in a phone box at the Ulster Hospital, just outside Belfast. Our father had had a massive heart attack, she said, and the doctors feared he might not last the night. Could I come home at once?

Dad was only 65, but he'd had two previous heart attacks and each one had left him weaker. I stammered something about calling British Airways or Lufthansa to see what could be organised at short notice. Bonn, the capital of what used to be called West Germany, offered only a handful of flights each day to London and none at all to Dublin – and it was a Saturday. I'd do what I could, I told her, and get back to her.

'Just hurry,' she said. 'He's been asking for you. It would make a real difference to him if you could only be here.'

I looked around me at the almost empty room in which I had been proposing to spend the evening. A small sofa was pushed against the wall next to the window and a cheap coffee table, piled with books and papers, occupied the centre of a threadbare rug. There was nothing else. The phone, like me, sat on the floor. There weren't even any curtains. Not much to say goodbye to.

Where was the phone book? I had no idea. Did I even have one? But then I remembered there were airline numbers in my contacts book, which was in the inside pocket of my jacket, lying on the sofa. British Airways answered straight away. I explained that my father was dying and that it was an emergency. The woman on the line sounded genuinely concerned (nowadays there would be no voice; it would all be done online: 'click here if bereaved'). There was a flight to Gatwick leaving in two hours, she said, but nothing after that. That was fine, but I needed a connection to Belfast. She consulted her screen and came up with details of a flight from Heathrow, also the last of the day. Heathrow? How far was that from Gatwick? About 50 miles, she told me, but do-able – just – if I jumped in a taxi.

Before I left, I had one other call to make. The poet James Fenton, who lived in my spare room from Monday to Friday, was, as usual, in Berlin for the weekend. James had taken over my job as the *Guardian*'s man in Germany less than three months after it was given to me, which was a severe blow to my finances as well as my self-esteem. But it was nothing personal; it was just that he needed to live in the Federal Republic for a year or so to work on his poem, 'A German Requiem', and to research some essays he had in mind, dealing with the aftermath of war. The *Guardian*'s foreign editor was pleased to help, as was I, apparently. James – something of a party animal in those days – wasn't there when I called his Berlin number, so I left a message that he had his key and should just carry on as usual.

He did. And so did *The Guardian* – which to this day owes me three months' rent.

Minutes later, after packing an overnight bag, I ran up the Hochkreuzallee, past the level crossing, to the taxi rank. Unusually, there was a cab waiting, a big old Mercedes, with a Turkish driver. When I told him my situation, he drove like the wind. We roared down the B9, past the British Embassy, over the Kennedybrücke and straight up the autobahn on the east bank of the Rhine to Köln-Bonn Airport. I started to sweat as I ran inside, looking for the check-in, explaining to officials and police officers in my imperfect German that my father was dying and I had to make the plane to London. Everybody rallied round. No one objected when I was rushed to the front of the queue.

Once in the air, the impact of what was happening finally hit me. I had been living in Bonn for less than four months, after leaving Dublin in pursuit of a doomed love affair. The last time I saw my father was in the first week of July. He was sitting in his armchair, with my mum stood next to him, in the living room of their new home in Bangor with its view out over the Irish Sea. After 50 years' hard labour, he had finally retired, with a weak chest, a bad heart and serious problems with his eyes.

He spoke wheezily, finding it hard to catch his breath. An unintended side effect of some new medication he was on was that his tear ducts had dried up, and every couple of minutes he squeezed drops into his eyes, sending the residue trickling down his cheeks, as if he were crying. He wanted to know if I was doing the right thing going to Bonn. Didn't I have a perfectly good job in Dublin with the *Irish Times*? And what about Rosemary, the girl I had lived with for the past four years? What about her? I didn't know what to tell him. That I was being stupid? That I was following my heart? That I couldn't stand being home in Ireland and preferred the prospect of life in Germany?

'I'll be fine, Dad,' I said at last. 'Don't worry about me, worry about yourself. You need to pay more heed to what the doctors tell you.'

Slowly, he shook his head. 'Ach, I'm finished, son. Before long, I'll be going to the Good Lord for a bit of peace.'

'Don't say that, Dad. You've got years yet.'

He smiled at me, squinting, and squeezed another couple of drops into his eyes. 'Aye, well, we'll see. At least I have your mother to look after me, God bless her. Sure I couldn't be in better hands.'

I hope I hugged him. All I know is that I left for the airport shortly afterwards. I was 29 and I never saw him again, alive or dead.

In a letter to me, written only weeks before his death, he told me how wonderful it had been to hear my voice on RTÉ radio the previous Sunday morning. He also expressed his gratitude to Joe Hayes, an Irish diplomat, now ambassador to the Czech Republic and Ukraine, who put me up for several weeks after my arrival in Bonn. 'Joe and his good wife have been wonderful friends to you,' he wrote. 'God bless them for their great kindness to you.' His mood then darkened. 'As for me, sometimes I feel great and at other times (like this morning) I feel that I am going to say goodbye to this world. I find it so hard to breathe and so intensely painful, but with God's help, and your dear mother's, I will plod on, hoping for the best.'

I should have known. I should have called every day, not once a week.

As the BA flight from Bonn gained height over Aachen and made its way past Brussels to the English Channel, I wondered what Dad would make of my new life. Rosemary had been abandoned; the girl from Hamburg for whom I had given up everything had abandoned me; and I lived in a desolate, half-empty flat in Bonn, struggling to make ends meet as a freelance for *The Observer*.

Two lines of James's 'Requiem', not yet written, reflected my situation with bizarre percipience:

> *Yesterday the very furniture seemed to reproach you.*
> *Today you take your place in the Widow's Shuttle.*

Gatwick, on a Saturday night in late autumn, was half-deserted. But there was only time for the quickest of calls to Elaine. I ran through Arrivals to the taxi rank and babbled that I had to be in Heathrow in less than an hour. The driver, uninterested in my plight but mindful of the likely size of his tip, drove as fast as he dared. It was pitch black as we sped along the M23, but to either side I could see fires rearing up in the night, sending sparks into the darkness. Then a skyrocket whooshed up from a house nearby and I realised all at once that it was Guy Fawkes Night. The people of England were remembering the Fifth of November, Gunpowder, Treason and Plot. Children and their dads were placing rockets in milk bottles and lighting the blue touchpaper – just like I used to do with my dad, except that, being Irish, we lit our fireworks at Hallowe'en, on 31 October.

We pulled into Heathrow and drew up outside Terminal 1. I thrust money into the cab driver's hands; he didn't even offer to give me change. Inside, I ran to the BA check-in – but I was too late. The flight was closed, they said. The aircraft was waiting to depart.

'But you don't understand. It's my dad. He's dying. I've just got in from Gatwick after a flight from Germany.' Surely there was something they could do?

Hold on, they said. After a couple of minutes, a uniformed flight attendant told me the plane had been held and I should follow him. 'We've got to hurry, sir,' he said. 'We don't want to miss our slot.'

Did I speak to anyone on the flight to Aldergrove? I can't remember. All I know is that the journey seemed to go on for ever and that everyone around me seemed happy and cheerful and delighted to be heading home. Belfast is that kind of a place.

Elaine met me just as I reached the Arrivals gate. She looked shattered, and I knew the worst before she spoke.

'I'm sorry,' she said. 'Daddy died two hours ago. He was asking for you and I told him you were on your way.'

It was so unfair. I felt sorry for me, but I felt even sorrier for Dad. I couldn't imagine at that moment what it was like to lie in a hospital bed certain that you were going to die. One of the only comforts was surely the knowledge that your family was there with you, holding your hand. Dad wanted to see his son one more time, and I couldn't make it. I felt that in the hour of his death I'd let him down.

The funeral was held three days later. The undertaker gave me the opportunity to have a 'last look', but I couldn't do it. Dad was gone – to the Good Lord, he'd said. He'd been in so much pain and distress over the last year, but in the end it was golf that did for him. He was walking back to the clubhouse after winning a game against two of his oldest friends when he simply keeled over, clutching his chest.

Mum did her best not to show her grief, which I think made it all the harder to bear. The tears came later. Since the golf club rang to tell her what happened, she had been staying with my sister in Belfast, and now, in the first hours of her long widowhood, she fussed around in the kitchen, making tea, wanting to know if I was all right and what sort of a journey I'd had. She looked lost and understood little of what we said to her. I wanted to know if her religion was truly a comfort to her at a time like this, but I wasn't going to ask. I would find out one day, but now wasn't the time. In fact, there was never a good time.

When Dad was buried, in a cold, municipal cemetery, I felt as if my own childhood had died with him. I was inching closer to the front line and couldn't help wondering if losing a parent wasn't the point at which all of us truly come of age.

II

Starting as He Meant
to Go On

IN THE AUTUMN of 1948, as my mother went into labour, a spectacular comet raced through the heavens, finally exploding into view in the middle of a solar eclipse. Needless to say, this mighty harbinger, known as the Eclipse Comet, had nothing to do with me.

I have no memory of being born – though I'm sure I resented the extrusion. The only mildly unusual thing about my birth was that it didn't happen in hospital but in a private nursing home. I was delivered in a turn-of-the-century establishment in Ardenlee Avenue, east Belfast, close to the River Lagan, arriving just in time for breakfast. As nurses in stiff white uniforms tended to my needs, tea was brought to my mother in a china cup along with a McVitie's digestive. I doubt I was breastfed. My mother would have considered such an act unutterably vulgar. The only reason she dunked her McVitie's was that she'd read the Queen (later the Queen Mum) did it, and that made it OK.

Within a few years, with the development of the National

Health Service, most of Belfast's private nursing homes shut down. My birthplace ended up being sold by its owners to the Reverend Ian Paisley, the celebrated Protestant firebrand, who today, in his 80th year, still dreams of transforming Northern Ireland into an evangelical theocracy. Paisley promptly demolished it and built in its stead his Martyrs Memorial church, billed as the largest place of worship constructed in Britain or Ireland since the Reformation. To the Free Presbyterians who fill its pews each Sunday, it is the stairway to heaven; to Catholics, the hellmouth. To me, it is the Church of the Nativity.

My early years are a bit of a blur. Harold Macmillan, one of the more entertaining British prime ministers, is said to have remembered being stared down at in his pram when he was just a few weeks old. He vividly recalled public events, such as Queen Victoria's Diamond Jubilee in 1897, which happened when he was three. I find this astonishing. My first 'big' memory, and even this is questionable, was the visit of the Queen and Prince Philip to Tonga in 1954. I was six at the time and copied out an article for the school magazine, complete with drawing, notable for its description of Their Majesties touring the island 'in a van'.

This was sloppy journalism. In fact, the redoubtable Queen Salote – all 18 stone of her – used her official car, as one would. How she got into it and still left room for all her guests is another matter.

Certain images of myself as a young child stubbornly persist; what is missing is any sense of a continuous narrative. The few tiny black-and-white photographs of me that survive from the period show a small boy with curly hair seated on a tricycle, or standing next to my father (also called Walter – a sad family trait), or crouched down by the front door of the garage, staring into the camera. It's me all right, but any sense of a connection between the me writing these words and the me then is almost completely absent.

If I had been abused, or cruelly deprived, or had suffered from mental illness, the explanation for my sense of dislocation would be obvious: I would have 'blocked out' my bad memories, not wishing to revisit the experiences. Unfortunately (as I have said), that is not the case here. Perhaps I was just bored. The cliché goes that everyone remembers where they were when Kennedy was shot (though, in fact, I don't). Even if it's true, what does it prove? That some days stand out and others don't? Who remembers what they were doing the day before Kennedy was shot?

The other explanation is that we grow out of childhood much as a butterfly grows out of being a caterpillar. Having left behind the constraints of infancy and pre-pubescence, the new us that emerges forgets the early years, preferring to concentrate on the intriguing and seemingly permanent us that has so dramatically burst onto the scene. The old us, once sloughed off, is discarded and forgotten.

But its ghost haunts us.

My first home, bought by my father in anticipation of my arrival, was 26 Holland Crescent, a small red-brick 'semi-villa' in Ballyhackamore, east Belfast. Elaine, who knows about such things, says it cost £1,600 and Dad was worried he might never pay off the mortgage. Ten years later, he sold it for precisely the same sum, which gives an indication of how stable, and tiny, the Northern Ireland economy was in the long, sleepy run-up to the Troubles.

Our domestic arrangements were typical of the period. The house had a front hallway leading to a long kitchen at the back. Off the hall ran the living room and the sitting room, both small with fireplaces. The sitting room had a bay window overlooking a tiny front lawn and privet hedge. At the top of the stairs was the bathroom and toilet. My parents' bedroom was at the rear of the house, directly above the yard with its central drain. Elaine's room was at the front with a double window. I had the boxroom, about nine feet by six, over the front door.

Childhood homes share some of the characteristics of the womb. They are warm. They nourish and protect you. They are where you feel safe. They *contain* you. My boxroom, where I lay in bed reading Just William and Biggles and, later, the fantasy romances of H. Rider Haggard, was somewhere where I did not have bad dreams and never feared the Bogeyman.

I kept my toys in my room. There was a big box with my Tri-ang railway set. I had a Canadian diesel locomotive and a shunter; both had headlamps. My dad told me that when something went wrong and the train wouldn't go, you pressed the little red button on the control box and the men back at Tri-ang put it right. This seemed to work. The only thing they couldn't do was connect the track; you had to do that yourself. One of my favourite toys was a red plastic spaceship in which I travelled the universe. It was made in Hong Kong. Another was my gangster-style sub-machine gun with its round magazine that made a rat-a-tatta-tat sound when you drew back the bolt and pressed the trigger.

Before William and Biggles, I read Little Noddy and Big Ears. I liked the Gollywogs and Bumpy Dog. Later, I was a huge fan of Count Curly Wee, a rather exotic gentleman pig, whose adventures, so far as I know, appeared first in the *Irish Mail* in Dublin. Dad bought me Wee's annual every year, enjoying them, I suspect, almost as much as he enjoyed the stories of P.G. Wodehouse. There was something about the Count. He spoke in verse, he dined by candlelight; he wore tails (other than his own) and he was always up against it, yet never betrayed the slightest anxiety. I wanted very much to be like Wee. The problem was that I lacked not merely his savoir-faire but also his admirable sangfroid. Though I tried to take life in my stride, I was filled with uncertainty. I didn't fear the Bogeyman so long as I was in my room and my mum and dad were downstairs, but I often felt his footsteps out of doors – especially after it grew dark.

Belfast in the 1950s was as much an Edwardian city as a post-war metropolis. Our street was lit by rows of cast-iron gas lamps spread out at 50-yard intervals. Employees of the city corporation known as 'leeries' kept an eye on the lamps, which each had a four-sided glass lantern and meshwork mantle. Sometimes, the lamp refused to light properly and you could see the mantle glowing red. That was when the leerie would place his short ladder against the lamp-post's shoulders (otherwise used to support our makeshift swings) and begin tinkering. After a while, the gas would hiss and go *whoosh!* and the street below, where we were standing gawping, would be bathed in a gentle yellow light. If you had told me then that I would end up typing on a laptop computer connected to the Internet by Bluetooth, I would have thought you a visitor from another world, or possibly America.

But if the prevailing technology was primitive, retail services were friendly and efficient to a degree that today would be considered irresponsible and profligate. Horse-drawn carts delivered coal for the fire. While the horse tucked into the contents of its nosebag, the coalman – black-faced, wearing a shiny leather jerkin – would place a sack on each shoulder and heave them round to the 'wee house' at the back, where he emptied them with a satisfying crump. The last two bags were of slack, tiny pieces of coal and dust that were used to tamp down the embers each night and preserve the basis of the next morning's fire. Tamping was my dad's job – the last thing he did before retiring for the night – and, up in bed, I would often hear the rattle as he shut the vent and placed the layer of slack on the hot coals. It felt cosy and reassuring.

Tradesmen had almost to stand in line to get to our front door. My mother's preferred baker was Inglis, whose massive premises dominated Cromac Street next to a tannery. Each day, the Inglis breadserver would arrive outside our house. The doors at the back of his electric van would fly back and he would draw out the huge wooden drawers on their aluminium runners. Inside, as we crowded round, was every kind of Irish bread: from the straightforward sliced pan to Barmbrack, a sticky, spiced confection with currants that would leave you licking your fingers for minutes afterwards, via malted 'Veda', soda, wheaten and potato. There were also cakes and biscuits and Jacobs crackers and all sorts of speciality treats, a selection of which the breadserver would place in a large wicker basket that he would then transport to the front door, where my mother would be waiting.

The arrival each day of the horse-drawn milk cart was an important event, especially in the growing season. Housewives, armed with shovels, followed it down the street, seeking manure for their roses. It was a competitive business, as demand far exceeded supply. Mrs Whitaker − related, someone once told me, to an eminent former governor of the Irish Central Bank − was one of the principal shit shovellers. Another was her neighbour, Mrs Bloomfield, whose son, Ken, an Oxford man, ended up as *Sir* Kenneth, head of the civil service at Stormont. My mother kept out of it; her roses suffered, but at least she had her dignity.

Towards the end of the '50s, when horses were replaced by electric floats, the milkie, Mr McQuillan, let me ride in the cab with him and maybe even take the wheel. Saturdays were his busiest day, since the delivery included cream and buttermilk, as well as eggs and butter. I helped him on our street and, so long as I didn't drop any of the bottles, he would hand me tuppence for my trouble. At the corner, another boy would take over on the same basis, and so on all the way back to the depot.

Ken Bloomfield was a stocky bugger, who kept himself fit. He cycled everywhere. I suspect he looked at the rest of us as a department he had yet to take charge of. In the summer, he played tennis in immaculately pressed white shorts, achieving the kind of tan that normally required a fortnight in the Costa Brava − wherever that was. But there was another young man − I didn't know his name − who actually went jogging through our streets, which made him something of a pioneer. When we came across him, puffing and wheezing up the hill, his loose cotton shorts flapping in the wind, we would call out after him, '*Skinny-Malink-Melojun legs!*'

Summer didn't exactly arrive with a bang in Northern Ireland. It crept up on you, taking you unawares. Sometimes, it forgot to turn up altogether. But in a good year, as the temperatures crept up into the low 70s Fahrenheit, lemonade was big business. Coca-Cola had yet to make an appearance outside of coffee bars, and so Ross's, White City and C&C were the local companies competing for our custom. We at number 26 preferred Ross's, which dispensed its drinks in long, slender bottles with stoppers that incorporated what looked like a gorilla's nipple, with a pink rubber washer. The company claimed that its sparkling water came from a natural source and had an altogether superior fizz, yet its product range didn't run to white and brown lemonade (neither of them connected with lemon), the staples of soft-drink gastronomy in Belfast. For these, you had to slum it with White City.

Grocery shopping varied, depending on the quantities involved. If you only wanted a few things or had nothing else to do, you queued up and waited your turn. This was where you caught up on the gossip. For the 'big shop', home delivery was the norm at no extra cost. My mother would send me round with a note to the local grocery store detailing all the goods and foodstuffs she required for the week ahead. It meant that she could get on with the washing and ironing, or just listen to the wireless, while others did the heavy lifting. In the afternoon, a van would call and a smartly dressed young man would carry the box of groceries into the kitchen.

It was the same with fresh meats. The butcher's boy, called Frankie, would turn up from the high street on his bicycle, with its big metal carrier, and deliver the chops and sausages and minced beef in brown-paper parcels dripping with blood. He wore a proper butcher's apron with stripes, and the bottoms of his trousers were held free from the oily chain of his bicycle with a set of metal clips.

Everyone seemed cheerful and there was no bad language – or at least not within my hearing. But then, in the 1950s, even the local Teddy boys, in their velvet 'drape' suits and string ties, would say hello. So long as you didn't take a knife to them or call them names they were more amusing than intimidating.

A key routine that I observed with something approaching awe was that of my father counting his wages on a Friday night. A couple of huge white £5 notes, each as big as a handkerchief, led the way, followed by several single pounds, a ten-shilling note and a rattle of change: half-crowns, florins, shillings, sixpences and thruppenny bits. A sizeable portion of the total would be handed solemnly to my mother. 'That's your housekeeping, Molly,' he would say. 'Try not to spend it all at once.' Elaine, my sister, was given pocket money of two shillings; I got one and six (a shilling and a sixpenny piece, or 'tanner'). The remaining notes were carefully folded and replaced in Dad's wallet to be banked. Years later, I remember a friend telling me that it was always his ambition to earn £1,000 a year (about what my father earned when I was young). He gave up congratulating himself when his salary as a journalist exceeded 50 times that amount.

Ours was not a high-tech house. My mother had an electric boiler that looked like it belonged in a chemical plant in which she would 'steep' her weekly wash. Afterwards, she would put it through the hand-cranked wringer, with its hefty wooden rollers, in the backyard. Washing took up a massive amount of Mum's time. She washed the dishes, she washed our clothes, and she washed the floors in the kitchen and bathroom. Even then, it wasn't done. The dishes had to be dried and put away, the floors blocked off until they shone.

The upright enamel stove in our old kitchen was fuelled by town gas produced at the gasworks on the other side of the river. The gas was smelly and extremely dangerous and, as children, we were told in no uncertain terms to leave it alone. I tried to use it once to fill up a balloon, earnestly holding its plastic neck over one of the gas jets until I was giddy and the house was geared up to explode.

Compared to the clumsy machinery that littered my mother's domain, the family wireless was uncharacteristically compact. Tiny cream-coloured rectangles on the illuminated dial showed the supposed locations of Radio Éireann, Network Three (whatever that was) and stations in Frankfurt, Paris and Hilversum at the edge of the known world. As far I know, we only ever listened to Home Service and the *Light Programme* on the BBC.

Children's Favourites, presented by Uncle Mac (in real life, war hero Derek McCulloch), was a high point of my week. It aired on Saturday mornings and featured a virtually unaltered playlist throughout my childhood, extending from Burl Ives's 'Big Rock Candy Mountain' to 'Sparky's Magic Piano' – the world's first electronic music – by way of 'The Laughing Policeman' and 'High Hopes'. It seemed unnecessary to write in with a request, and I don't think I ever did. We all knew what was coming up anyway.

Locally, the most popular radio programme was *The McCooey's*, an early soap opera set in Belfast in which, it was said, neither politics nor religion ever intruded and all the characters were earthy, good-hearted and comical. I don't remember a thing about it, except that it starred Jimmy Young, Ulster's top comedian for as long as anyone could remember, and was written by Joe Tomelty, who, as an actor, had roles in scores of films, including *A Night to Remember*, *Moby Dick* and *Hobson's Choice*.

Tomelty (grandfather, I discovered, to the children of rock singer Sting) was a fine actor but not a star. If you look him up on the Internet, you will usually find against the names of his characters 'vagrant' or 'innkeeper' or 'Uncle Dan'. Not until Liam Neeson came along 30 years later did Northern Ireland have its own full-blown movie star. In my childhood search for home-grown celebrity, all I could come up with was Tyrone Power, whose family apparently came from Toomebridge. Power's ten inch by eight black-and-white photograph hung on my bedroom wall until 1958, when he died. Next to it was a publicity picture for Walter Pigeon, who, though unconnected to Ireland and distinctly B-list, was at least called Walter.

But back to the radio. At a quarter to two each day there was *Listen With Mother*, announced by its gradually ascending trademark chimes: *Donga*-dong, *donga*-dong, *donga*-dong – *Dong!* The programme itself opened with a song from the perennial George Dixon: 'This is the way the gentlemen ride, clip-clop, clip-clop, clip-*clop*.' The nursery rhyme followed and then the story, usually read by Daphne Oxenford ('Are you sitting comfortably? Then I'll begin'). Finally, there would be another song. It was a winning package, which I listened to before starting school and continued to enjoy in the holidays. But time doesn't stand still and by the time I was eight (all right, *nine*), I was ready for more adult fare. One particularly scary series that stays with me even today is *Journey Into Space* – more properly *Jour-ney In-to Spaaaace* – the adventures of Jet Morgan and his intrepid crew of spacemen. It was Jet Morgan and Dan Dare, of the *Eagle* comic, who first got me hooked on the mysteries of space travel. I have been mystified ever since.

Like I say, I find it hard after all these years to place myself inside this small child. I can no longer inhabit him, only observe him from the outside, like a museum exhibit. The boy I knew who felt this way and did these things is not altogether a stranger to me, but he's like someone who stayed a long time then moved away, leaving only a memory. When I visited Holland Crescent some years back for a series in the *Daily Mail* about childhood, I remember being slightly chagrined to discover that a message in blue chalk that I had written there beneath the hall window, reading 'Punctures Repaired Here', was no longer visible. I took off my glasses and squinted at the brickwork, looking for traces. It felt as if I was back there, just for a moment, marking the wall. I even felt around pathetically, hoping to find a rubber patch or a valve cover – anything that would prove to me that I had indeed lived there for ten years of my life.

I am forever retracing my footsteps, trying to work out where I went wrong, or simply curious, wondering if in some way I am still there, carrying on as before, trapped inside an inconsequential loop of time. Once, I went back to my apartment in Bonn, years after I'd lived there. It was on Eltviller Strasse in the suburb of Bad Godesberg, next to a supermarket that closed for two hours every lunchtime and shut down completely from midday on Saturdays until nine-thirty on Monday mornings. It was that kind of a place. James Fenton suggested to me as we went walking one evening that it was Hitler (a regular visitor) who had put the Bad in Bad Godesberg, but the way I saw it, it would have been more appropriate if he had renamed it Langweiligsberg – Boringville. Years on, I wanted to know if the same residents were still there and if I would recognise any of them. Unsettlingly, all the familiar names were still listed next to the doorbells: the dentist, the Syrian, the widow who always wore a headscarf. That was when I fled for good. I felt sure that if I stayed I would meet myself coming back from the shops.

The narrow hallway of our house in Holland Crescent was dominated by a black Bakelite telephone (Belfast 654201) with a drawer in its base that when pulled out dispensed an alphabetically arranged personal directory. For the first couple of years, we shared the line with another family up the street (on whose conversations I used to sometimes eavesdrop until they realised I was there and threatened to tell my father). The instrument, about as heavy as my mother's flat iron, sat next to a brass gong and, like the gong, was rarely used. It was only when my sister – by now wearing skirts splayed out by 50 yards with some kind of netting – became a teenager that our account was finally put through its paces.

Radio Luxembourg, the precursor of Radio 1, was growing in

popularity at this time and my sister soon acquired a tiny transistor radio, the signal from which fluctuated wildly. Sometimes the music disappeared altogether to be replaced by soaring atmospherics and when you fiddled with the dial, you were as likely as not to end up with Radio Moscow. The songs, spun 500 miles away in the Grand Duchy, were interspersed with adverts, which in itself was something of a novelty. The one I remember best was narrated by the lugubrious figure of Horace Bachelor, who described to listeners for a decade or more his amazing 'Infradraw' method for doing the football Pools. Those who wished to make it big in the business of predicting score draws were urged by Horace to buy into his unbeatable system. Sadly for those who did, 10 per cent of their winnings fell due to the system Lord, who lived, it emerged, in a 27-room folly in Keynsham, Somerset, like some sort of cut-down Howard Hughes.

Back in the sitting room, our black pre-war wind-up gramophone – an anachronism even then – played old 78s made from shellac, with all the weight and density of a discus. I doubt Thomas Edison would have been challenged by the mechanics. It was only with the emergence of Elvis Presley, Cliff Richard, Marty Wilde and their clones round about 1958 that Dad reluctantly splashed out and bought us a record player. His own musical preference remained with Irish ballads of the Percy French variety or even, God help us, his own recording of 'Westering Home', a traditional Scottish ballad:

> *Where are the folks like the folks of the West?*
> *Canty and Couthy and Kindly the Best.*
> *There I would hie me and there I would rest,*
> *At hame with my ain folks in Islay.*

What did this mean? I had no idea. I still haven't. There is a certain type of popular song that harks back only to an imagined reality, and I think these had a strong appeal for my dad. Or maybe it was just that it was a good tune. As my sister and I sat in the back seat of the car during the 'wee runs' we made each month in the car along the north coast of Antrim – which actually looks across the North Channel to Islay – my father's tenor voice invariably rose to the occasion, cheerfully evoking the sense of loss he appeared to feel at being deprived of his friends Canty, Couthy and Kindly the Best. Sometimes, he would turn round in the driving seat and require us to join in the refrain.

Westering home with a song in the air
Light in the eye and it's goodbye to care
Laughter and love are a welcoming there
Pride of my heart my ain one

The gravel on the path outside our house was made up of smooth white stones, not grey. They are gone now, replaced by tarmac. My mother saw them, I think, as a further mark of our distinction; I saw them as particularly suitable for my catapult. When I was ill in bed, I always had a cache of stones. I waited until there was no one around, then I opened the window, leaned out and sent the stones, one by one, hundreds of feet into the air. They fell to earth I know not where, but no one, so far as I know, ever complained. It must be the same when Palestinians fire their weapons into the air at weddings – hundreds of bullets fired straight up. You would think there would be reports of deaths and injuries from all over the place, or at least of windows being broken. But it doesn't work like that in Gaza and it didn't work that way for me.

At the end of the path, at the back of the house, was the garage, with its two big wooden doors, where I liked to hide. It was a place where I could be on my own and collect my thoughts, free from adult interference or the shrill querulousness of my friends. There was a knot hole in the wall between our garage and the one next door, owned by Mr Sinclair. Our garage smelled of paint; theirs smelled of bitumen. Sometimes, I would peer through, standing on an upturned flowerpot, hoping to witness something odd, like a ritual or a murder. But there was never anything. Mrs Sinclair or her son, Eoin, would maybe come in to fetch a shovel or a garden fork. Once I saw a mouse. But that was about it. Very disappointing.

Next to the garage, the 'lawn' was just a patch of grass over which my father would run his little cylinder mower once a week between March and October – until, that is, I grew big enough to take over the task. It was also a toilet for our various dogs: Beano, Nicky and Rags. Nicky and Rags were Yorkshire terriers, about the size of a lunchbox. Their predecessor, Beano, was big and burly – and a mistake. He was a boxer, with a lunchbox to match. He would attack other dogs and liked to pin me up against the wall, with his paws on my shoulders and his fangs just an inch from my face, daring me not to find him amusing. Beano was seriously deranged and hated it when his mistress left the house to go shopping. On one famous occasion, he pushed past me in my bedroom and jumped out of the open window to catch up with my mother in the street, barking like a maniac. He had to go, and downsizing to a sequence of Yorkshires seemed to my father to be the smart move.

At the rear of the garden was a large hawthorn hedge that flowered every summer. The flowers were tiny and white and attracted butterflies. It was hollow in the middle, so perfect for surveillance. But surveillance of what? On its far side was the near-identical back garden of a house on Enid Parade, the next street. Most of the homes there were given out to ex-service families and were painted in shades of institutional off-white. In the ten years that we lived in Holland Crescent I never found out who the people were on the other side of the hedge, only that they had no children and hardly ever used their garden. I didn't know their names or anything about them, except that the husband was ex-Army and never seemed to smile.

Our family had its guilty secret. My father, though of sound mind and body, and just 27 in 1939, had spent the war as a non-combatant, taking advantage of the fact that Northern Ireland, with its volatile republican minority, wasn't subject to conscription. To be fair, a lot of patriotic Protestants did the same. Some said there were more Fenians than Prods in the British Army. Whatever the truth of it, London wasn't asking and we weren't volunteering. The residual embarrassment this engendered meant, of course, that, like Basil Fawlty, we didn't talk much about the war. My father would praise Churchill when the occasion demanded (the Old Man was, after all, back in as Prime Minister) but otherwise gave the issue a wide berth. I asked no questions and was told no lies. Dad, I later discovered, had been an air-raid warden during the intermittent Belfast Blitz and had on several occasions pulled the dead and injured from burned-out buildings after German raids. If they had given out medals for that, he would have qualified. (Years later, I asked my mother what it had been like during the war. She looked blank. 'Oh, I don't remember, dear. I never took much interest in that sort of thing.')

For Uncle Norman, married to my mother's sister, Nancy, it was very different. A resentful, quick-tempered man, who delighted in teasing my sister and me, he had fought on the beaches at Normandy and was commended personally by Field Marshal Montgomery for his 'right trusty' service. He also won the Croix de Guerre, which meant that an official communication from the French ambassador was read out at his funeral. Uncle Norman was not an easy man to live with and I think my Aunt Nancy was quite relieved when he finally fell off his perch. He demanded 100 per cent obedience from his wife and their daughter, my cousin Norma, and total, unwavering dedication to hygiene. Aunt Nancy bathed him every Friday night using Lifebuoy antiseptic soap. She also had to polish his golf clubs and ensure that his vast collection of *Reader's Digest* condensed books was kept in alphabetical order, like returns in an accountant's filing cabinet. Sometimes, she told me years later, he would wake up in the night screaming, believing that someone was about to stab him with a bayonet. The war never left him. But it wasn't the Germans that killed him, it was cigarettes: a salesman most of his life for a series of tobacco companies, he smoked 50 untipped a day and died of cancer in his late 60s.

Occasionally, the two families went on holiday together. The signal for this was usually a violent downturn in the weather. One August afternoon we sat in my father's car looking out over the beach at Portstewart, not far from the Giant's Causeway. The wind was blowing and it was raining so hard that the sea was just an angry blur. My mother passed round tea from a thermos flask and distributed startlingly white sandwiches filled with Spam and tomato and slivers of limp lettuce. Uncle Norman and I ate distractedly as we pored over my *War Picture Library* comics, detailing the derring-do of a series of barrel-chested British commandos who made short work of Gerry while uttering the immortal phrase, 'Take that, Fritz!' My father, I noticed, preferred to read about golf.

I don't know when Dad gave up the grocery business (to which he would return in later life just in time to give himself the first of a series of heart attacks), but at some point in the early 1950s he became a commercial traveller for Pratt & Montgomery, a Belfast company owned by Twinings of London, whose warehouse and offices were next to the RUC barracks in Musgrave Street. Each morning, he would put on his trilby hat and a 'shortie' overcoat that gave him shoulders like an American football player, and set off on one or other of his routes. The boot of his Ford Anglia, with its long, bendy gear lever, was filled to the gunwales with multipacks of tea wrapped up in brown paper, which he would tout around the 50 or so corner shops on his list. A typical order would be one pack of Namosa (mainly for the better off), two of Nambarrie (for those who hoped one day to be able to afford Namosa) and three each

of the sublimely juxtaposed Orange and Green labels for the
working classes. He was fond of his tea, my dad – 'He always likes
a cup in his hand,' my mother would say – and he was a supremely
gifted salesman. But he believed, justifiably I suspect, that he should
have been promoted into management and he resented it when his
friend, Fred Allen – who sold less of the product but had a more
plausible executive face – was appointed a company director. That
was when Dad went back to boning bacon.

My father played the mandolin and the banjo and for several
years – oh, dear, the shame of it! – was the 'darky' of a black-and-
white minstrel show. It turned out he led a secret life: snuggled in
beside the plectrums in the banjo case beneath his bed were his
woolly wig and burned cork, and the words of his trademark song:

Way down upon de Swanee Ribber,
Far, far away,
Dere's wha my heart is turnin' ebber,
Dere's wha de ol' folks stay.

Shades of Westering Home! What was my dad looking for? I knew
that he had been born on a farm and that things hadn't been easy for
him as a young man; what I didn't know until long after he was gone
(we were that close) was just how hard it had been. My dad's father,
yet another Walter, farmed a hundred acres in Hillhall, close to the
market town of Lisburn, where he owned, in addition, a large and
thriving public house. He had another farm in Ballinderry, some 20
miles away, and a second pub in the Catholic Smithfield area of
Belfast. How he came to own this rather impressive portfolio I have
no idea, though I imagine inheritance played the biggest part. It is
odd to think that if Grandad had not been a serious drinker and
gambler, my dad would have copped the lot and, in all probability,
not met my mother. Thus, I would not have existed – or if I had, I
would have been someone else. The fact is, Grandad drank copiously

behind his own bar and then accounted it sensible practice to bet the week's takings on the 2.30 at Leopardstown.

The inevitable happened. My father, then aged fourteen, found himself loading up a jaunting car with the family's remaining possessions, plus his mother and three sisters and his father asleep in the back, and driving the fifteen miles into Belfast to look for somewhere to live.

> *All up and down de whole creation*
> *Sadly do I roam,*
> *Still longin' for de ol' plantation,*
> *And for de ol' folks at home.*

During their glory years, the Ellises had owned, in addition to everything else, a substantial 'gentleman's residence' in the Dundela district in the east of the city, close to the Lewises, whose son, C.S. 'Jack' Lewis, would go on to be one of the most celebrated Christian apologists of his age. Did my grandfather know the author of *The Lion, The Witch and The Wardrobe* and *The Screwtape Letters*? They were probably on nodding terms, but it would not only have been the difference in age (Lewis was at least a decade younger) that would have prevented a friendship forming. Lewis was a sensitive intellectual; my grandfather was a drunk. Either way, the question is moot, as all such associations were now lost. Home in the lean times that followed the fire sale of our family patrimony was not the gateway to Narnia but a grim terrace house in Madrid Street on the borderline between Protestant east Belfast and the fiercely Catholic and nationalist Short Strand.

There was real sacrifice here. My father had to give up a scholarship to Friends' School, Lisburn, one of the finest grammar schools in Ireland, when the crisis hit. This meant that instead of going on to be an accountant (his dream job) he became an apprentice grocer, working long hours to pay the rent in Madrid

Street while his father, who would eventually die of a combination of alcohol abuse and gangrene, railed against the injustice of the world. I can only imagine how hard it must have been. My father served all seven years of his apprenticeship and ended up, in the way of those days, a Master Grocer. The one permanent memento of his artisan servitude was the missing little finger on his left hand – the result of not, as I once thought, some peculiar Masonic ritual but a horrific encounter with a bacon slicer.

Here I should digress for a second. A few years ago, while reading *Reflections on a Quiet Rebel* by the journalist Cal McCrystal, I was astonished to learn in an account by Cal of his father's life in republican Belfast that his grandfather, a hardened drinker, had declined disastrously, then died prematurely of 'heart strain', obliging his son, James, to give up his scholarship to the prestigious St Malachy's College in order to look after his sisters and brothers in their newly reduced circumstances. James became – you've guessed it – an apprentice grocer and inflicted permanent injury on his left hand with a bacon slicer.

Very odd. Sure what were the chances of that?, my uncle Tommy would have said. My dad and Cal's father did not lead parallel lives; fate doesn't work as neatly as that. Yet they were more alike than I would have supposed. James McCrystal flirted with the old IRA and was a lifelong republican and Gaelic scholar. But he dreamed of the day when the two religious communities could come together and agree on a shared future. My father was a dyed-in-the-wool unionist who, in 1974, played a walk-on part in the Ulster Workers' Strike. But, as I was to discover after his death, he was simultaneously a member of the moderate non-denominational Alliance Party. For years he lunched twice a week at the Tea Cosy Grill with Canon Pádraig Murphy, a leading Catholic priest from the Falls Road. Sometimes, usually on a Saturday, I would get to meet Father Murphy and we would discuss the politics of Dublin as relayed to us by the *Irish Times*.

Religion is famously divisive in Ireland. But contrary to the frequently expressed view that Catholicism has the final word on misery, it seems to me that belief dispenses its gloom in an admirably ecumenical fashion. It was certainly a deadly serious business when I was a boy. The Good News, so far as I could make it out, was that God had an inexhaustible appetite for flattery, which required a willingness on our part to engage in non-stop devotion. There would be no fun in heaven. Angels didn't laugh; they 'adored'. Far from being a joyous reunion of the Great and Good freed from pain, temptation and despair (perish the thought), the afterlife conferred eternal membership of a celestial chorale that sang the Lord's praises twenty-four hours a day, seven days a week, for ever – with no time off for good behaviour. That's what we had to look forward to. But until that blessed – and endless – day arrived, there were lots of tasks to be performed here on earth.

My father was an elder of our local Presbyterian church, Kirkpatrick Memorial, in Ballyhackamore, so he was one of those offering advice and counsel to the minister. He was, in addition, treasurer of the church committee, made up of local traders and bankers, which gave him the chance to practise his bookkeeping skills. Once a year, as I grew older, I would help him to tot up the amounts given to the weekly collection by each family in the congregation. A street-by-street table would then be compiled, showing who were the biggest donors and who were the tight-wads. This table was widely distributed and keenly read.

But that was the catch, wasn't it? Charity, though competitive, was not the key to success. Grace was the real bugger. As implied in the regulations governing the 'Choir Invisible', you could do all the good deeds you liked, but you still wouldn't get in unless God liked the cut of your jib. And that meant a lot of prayer and non-stop buckets of praise. Years later, after my father died, my mother, in the midst of her grief, gave me a Marked Testament with underlined texts and little red fingers that pointed towards key phrases. In the front of the Testament, after reminding me that one of Dad's favourite texts was Romans 8:38–9, in which Saint Paul speaks of the certainty of God's love, she also wrote 'Phil 3:8'. I looked it up.

> Yea, doubtless and I count all things but loss for the excellency of the knowledge of Christ Jesus my Lord: for whom I have suffered the loss of all things, and do count them but dung, that I may win Christ.

Dust we are and unto dust we shall return. But *dung*?

My mother clearly saw in this a way of assuaging her loss through a realisation of its irrelevance in the great scheme of things. But I found it hard to understand. The idea of life as an audition for everlasting membership of the Mormon Tabernacle Choir struck me as odd when I was a child. It seems just as strange today.

But perhaps I am being unfair. Religion, in any case, was far from being all-pervasive back then. During the week, we could relax. There would be prayers at school, the odd bit of hymn singing, religious holidays to watch out for, but nothing too heavy. It was the Sabbath that set the pulses racing. The Lord's Day didn't get its possessive for nothing.

It began deceptively enough. We would get up later than usual, at about eight-thirty or nine, and wash ourselves until we shone. My mother would prepare a 'fry' – eggs, sausages, bacon, tomatoes, soda bread and potato bread – preceded by cereal and followed by toast and marmalade with lashings of tea. Afterwards, we would brush our teeth and make our way to the car.

It was then that life threw on its handbrake. Morning service was like a bout of constipation: to be endured until relief came. Our minister, the Reverend A.W.E. Forbes, was tall and predatory and remote, his tonsure ringed by a thicket of black oily hair. He liked to survey his flock from the pulpit, as if at any moment he could call down God's holy retribution. He wasn't someone you would go to for solace. There was no reassurance in the ritual he offered and I suspect he was often bored. Like other Presbyterian clergy, he lacked proper vestments (though on family visits he affected black britches and gaiters): all he had was his dog collar. On Sundays, in order to put on a show, he made up for his sartorial lack by wearing his academic gown and the black-and-white furry hood of a Bachelor of Arts from Magee College, Londonderry. God was not only great, he was a university man!

Lord love him, but Mr Forbes's sermons were unspeakably dull. Unfortunately, this did not mean that they were not spoken. I can't remember a word of anything he said, in spite of more than a decade of regular attendance, only the baritone monotony of his voice. I would be constantly looking around me, at the white walls and the polished wood, and the doors leading out, covered with thick velvet curtains the colour of burgundy. The choir's repertoire of hymns and psalms was as unvaried and lifeless as a privet hedge. When they came up with some new arrangement of a familiar psalm, maybe with a hint of harmony, there would be a brief flicker of interest among the congregation, but it soon died down again, like a tamped fire. The Bible readings (something Old, something New) made no sense to me; the prayers were interminable, the benediction vaguely threatening.

My mother, like my father, had a strong voice and loved to sing, so I was obliged to listen, cringing with embarrassment, as their voices soared over those around me during the hymns. All the time, my eye was on the clock. It had to be half-twelve. Jesus, it *had* to be!

Once a month, before Holy Communion, the children would be ushered out to the church hall, leaving the adults to roll up their trouser legs, bear their breasts and drink blood, or whatever it was that made sitting on oak pews for two hours listening to Mr Forbes an entertaining prospect. I lived for this moment: sweet release. Non-communion mornings were a penance. Once, I tried bringing comics in to relieve the tedium, but my father's righteous anger, involving a slap in the face and, later, his toe in my arse, made this an ill-advised tactic.

Sunday School, which took place after lunch in the Toland Hall next to the church, was another pain in the arse that I endured. Each group of children had its own small circle of chairs, in one of which the 'teacher' sat with his illustrated Bible and catechism. At the front, the prayer leader would beseech the Lord to gift the children here assembled an understanding of His holy word, while we, the assemblees, consulted our Mickey Mouse watches, praying the rain would stay off long enough for us to get home without getting soaked through. The catechism, with its joyless language and arid definition of the Faith, played a central role in our instruction. We were tested each week on our knowledge and, I have to say, over the years I won several prizes for my performance. Today, beyond the catechism's melancholy opening, reminding us that the 'chief end of Man is to glorify God and enjoy Him forever', I can't recall a word of it. A flavour of its essential ethos is, however, contained in *The Shorter Catechism of the Westminster Assembly Explained and Proved from Scripture* by the seventeenth-century divine Thomas Vincent.

Vincent was writing in the age of Cromwell, which meant that, by the standards of Ulster Presbyterian thinking in the late 1950s, he was bang up to date. What, he asked of us, was the doctrine of the 'papists' concerning the number of the sacraments of the New Testament? His answer, couched in the language of the 39 Articles, was chillingly measured and harsh.

> The doctrine of the Papists concerning the number of the sacraments is, that there are seven sacraments under the New Testament. Unto baptism and the Lord's supper they add confirmation, penance, ordination, marriage, and extreme unction: which, though some of them are to be

used, namely, marriage and ordination, yet none of them in
their superstitious way; none of them have the stamp of
divine institution to be used as sacraments; none of them are
seals of the covenant of grace; and therefore they are not
sacraments, but Popish additions, whereby they would seem
to make amends for their taking away the second
commandment out of the decalogue, as contrary to their
image-worship; whereas both such as add and such as take
away from God's laws and institutions are under a severer
curse than any of the anathemas and curses of the Popish
councils. 'If any man add to these things, God shall add unto
him the plagues that are written in this book: and if any man
shall take away from the words of the book of this prophecy,
God shall take away his part out of the book of life.'

I can't think of a word of the above with which the Revd Ian
Paisley, preaching as he does in the church of my nativity, would
disagree. Vincent was a man for whom plagues were a judicial
instrument and eternal damnation was the inevitable fate for a
majority of the world's Christians. He was a Puritan zealot who
believed in witches and ducking stools and the inestimable
pleasures of the Wrath to Come. But to Paisley and, I would say, a
majority of Northern Ireland Presbyterians during my childhood,
he spoke no more, and no less, than the truth.

Today, as an adult well into middle age, I am re-examining my
antipathy to religion. But I doubt that I shall come to any other
conclusion than that reached by Philip Larkin in his great poem
'Aubade':

> *That vast moth-eaten musical brocade*
> *Created to pretend we never die*

As a child, I don't think I ever doubted God's existence. For some
reason, I even believed that he wore a chef's hat, as if he had just

whipped us up like a soufflé or popped us in the oven for six days at regulo five. But He didn't seem important to me; He was irrelevant to the life I led. Looked at the other way round, I thought the things we did in church – the singing, the praying and the Bible readings – had nothing to do with God, who surely couldn't be so banal, so *ordinary*, as to want to spend His Sunday mornings with Mr Forbes.

What was lacking, almost brutally, from our church and thousands like it, was any sense of mystery. We had the answers right here in this book. There was no question the Bible couldn't answer. It even explained why we gathered each Sunday morning to bore ourselves rigid. That was what God wanted. Well, if that was the sort of God He was, then He would have to learn to get along without me.

And I still feel that way. The difference now is that I feel the absence: the bugger's not there and He ought to be. Without Him, it all seems like a waste of time.

The most vital things in life are, of course, rarely the most important. Away from the covenant of grace, golf was Dad's real passion. He remembered the heroics of Fred Daly from Royal Portrush, the only Ulsterman ever to win the British Open. He was also a big fan of Irish ace Christy O'Connor and once took me to a tournament to get his autograph, which I held on to for years but have now misplaced. Once or twice a week – three times in the summer – he would head off to his club, set in the former estate of The O'Neill of Clandeboye, one of Ulster's last Gaelic chieftains, to play as many holes as he could before it grew too dark to see. O'Neill, a vigorous opponent of England's scheme to sweep away the native Irish from their lands, 'except for "churls" to plough the soil', would have wondered what the hell was going on. Where were the churls, and who were these eejits with sticks? Dad's lowest-ever handicap was, I think, 12, and he normally played off 18, which put him comfortably in the bottom 10 per cent of the club's top 100 golfers. On Saturdays, after a typical 27- or 36-hole marathon, he stayed late, ingesting a spectacularly high-cholesterol 'tea', and played poker in the bar until the early hours, when he would weave home reeking of whiskey.

For years, against all the evidence, my mother believed my father didn't drink. I thought this too, or at least took her word for it. Once, when we were on holiday in the seaside town of Donaghadee, he bought me a glass of Guinness. I nearly retched at the bitter taste of it in my mouth. 'Ah,' said my father, with a brave show of naivety, 'that'll do it – sure he'll never touch another drop now.' It was Uncle Norman, a brandy and ginger man, who much later revealed that Dad was, in fact, partial to a wee Ballantine's or a Chivas Regal. Frankly, I was relieved.

Mum never took to golf. She resented being left on her own at weekends while, as she put it, 'your father goes off gallivanting'. On the not infrequent occasions when Dad's pals turned up before a game and he announced, 'Molly, get the pan on, the boys are here,' she would slam the kitchen door and rattle the saucepans, slashing the empty air with a breadknife.

She didn't care much for holidays either. During the same week-long stay in Donaghadee at which I apparently foreswore drink, she refused to come with us on a boat trip to the nearby Copeland Islands. 'It looks a bit rough,' she announced. 'What would happen if the boat sank?' And then she waved us all off to our doom.

I think her insecurity and recurring timidity resulted from the fact that for much of her childhood she and her family were frequently close to ruin. Stability was something she never took for granted. The fact that her father, Jimmy Glenn, though a man of natural wit, style and discernment, spent most of his life as a cowherd, getting fired from job after job for drinking and rowing with his bosses, demonstrated the unremitting nature of fate. But while she regretted the lack of stability in her background, she never doubted that she was descended from a proud tradition in which reading and learning were respected. She often told of how one of her father's ancestors had been a preacher, with several books of theology to his credit, and another a private secretary to the Earl of Antrim during the 1745 Jacobite Rebellion. I never disputed this and, indeed, one of my nephews owns an impenetrable volume of reflections by the Reverend James Glenn from Victorian times, which occupies a place of honour in his front room next to a leather-bound volume of Longfellow. My own faint memories of Granda are of an old man with next to no hair and only one front tooth wearing a brown suit with white pinstripes, leaning on his walking stick as he tapped his foot to the music on the wireless.

Granny was another matter altogether. Hetty Baines was born in 1884 in Beltra, County Sligo, a little north of Collaney, overlooking Ballysodare Bay, and liked to claim descent from Spaniards shipwrecked in Ireland after the Armada. Her own mother spoke Irish, which was rare for a Protestant (and a Spaniard), and used to translate official correspondence from Dublin for the locals. Granny grew up with Irish and retained phrases and expressions from that time that in later life set her apart from her neighbours. She had the kind of class that has nothing to do with learning and affectation and everything to do with having a sense of who you are and what you are worth, regardless of wealth or fine clothes.

The poet Yeats was one of those Granny came across as a girl. She remembered him from his annual summer visits to what would later be known as the Yeats Country but to her was simply home. 'He had manners on him,' she recalled in her lilting west of Ireland brogue. 'If he passed a lady in the street, he would tip his hat.' She approved of that.

Sometime around 1905, as a 20 year old, she moved to Belfast, where she worked as a skivvy in various mansion houses overlooking the Lough. One of her early employers was painter Sir John Lavery's wife, Hazel – a famous beauty whose image, as Kathleen ni Houlihan, for years adorned Irish banknotes. Another was the owner of the Belfast *News Letter*, the world's oldest continuously published newspaper in English, founded in 1737. Yet another, this time at Cultra Manor (now the administrative headquarters of the Ulster Folk Museum), was the former diplomat and Minister Resident in Montevideo, Sir Robert Kennedy. Granny's first task each morning at the Manor was to iron the *Irish Times*, fresh off the train from Dublin, and stitch it together before presenting it to Sir Robert on a silver tray. She must have been a tweeny by then, meaning that she was not confined to the basement and ground-floor areas but able to mount the stairs. Upward mobility – that was the secret. All in the blood, of course. As Granny herself would have put it, we were no goat's toe.

Granda, whom she met during the First World War when he was a groundsman at the Manor, was by nature itinerant. He was from Newtownards, County Down, where, according to my mother, he was 'well known' – though for what she didn't say. He must have had something – charm, I should imagine. Some while after their marriage, they moved to County Louth, south of Dundalk, where my mother's younger sister, Ina, was born, only to be driven out in 1922 when the local IRA burned down the Big House. These were bad times for Protestants in the infant Free State and it made sense to get the hell out. They retreated north of the newly established border, to Cushendall, County Antrim, which turned out to be home for the longest period in my mother's childhood. Here, within sound of the sea, she and her sisters went to school and lived, by their own account, an idyllic life, marred only by Granda's tendency to spend his wages on the horses.

On one occasion, he was sent out to do some grocery shopping. Not for the first time he had been given a tip about a 'sure thing' that day and placed most of the money on a nag instead. The horse duly lost, and with allowance for the amount of Guinness consumed in the interval, the remaining cash was just enough for a pound of sausages. Granny was not impressed. She threw him out of the house, and the sausages after him. 'Sausages!' she roared. 'I'll give you sausages.'

Happy days – so long as the sun shone.

But Granda blew it. He got himself sacked. Again! Moving to Gilnahirk, just outside Belfast, was a blow to the family's esteem from which I suspect Mum never fully recovered. Granda took on his last job there, as sexton (i.e. gravedigger) in the parish church, while Granny became housekeeper to the minister, Mr Best.

In retirement, Granny habitually wore an apron and spent practically all of her time making soda bread, potato bread, scones and apple tarts rich in butter – all baked or griddled on an anachronistic coal-fired 'range'. Even in the war years, there was apparently no shortage of food. Granda and Uncle Willy (Granny's brother, who had been gassed in the Somme and hadn't really worked since) would take the bus to Monaghan, over the Irish border, where rationing was not imposed, and return weighed down with butter, eggs and sides of ham. The three of them, including Uncle Willy, lived on a council estate in what is now the loyalist stronghold of Ardcarn supported by my aunt Ina, a civil servant who was destined never to marry and died of muscular dystrophy not long after her parents passed away.

I loved going to Granny's. Granda didn't say much, but he was always cheerful. He found politics ridiculous. Marooned in the city, he missed his beasts. When he got bored, he would take the bus to Paddy Lamb's pub, where he would wait for news of how much he had lost on the horses. Old habits died hard. Granny, for the same reason, was constantly busy. No sooner would visitors be in the door than there would be a cup of tea in front of them and a plateful of scones.

'Walter, darlin',' she would say. 'Sure God love you and wouldn't you like somethin' to eat, just to take the edge off your hunger? What about a slice of tart with fresh cream?'

I couldn't say no. I still can't. I would sit in the front room, reading the *Sunday Post*, stuffing myself with bread and cakes while Granny told me stories about growing up in Beltra at the foot of Slieve Gamph, carrying home turf for the fire and helping her father with the harvest. She even gave me a florin to take home with me when I left. Sometimes, if I was lucky, it would be a half-crown.

When I was 12, we paid a family visit to Beltra. Our cousins, the Blacks, still lived at the bottom of the lane, just off the main road, but what remained of Granny's childhood home was further up, marked only by what was left of its foundations. The scent of turf and wildflowers filled the air. The bare peaks of the Ox Mountains rose above our heads. Across Ballysodare Bay, on the summit of the hill of Knocknarea, a massive cairn, said to be the burial place of the Gaelic chieftain Queen Maeve, dominated the horizon. Huge waves, big enough for surfers, raced towards the white strands that fringed the bay. Below us, on the other side of the road from Sligo to Ballina, lay the parish church, now all but abandoned, in which my ancestors had worshipped for centuries. It is the region deemed by Yeats as the Land of Heart's Desire, and if I ever felt I belonged anywhere, I felt I belonged there. I took one of the hearthstones and brought it back to Granny. It made her cry. She hadn't been 'home' in 60 years.

The visit also brought tears to my father's eyes. My cousin dug up a jar of poteen and offered him a taste. It went down as smooth as a glass of acid. My mother was horrified. Decades later, she still smiled at the thought of it.

Looking back, I am surprised by how often we went as a family to the Republic. Dad, as I have said, was a convinced unionist, brought up to believe in the strength and integrity of the 'Orange' position. He had seen a lot. On 22 August 1920, when he was eight, he witnessed the assassination in Lisburn of Detective Inspector Oswald Swanzy of the Royal Irish Constabulary (RIC). Swanzy had been identified by Michael Collins, the IRA chief-of-staff, as

the leader of the gang that had murdered Tomás MacCurtain, the
Lord Mayor of Cork, a hero of the republican cause. Following
MacCurtain's death, Swanzy, a Monaghan man, moved north, but
Collins' agents tracked him down and late on a Sunday morning, as
he left Lisburn Cathedral after morning service, he was shot twice
in the chest and died in an instant where he fell. The IRA squad
responsible kept firing as they ran from the scene, sending
onlookers diving for cover. They made their way to the local
technical college, where, however improbably, a taxi was waiting for
them, its meter no doubt running, and made good their escape to
Belfast.

It was a pivotal moment in my father's young life. He had seen
Swanzy slump to his knees in the Market Square close to his father's
pub and remembered how, in the tumult that followed, Catholic
businesses were burned out and suspected nationalists hunted down
by the mob. I wonder what his father thought of the slaughter. I
would guess he saw it as God's good justice. A total of 22 people
died. The Troubles that resumed 50 years on were to Dad a reprise
on a larger scale of those terrible events. He hated the violence, but
he hated attacks on the police even more. To him, the Royal Ulster
Constabulary, the successor to the RIC, was all that stood between
decency and madness.

You might think he would have turned his back on the Republic
after what had happened, yet when he and my mother were
married in June 1944 – just 48 hours before D-Day – it was to
Dublin's Shelbourne Hotel, looking out over St Stephen's Green,
that they went on honeymoon. In later years, the Shelbourne
transformed itself into a magnificent five-star establishment,
boasting one of the finest restaurants in Ireland. Back then, it was
best known as the location in which Collins and his nationalist
cohorts drafted the first constitution of what became the Free State.
Not far away was the German Embassy to which Prime Minister
de Valera later sent condolences after the death of Hitler.

Ireland! Neither of my parents could quite make up their mind about the place. They happily proclaimed their Britishness and loyalty to the Crown. Members of both families appended their names to the Ulster Covenant of 1912, pledging themselves to use 'all means which may be found necessary to defeat the present conspiracy to set up a Home Rule Parliament in Ireland'. My mother may even have believed in the Divine Right of Kings. On the other hand, apart from a brief two-day visit by my father to Twinings of London, neither of my parents set foot in England until I was well into my teens. They thought of it as 'foreign' and quite possibly degenerate – certainly not somewhere they would ever have considered living. Conversely, they always spoke fondly of times they spent south of the border. Trips to Donegal and Dundalk, even Connemara, were almost routine, involving a lot of staring at mountains shrouded in mist and the accumulation over the years of various small objects, such as a miniature Celtic cross in a granite slab and a music box in the form of a thatched cottage that played 'An Irish Lullaby'. To my parents, the Republic was their natural hinterland. Dublin was not so much the capital of Ireland as 'second city of the Empire'.

When I was seven, we spent a week at a Butlin's holiday camp in Mosney, County Meath. Dad said we'd love it. Everything was laid on, including, apparently, Dave Allen as one of the 'turns'. There were magic shows and puppet shows and singing and dancing 14 hours a day, and once you were inside the perimeter fence you didn't have to spend money on anything, not even food.

I hated it. Each morning, we were wakened by loudspeakers outside our cabin window and summoned to breakfast like soldiers. I wanted to keep on sleeping, but as soon as he heard 'Good morning, campers!' ring out, Dad shot out of bed. There were two servings at breakfast, early and very early, and if you missed out you went hungry until lunch. I couldn't see the point of being there. It was like the Boys' Brigade, only worse. Hundreds of us queued up, yawning, in a vast hangar-like structure, then sat down to eat at a table with our number on it. Strict rations of bacon and eggs, with precise allocations of toast and butter, were consumed in a given space of time to the accompaniment of the Andrews Sisters or Mantovani and his orchestra. And then the true torture began: the entertainment. The week, during which we survived innumerable talent contests and the omnipresent bonhomie of the Redcoats, reached its low point for me when I fell, fully clothed, into a swimming pool. I was wearing sandals with little tear-shaped holes in the toe. I remember thrashing my arms and legs around and seeing one of my sandals come loose. As the water, sharp with chlorine, entered my mouth and nostrils, I was hysterical with fear. It wasn't a case of my whole life flashing before my eyes – that wouldn't have taken more than a few seconds anyway – it was more that time for me appeared to have slowed down, while for everyone else it speeded up. In the event, a lifeguard rescued me after less than 30 seconds and it is probable that I was never in any real danger. But I was determined I wouldn't go through that experience again: I have been nervous of the water ever since and have never even learned to float properly let alone swim.

Back in Belfast, life continued uneventfully, centring on school, friends and family. Aunts and great aunts were especially plentiful; like Bertie Wooster, I seemed to be surrounded by powerful women. Great Aunt Sissy, one of Granda's sisters, was the one of her generation, other than Granny, that I knew best. She had found a job in the ropeworks – the world's biggest – back in the 1920s and held on to it until she retired more than 40 years later, unmarried, with only her cat for company. In her fairly extreme old age, with the Troubles in full swing, she began to go ga-ga. My mother and Aunt Nancy tried to help but short of placing her in a home – to which she was vehemently opposed – there was little to be done. What followed was entirely indicative of the times. Tradesmen and local youths, 'loyalists' to a man, took advantage of my great aunt's senility and made off on a regular basis with her good china and bits and pieces of furniture. By the time it was agreed that she had to be taken away to a charitable institute, where she later died hardly knowing her own name, her once crowded home had been stripped bare. This, I think, was what was meant by a sense of community.

Then there was Great Aunt Fanny and her husband, Uncle Willy Pogue. They lived in a tiny terraced home about half a mile from us and always had a fire burning in the hearth and a tin of toffees on the table. Uncle Willy Pogue (so-called to distinguish him from my other Uncle Willy) always wore a vest and a shirt without collars, and smoked what seemed like hundreds of cigarettes a day. My dad said he had a chest like a bag of nutty slack.

Aunt Ina was a tragic case. She had been good-looking and fun-loving when young, and her happiest times by far were spent in the Orkneys during the war when, as one of those girls who moved pieces around the RAF's operations boards, like a croupier in a casino, she was apparently a heartbreaker, out dancing every night with her crimson lipstick and home perm. For her, as for many others, the defeat of Germany marked the end of the good times. She came home to Belfast, found government work at Stormont and looked on, puzzled, as the world sped off in mysterious directions.

Ina would sit in the front room at Granny's of a Sunday night, exchanging platitudes with her gormless long-standing boyfriend, an eejit who couldn't summon up the courage to propose and in the end just stopped calling. As late middle age overtook her, she eventually gave up the struggle to regain her own life. She told my sister one night that she was still a virgin and, more bizarrely, that she believed children were born out of a woman's navel – presumably after it was unscrewed, like the lid of a jam jar. She would sit in her favourite chair at the end of the week with the wireless on, listening to *Friday Night is Music Night* with the Mike Sammes Singers. I didn't understand it at the time; to me, a ten year old, it seemed so boring. But the music on the radio was 'her' music: the music of the war, when she had been happy and in demand – before she threw it all away. I am convinced that when she finally died, lost in the past, surrounded by a society in torment, weighing no more than six stone, it was actually a blessed release.

'Gran' Ellis, my father's mother, was from another world. Gran – never Grandma or Granny ('none of that rubbish') – had a moustache. She wore her white hair in a hairnet and I never saw her dressed in anything but widow's weeds. I think she felt a mild disdain for us all rather than affection. She remembered better times. She recalled what it was like to have servants do her bidding. Her grandchildren were 'received' by her and if they pleased her, she offered them sixpence. But there was no love in her. Even the fact that my father had paid for the house in which she was living made no apparent impact on her. It was no more than she expected. As far as she was concerned, everything since that far-off day when she had climbed up on the jaunting car to come to Belfast had been a comedown for which my father was, at least in part, responsible. She was that kind of woman.

Originally, Dad had five sisters, but two had died: one, who may have been his twin, shortly after she was born; and the second when she was, I think, 19. Such attrition was not considered unusual in those days. It was one reason – apart from the lack of effective contraception – why women right up until the 1950s chose to have large families.

Of Dad's surviving sisters, Aunt Wilma was the most severe. With her blue-rinse hair and horn-rimmed spectacles, she looked like Dame Edna Everage – but with a more caustic tongue. Her excuse for her harsh outlook was that she had a school to run and when she got home of an evening all she had to look forward to was Gran sitting in her chair in the corner next to the budgie in its cage. It must have seemed to her a cruel and unnatural punishment. Late in life after her mother's death, Aunt Wilma finally married a retired shopkeeper with a penchant for loud waistcoats and began swanking around, going on expensive holidays to Australia and Canada. We hardly saw her after that. In her will she left everything, including the house Dad had paid for, to her step-daughter, who lived in England.

What was truly surprising was the affable demeanour in adversity of Aunt Irene, the oldest sister, whose life was one long catalogue of tragedy. Aunt Irene and Uncle Tommy lived in a bungalow, surrounded by chickens, in Carnalea, about ten miles east of Belfast. They worked hard and were pillars of their local community. Uncle Tommy was a carpenter and once carved a wooden eagle with outstretched wings to hold the big church Bible. Aunt Irene visited the sick and gave us all eggs. But they got no thanks. Their daughter Myrtle and son Tom died of diabetes as teenagers. (They were practically blind towards the end and I remember watching, fascinated, as they felt around for a vein before injecting their arms with insulin.) Bonded to each other, they knew their fate and seemed reconciled to it. Both died choking on food.

But misfortune didn't end there for Aunt Irene. One of her other sons became an alcoholic; another was an inveterate gambler. Both ran away to England to escape their creditors and never came back. So she lost them, too. The surviving daughters emigrated to Canada when still in their teens, raising their families 3,000 miles from home. No wonder Uncle Tommy, who was forever kind and always went out of his way to make me feel at home during visits to Carnalea, used to observe wryly, 'You know my trouble, son? Sure everything in my favour's against me.'

Aunt Sadie, Dad's youngest sister, was my favourite on his side of the family. She ran a small grocer's shop on the Cregagh Road, just around the corner from where Cal McCrystal grew up. Her husband, Cuddy, had left her years before, stealing her savings on the way out of the door and leaving her to bring up their daughters, Pearl and Iris, on her own. I don't remember Cuddy at all, but my sister tells of how my father, who at the time drove a three-ton van fitted out as a mobile shop, once gave him a tow after his car broke down some miles from home. He attached a rope to the rear of the van and threw the other end to Cuddy. Then, climbing back into his cab and starting the engine, he gradually took up the load and set off. Throughout the journey, with Elaine in the seat next to him, he deployed exaggerated hand gestures through the open driver's-side window, shouting out instructions about upcoming bends in the road or approaching traffic. It was only when they reached Aunt Sadie's that he realised Cuddy hadn't joined him on the journey but was still back at the starting point. He had fitted the rope badly and as the van drew away it came adrift. My father's view of this phantom manoeuvre went sadly unrecorded. He never spoke of it.

Aunt Sadie worked hard and did her best over a long life to be self-sufficient. But she didn't drive and in the new age of the supermarket, which was then just beginning, the only way she could get deliveries of goods to her tiny shop was to pay wholesalers the full price: a ruinous practice. Dad did what he could to help. Twice a week, he bought groceries in bulk for her from a cash-and-carry depot on the far side of the city and unloaded them into the back store of her shop from his van on the way home from work. Without him, she couldn't have turned a profit – a fact she never denied and for which she was always grateful.

By now we were city folk, cut off from our rural past. But out in Ballinderry, close to Lough Neagh, relations of ours worked land that had once been owned by our branch of the family. The farm had changed hands at auction a generation before, following Grandad's drink-and-gambling crisis. Our cousins, in the Irish fashion, had persuaded other potential bidders to stay away, thus depressing the price. To compound the injury, there was talk that the money was never paid. I don't know the truth of any of this, but it is likely Grandad would have been too far gone to sue.

I liked my cousins. When we visited, there would be ham and boiled eggs and soda bread, and Daddy would play the pipes and the mandolin while the crickets sang in the hearth. I liked the smell of the cows in the byre. And the pigs were funny but frightening. Once, I climbed up on the tractor and inadvertently released the handbrake, so that it rolled backwards into a wall, causing some minor damage. No one, except for my father, seemed to mind.

Further north, my long-widowed Auntie 'Pa' (we never knew her real name) held sway. The undisputed matriarch of the Ellis family, she was a woman of substance. She owned a large house filled with dark furnishings and gloomy paintings that looked out over the boglands of Broughshane inland from the Glens of Antrim. The belief was that she had a fortune in the bank – and she may well have done; in her younger days there had been servants as well as farmhands. But as the years passed, Pa turned into Ulster's Miss Havisham. She took to living permanently in her kitchen, where she ate only porridge from a large black pot that bubbled on the range, and complained bitterly about the waste of her life and the selfishness of her ungrateful relations.

As it turned out, we had much to be ungrateful about. When she eventually died, aged 90, the money and the house went not to relatives clustered about her coffin, but to her doctor, who had pandered to her hypochondria for years. All those visits, my father reflected bitterly, and we didn't get a penny!

But, of course, family is only part of the story of a boy's life. There is much else to be misunderstood and forgotten. My best friend when I was young was called Howard. He lived at the bottom of the street, just where Holland Crescent gave way to Kirkliston Drive, and was a year younger than me. His father, a foreman at the

Harland & Wolff shipyard, wore a bowler hat, drove a black Ford Popular and hardly ever smiled. In his cellar, he had two huge lathes that once belonged to the shipyard – but didn't appear to any longer. He never used them but kept pictures on the walls next to them of girls in swimming costumes, with bright ruby lips and huge breasts. Perhaps *they* made him smile.

Howard's mother wore big frocks with floral prints on them. She had brown hair and glasses. Before she had got married, she had been a hospital matron, and in the afternoons she listened to *Mrs Dale's Diary* on the wireless, a saga about a doctor and his family. She pulled the war blinds down while her 'wee story' was on, so she could concentrate, and no one dared enter the room and disturb her.

At five o'clock it was our turn. Howard's parents had the first TV of anybody I knew. Their set, encased in dark heavy wood, was made by the Pye Company and had a tiny 12-inch screen. You would turn it on and wait for up to a minute while it warmed up. We watched BBC children's television. I used to know the programme schedule by heart; indeed, it hardly changed over the years: *Andy Pandy* was on Tuesdays, *Rag, Tag and Bobtail* on Thursdays and *The Woodentops* on Fridays. *Tales of the Riverbank*, with Johnny Morris, fitted in somewhere, as well as *Larry The Lamb* ('And how are you today, Larry, my lamb?' – '*Baaaaa!* Very well, thank you, Mr Mayor.'). Eamonn Andrews, later to make his name as a grown-up talk-show host, presided over the children's variety show *Crackerjack*, so weak it could have been knocked over by a rolled up copy of *Creationism Today*. I loved it.

But there were also Westerns (*The Cisco Kid*, *The Range Rider*, *Hopalong Cassidy*); school stories (most famously Billy Bunter, 'the fat owl of the Remove'); and children's 'classic' serials (*Oliver Twist*, *David Copperfield*, *The Count of Monte Cristo*). All in black and white, of course, and broadcast on 405 lines, which meant it was like looking at a photograph through cling film.

Actually, contrary to my claim about the Queen of Tonga (you see what I mean about accuracy), my earliest 'royal' experience was in 1953 when the Coronation of the new Queen Elizabeth was aired on TV. I was five and we watched the four-hour-long broadcast in the church hall in Gilnahirk. The tiny receiver was placed on the edge of the stage, I remember, and at least 200 people sat on hard chairs throughout the performance, eating Spam and tomato sandwiches and waving tiny Union flags.

In 1957, when Ulster Television, the local version of Independent Television (ITV), arrived to give the BBC a run for its money, my father finally bought a set. It was made by the Pilot Company. The channel switch had 13 available options, which I would click through, hoping against hope to discover something new and exotic. But until the arrival of BBC 2 some years later, the choice was restricted to channels 1 and 2. UTV's first blockbuster programme was *Robin Hood*, starring Richard Green, shown in chunks between adverts for Daz and Omo and Bord na Móna peat briquettes. I was very excited. *Robin Hood, Robin Hood, riding through the glen* – it would become one of my favourite songs. As ill luck would have it, Robin's debut clashed with *The Archers* on the radio, which that night featured the death, in a stable fire, of Grace Archer, first wife of apprentice patriarch Phil. My father insisted on listening to the wireless, horrified by the immolation of poor Grace, while I stared in frustration at the muted screen of our Pilot.

Howard hated to get his hands dirty. He wore ties even when he didn't have to and avoided rough games and fights in case he got hurt. But there was something – an underlying decency – about him to which I responded, and we were best friends for seven years. Maybe it was the fact that neither of us played football – though we weren't the only ones. In fact, when you think of it, there were probably enough 'slackers' to make up a reserve team. At one point, he and I developed a real interest in astronomy. We made models of the planets (Saturn was a tennis ball with a plasticine ring) and put on slide shows at a penny a go, in which we projected View-Master pictures of star clusters and the like onto the walls of Howard's cellar, with learned commentary by me. Down the road, at the bottom end of Kirkliston Gardens, lived Mr McElderry, a retired civil servant who had a four-and-a-half-inch refractor telescope with which we would greedily survey the night sky. Mr Mac lent us books on astronomy and once gave us photographs of the moon he had taken during a total eclipse. Years later, it turned out that these were ordinary pictures of the full moon with the middle blacked out by an old penny, creating an apparent corona. But we were believers. 'Look!' I remember saying to Howard one overcast night. 'There go the Magellanic clouds.'

Howard's brother was two years younger and an eccentric by anyone's standards. He was clever, we were told, but the truth is he lived in a world of his own. He rarely joined in our games, preferring to look on with disdain, occasionally correcting any assertions we made by reference to something he had read. He was particularly noted for stuffing his face with his lunch and then holding it all in his cheeks like a squirrel. In fairness, he never did anyone any harm.

Next door lived Trevor Lloyd – my age, or maybe a year older – who played with us when he felt like it but a lot of the time lived a quite separate life that we knew nothing about. Mr Lloyd worked for Denny's Sausages; Mrs Lloyd was very small. My sister liked Trevor's brother Charlie, but I don't think they ever went out.

Right on the corner, in the last house on Holland Crescent, lived the Bothwells, whose garden was vast, extending over at least an acre of ground. Gordon Bothwell was small and wiry; his sister, Sharon, would show you her knickers for a penny. Whenever we got bored with the street or the restrictions of Howard's back garden, we would go to Gordy's and light a bonfire, baking potatoes on the ends of sticks, sometimes throwing in a penny banger or maybe even the body of some small animal just to observe the effects.

Some time later, when we were about ten, members of our gang would lie flat on the tracks of the doomed County Down Railway and let the trains thunder over us. They were hulking Irish gauge trains and high off the ground. Even so, it was terrifying. Gordy was the most fearless at this activity; he would do it at the drop of a hat. Once was enough for me. I think I shat myself.

The past is not a file index. Establishing connections is the trick. First time around, you were already wasting time (the essential condition of Man). If you can't make sense of it all later, then you're wasting time twice over. You have to concentrate to restore what went before in anything like its true form, with the proper sequencing, and even then truth can easily give way to fiction or a convenient rearrangement of the facts. Memory rots like a corpse: the flesh corrupts and the worms come through.

The past was once, of course, the present. Before that, it was the future. When I was young, I thought my friends and I would go through the whole of life together. So in 1960, when my dad told me we were moving house, I broke down in tears. Three months later, I had forgotten all about the old crowd. I could barely remember their names. This would be a recurring theme in my life.

Yes, but were you a happy child? That's the question people like to ask, as if all else that is meaningful must flow from the reply. The fact of the matter is, I don't know. It was a long time ago. I can only say that things probably tended to go downhill the older I became. I became annoyed, even indignant, that I couldn't play football and appeared, as my father put it, to have two left feet. Nothing at primary school is so isolating. But in between times – which was most of the time – I was fine. I wished that life was more exciting, more interesting . . . more *entertaining*. And I frequently preferred my own company, or that of a good book, to that of my friends and family. But happy or unhappy? How do you judge these things? What factors ought I to consider?

Was my father a brute? No, he wasn't. He had led a hard life and was often impatient of his children's idleness. He would shout at my mother and me and, sometimes, in a rage with my sister and me he would 'tan our hides'. But if there had been a competition for such behaviour among the men of the neighbourhood, he wouldn't even have made the finals. Was Mum aloof from her children? Possibly. At times, certainly. Photographs of her hinting at a truant mind are not, I think, wide of the mark. She lived within a marriage in which her husband was the unquestioned and unimpeachable authority. And I think she was nervous at times, puzzled at others. But she was always kind and considerate and never did any less than her best for Elaine and me. Notwithstanding the Copelands incident, I think if anyone had attacked us, she would have been like a vixen defending her cubs. She liked routine and knew its value. At night before I went to bed, she made me a cup of tea and slices of toasted Veda with marmalade, and I always had clean pyjamas. I know she cared, and I was grateful for it.

What about my friends, then? Were they too undemanding? Too 'ordinary'? Too 'normal'? Oh, come on! They weren't Yeats and Wilde. They weren't Crick and Watson. But they were perfectly nice. We played together without rancour.

In his terrifying 'Prayer Before Birth', Louis MacNeice, born and raised in Carrickfergus, once thought of as the third member of a triumvirate that also included Auden and Spender, took adult fears and gave them precognitive expression.

> *I am not yet born; rehearse me*
> *In the parts I must play and the cues I must take when*
> *old men lecture me, bureaucrats hector me, mountains*
> *frown at me, lovers laugh at me, the white*
> *waves call me to folly and the desert calls*
> *me to doom and the beggar refuses*
> *my gift and my children curse me.*

I was shocked when I first read that poem. But it was the shock of the new, not the shock of the familiar, which is so much more disturbing. MacNeice's amniotic angst was not for me. If it had really been like that, I would have gone mad. Uncle Tommy used to say, 'There's no strangers here, just enemies you haven't met yet.'

Yet surely, you must think, there is something missing here. Mine was an Ulster childhood, and I've hardly even mentioned the F-word: Fenians. But then, why would I? Hardly any Catholics lived in our neighbourhood, which meant there was no tension or conflict. Just around the corner from us, it is true, next to Simpson's sweetie shop, was St Joseph's RC School and next to it St Colmcille's Parish Church, with its unfinished West Front. There must have been 600 pupils at St Joseph's and each Sunday morning the car park of St Colmcille's was filled with cars. Yet during the ten years that I lived in Holland Crescent, I never once entered either establishment. Like a vampire that hadn't been invited in, I couldn't cross the threshold. Nor did I know a single Catholic. Where they came from, where they lived, what they felt about their situation, remained unknown to me throughout my childhood.

But there were things I *did* know. I knew myth. Each 11 July, on the eve of the annual commemoration of the Battle of the Boyne (the defeat by William of Orange of the Catholic King James in 1690), a huge bonfire was erected in the street outside St Joseph's on top of which would be placed an effigy of the Pope. There we would noisily proclaim our loyalty to Britain and our detestation of Rome and all it stood for (whatever that was). I quite enjoyed this; it was a spectacle, after all. It was history.

Next day, on the 'Twelfth', our Billy Boys would join others from all over Ulster to celebrate our people's ancient, fly-blown triumph. My father would take me to the Lisburn Road on the other side of town to watch the bands and 'Brethren' of the Orange Order as they headed to the Balmoral Showgrounds, where speeches rubbished our Catholic fellow citizens and proclaimed the right of

Protestants to eternal dominance in conformity with God's laws. The Orangemen wore bowler hats and white gloves and carried Bibles. A few of their banners were in Irish, which surprised me, but most showed Protestants being martyred or besieged, or else Catholics ignominiously fleeing the scene of battle. One, under the rubric 'The Secret of England's Greatness', showed a group of Indians and Africans prostrated at the feet of Queen Victoria – later characterised to me by a friend as 'the wog on bended knee'. The faithful would pray and sing hymns and cheer each intemperate outburst of their leaders. Then they would go home and get drunk. All a bit of fun, really.

'Sure where's the harm, eh?'

My childhood passed slowly – or so it seemed at the time. Every day lasted a week, and I resented this. I was impatient to grow up, little realising the agonies of adolescence that had first to be endured, like purgatory.

I didn't start school until I was six. This was because I was born on 7 September 1948, and 5 September was the cut-off point for each year's registration. My parents could, I dare say, have argued the point, but they didn't. As a result, instead of being the youngest child in the class at Strandtown Primary, I was the oldest. Was this a good thing or a bad thing? I have no idea. All I know is that in my first week in class I was caned for not being able to print my name. 'Any six year old should be able to write his name,' Mr Martin, the headmaster, said. He was tall, with thinning hair and an unpleasant moustache. He wore sleeveless jumpers. He had come to our junior infants classroom to introduce himself and started as he meant to go on. I remember as if I were writing my autobiography how the thin bamboo cane stung my palm and the welt it left behind.

My sister tells me that my mother accompanied me to the school gate each morning in the early weeks and cried as I was forced to go on alone. If I were a film-maker, this would be an easy scene:

the tears trickling down my mother's face in close-up; my tiny hand stretching backwards towards hers; then the noise of the other children and the schoolyard bell sounding. Cut to me in my classroom, bent over my Janet and John reader, watching out for Mr Martin on the prowl.

Mr Martin's secretary was called Miss French. She was trim and prim. She wore tweeds and kept her hair in a bun. When you were sent to the headmaster to be caned, Miss French would direct you to a hard chair next to the wall where you waited for the sound of the heavy footsteps on the chequer-board tiles outside. Miss French would carry on typing. I suspect she typed through the punishment as well – which always took place right in front of her – drowning out the swish of the cane and the resulting howl with a deft transcription of her boss's latest communication to the Ministry.

Opposite the headmaster's office was the medical room. It smelled of disinfectant. Several times a year, we lined up outside the medical room to have our hair checked for nits and head lice. The nurse would run a metal comb through our hair and peer at our scalps before dipping her comb into a jar of Dettol and calling the next person forward. I don't think I ever had nits, but some of the other children did. They were given notes for their parents and a prescription to take to the chemist's: it was a mark of shame.

I made lasting friends at school. I've never seen them since. There was John Brown, strong and capable, with his shock of red hair, who would have made an excellent Army officer – and probably did. There was Fergus Patton, about whom I remember nothing except his name and the fact that he wore a grey jacket and matching grey shorts; Sam Jordan, big and beefy; and Billy Kelly, small and dark, with hooded eyes constantly on the lookout for trouble. There were girls, too: Madge Bryce, who used to wet herself, causing hoots of laughter among the boys; Victoria Stockman, who reported me to the teacher when she discovered I had stolen toys from a local shop; Doreen Stitt (was that her name?), who was good at knitting and showed me how to weave a rug. I've no idea what happened to them – and I don't want to know. They are frozen forever in my mind as they were then. What they are now has no significance for me, but I hope they are alive and well.

Crucially, as I have said, I was useless at sport. At primary school, I only ever played one game of football. Mr Moffet, a young form teacher who drove a red MG, insisted one afternoon on his right to force me into a pair of boots. He refused to listen to my protest that I couldn't kick my way out of a paper bag (an odd occupation) and made me play left-back against some visiting team, from Lisnasharragh I think it was. He was outraged when all I did was stand there with my arms folded, looking despondent and staring at him. He didn't know it, but I would happily have gunned him down that day.

Yes, but what was it like? What was it *really* like being the young Walter Ellis? Tell us how you *felt*.

I'm walking up Holland Crescent in June. I have red hair and a gap between my two front teeth and my legs are thin. I'm wearing a pair of grey shorts and a pale grey shirt. I'm off to school, so there's a schoolbag on my back, worn properly not slung casually over one shoulder like the older boys. It's Monday morning, so I have a florin in my pocket to buy the tickets I need for my week's dinners. On my way, I'll call in at the Wee Shop and buy four Fruit Salads and four Black Jacks and maybe a penny chew. Or I could get one of those 2d strips of Cadbury's chocolate, the one that doesn't come in chunks but is a long, thin bar – too thin for 2d, John says.

When I get to the main road, I wait for the lollipop man to show me over. He was in the Army and the skin on his face is full of folds. Where I cross, at the corner of Holland Drive, is where Fusco's ice-cream parlour is. Mr Fusco is Italian. He goes to church in St Colmcille's right opposite. I go to the parlour with my dad in the summer and we buy two pokes, one for me and one for Elaine, and a slider for him. If I was getting a poke today, I'd have raspberry juice on it. Maybe another day I'd ask him to dip it in his big bowl of hundreds and thousands and then we'd sit in one of the big wooden booths with the mirrors on the wall and the framed photographs of Italy, with ice cream running down our chins. But I'm not going to Fusco's today, I'm going to school. So I don't go right, I go straight on down the street by the Bank of Ireland towards the school gates that I see ahead of me. The gates are open and the school lies beyond.

I've got a few minutes, so I nip down the back entry behind the houses. The entry's dark, with trees hanging over from the back gardens down the two sides. At the bottom, just before the turning that brings you back out onto the road, is the house where the old ladies live who sell you apples for a ha'penny or a penny, depending on the size and the state of them. Walking through the gates, I see a couple of football games going on and girls skipping or playing hopscotch on the path. There's a lot of noise and yelling, the girls screaming and the boys shouting. I see John and I call out to him, 'Hey, John, do you want a Black Jack?'

He and I walk in together, under the brick archway into the playground, next to the toilets where Sam Jordan says he can piss right over the top wall. There's more football and a group over there are playing rounders. I'm not worried. There are no enemies, no obvious bullies, waiting for me in the playground. If someone wants to beat me up, they'd better be ready for a scrap. My friends are there – John and Fergus and Billy Kelly and Sam Jordan and the rest. They like me. I won't play football in the yard with them, but that's OK. I'll just sit and eat a bag of Tayto cheese 'n' onion until the bell goes and we head into class. Arthur Acheson doesn't play either; he doesn't even play tig. He's always clean and neat, like Howard. He sits with his arms folded.

I look at everything that's going on, taking it all in. I see the swallows up high in the air, in the shape of Vs, diving and shooting back up. I hear a door slam and a toilet flush and a window shut too hard so that the glass rattles in the frame. Then the bell rings and we all line up like regiments of soldiers, our class over there to the left, next to the huts.

One of the teachers says something, but I'm not listening. I'm looking way out past the playing fields to North Road, where I can see the traffic rushing past. There's a Territorial Army barracks down there to the right and if you keep going, after the football ground with the gaps in the fence, you get to the Strand Cinema, where I'm going to the ABC Minors on Saturday with Howard and his brother, William, and Elaine and her friends. I like it when it's Tom and Jerry. I hope when we get to class it isn't sums. I wish we didn't have to keep on doing sums. I don't like sums. I'd rather have more history and geography. What are the main rivers of Ireland? The Shannon, the Liffey, the Foyle, the Blackwater, the Nore, the Suir, the Bann and the Lagan. And the Boyne, where King Billy, of glorious, pious and immortal memory, crossed over the water on his horse to beat King James and win us all our freedom. I turn my head back to the front, but the sun is shining into my eyes and it makes me squint. There's an apple in my schoolbag and four Fruit Salads in my pocket and two Black Jacks. The teacher is still talking. She is wearing bright red lipstick and her hair up in a bun. Mrs Ferris standing there, lips pursed. And Miss Simpson behind her, looking fierce, her eyes half-shut, no more than slits. Miss Simpson was our class teacher last year. I don't like her. Mummy says she's an Old Maid. She used the cane on me – Mrs Ferris just hits me with a ruler.

Miss Simpson says it's time for us all to march into school. Mr Moffet starts up 'Colonel Bogey' on the big wooden gramophone that is brought out each morning on a trolley. A prefect clicks the clapper against the inside of a handbell to mark time and we wheel right or left, our arms swinging, bustling into school to face the morning.

An ordinary day; nothing special. I don't look forward to it because I've got other things on my mind than schoolwork. I'm thinking about space and going to the stars. I'm wondering if I remembered my recorder. It was in its box in the hall. Mum covered the box in red Fablon. She said not to forget it. I look over and see Madge Bryce. I hope she doesn't wet herself again. But I'm not afraid. Not anxious at all. I just want it to be over.

I wanted it all to be over.

When I was ten, we went on a school trip to La Panne in Belgium. I had never been out of Ireland before and didn't know what to expect. We boarded the overnight ferry from Belfast to Heysham, Lancashire, in good spirits. On the train that took us to London, where we made our connection for Dover, I remained optimistic. It was the next day, when we settled into our hotel rooms overlooking the grey misery of the English Channel, that, without warning, I fell into a depression too deeply felt to be mere homesickness. I sent my mother and father a cringe-worthy postcard telling them how unbelievably unhappy I was, which fortunately didn't arrive until we were ready to begin the return journey. I felt as if an unnamed dread that had been stalking me for months had suddenly made contact. What was odd about it was that no one, neither teachers nor fellow pupils, did me any harm during the trip. We played on the beach; we rode huge tricycles along the seafront; we visited medieval Bruges. I have no explanation to offer for the despair that overwhelmed me. Years later, when I worked for the *Irish Times* in Brussels, I drove down to La Panne to work out in my mind what had gone wrong. I even checked into the same hotel, the Grand Hotel du Sablon. But nothing came to me. The town and the hotel seemed entirely benign. Whatever dark connection there was between the me of that time and the new 'me' that had since emerged was effectively concealed. It remains so to this day.

My last year at Strandtown Primary sustained this mood of gathering melancholy. I had always felt myself popular among my peers and rarely had difficulty making friends. I could also, if pressed, put up a decent show against bullies. Now, with the end looming, I became unaccountably uncertain about myself. It was as if everybody else had worked out where they were going and what they would be doing, and I was being left behind to brood. At one point, like I say, I took to stealing toys and other small objects from a local shop and giving them away to my friends. Why I did this, I don't know. Perhaps I wanted to buy their respect; perhaps I enjoyed the thrill of it. I turned out, at any rate, to be an accomplished thief. No one suspected a thing. When I was eventually found out – exposed to our class teacher by Victoria Stockman – I was plunged into grief and rage. I had to apologise to the shop and undertake to behave better in future. The feeling of criminality that enveloped me at this time did not disappear for many months.

In Ulster, then and now, the biggest test of any young person's life was the 'Qualy' – the qualifying examination (known in England as the 11-plus) that determined whether or not you went to grammar school. I failed. My problem was that, though I could write up a storm, I couldn't do sums. Infuriatingly, I *almost* passed. If I had only managed one more right answer in the long-division section of the maths paper, my life could have taken a completely different course.

But I didn't.

I ended up at Orangefield School – or, as it was billed in its prospectus, Orangefield Boys Secondary Intermediate School. The two-storey, red-brick complex squatted in a shallow valley between a park and a housing estate, surrounded by football pitches. Up the hill, set amid private houses, was Grosvenor High, the local grammar school, where those who had passed the Qualy went.

Oh, was I bitter! Grosvenor boys and girls dressed smartly. They learned French and Russian and even got to play grown-up instruments in an orchestra. Many went on to Queen's University;

a few even to Oxford and Cambridge. Orangefield boys, by contrast, left school at 15 without serious qualifications to work in semi-skilled jobs in failing factories or, if so inclined, to throw ball-bearings at Catholics in the shipyard. None, prior to my year, had ever made it into higher education.

It could have been worse. And in the end, the problems that arose almost overwhelmed me. But the early months were not without hope. The headmaster, John Malone, a firm believer in giving a second chance to the rejected, placed me in the newly established 'G' (for grammar) stream, which, notionally at least, meant that I was being groomed for O levels, A levels and – who knew? – *university*. He believed in me, even if the system didn't. I made new friends and encountered several teachers who shared the head's vision – people who were destined to make a lasting impression on me. Tragically – and I think tragic is the right word – it was at this point that Ronnie Bunting entered my life.

III

The Butcher's Apron

J.R. HORNER, my first-year form teacher at Orangefield, was a clearly recognisable type. I'd never seen anything like him. Twenty-six years old, 5 ft 9 in. tall, he wore the most brightly polished shoes of his generation. He said he used 'blacking' and the back of a spoon, and I believed it. His dark hair was cut short with a severe parting. His eyes, beneath a furrowed brow, were constantly in motion. The ties he wore put me in mind, even then, of public schools and clubs in Pall Mall. There was nothing casual or accidental about Mr Horner. Everything was minutely observed, including his accent, which was not quite Ulster and not quite England but somewhere between the two – perhaps the Isle of Man. Each day, it looked as if it he had just taken delivery of his sports jacket, or blazer, from a reputable tailor, and you could have cut your finger on the crease in his flannels. Unusually – or so I thought at the time – he rode a glistening green motorcycle to school. He was very erect, like a police outrider, as he sat in the saddle and his crash helmet was of the old-fashioned kind, with a steel dome and leather sides that clipped neatly together beneath his chin. On wet days, he completed his ensemble with a long rubber coat.

Today, in a more cynical age, you might have your doubts about Mr Horner. Why did he want to spend so much of his own time with his pupils? Was he a pederast? Did he spend his weekends trussed up in leather straps, suspended from a hook in the ceiling? Was he hoping to draw us into a bizarre religious cult? None of the above. He was, quite simply, a hard-working, sophisticated and dedicated teacher, whose mission in life, however eccentric it might seem, was to drum some sense of culture, discipline and civilisation into the young heads of those who stumbled into his care. Few men, and fewer women, that I have known in my life ever did me as much good.

On our first morning, with the rain rattling the window panes, he sat on the edge of his desk, flashing his toecaps. Each of us was to introduce ourselves, Ulster-style, by way of name and religious denomination. I was a Presbyterian, as were many others. Numerically, members of the Church of Ireland came next, followed by Baptists, Methodists and Paul McClinton of the Plymouth Brethren. Ronnie Bunting claimed to be a Methodist. There were, of course, no Catholics, for this was a state foundation and the Taigs went to church schools.

Friendships are quickly formed and as quickly lost. It is hard to know what brings any group together. In our case, I was thin and freckled, maybe a wee bit reserved. My front teeth stuck out and my hair, though less rawly red than when I was at primary school, remained a vivid auburn. Alan Kirker, a fellow Presbyterian, was tall and sturdily built, with broad shoulders and thick, blond hair, offset by Michael Caine-style black-rimmed spectacles. Mervyn Watson, from the Church of Ireland parish of St Finian's, was small and wiry with black hair and coal-black eyes. He liked to think he had Latin looks, but to his pals he was always the 'Wee Man'.

And then there was Ronnie.

Ronnie was a year older than the rest of us. His father, Major Bunting, a maths teacher at Belfast Technical College, had recently returned to Northern Ireland after 20 years in the Army with the Royal Electrical and Mechanical Engineers. This meant that Ronnie had grown up in Malaysia, Germany and Cyprus, where his education, for whatever reason, never quite took hold. Though he admired Army discipline, he also resented it. According to what he told us, he hung around with 'bolshy' recruits and disappeared whenever he could into the local towns to escape supervision. By the time the family returned to Belfast, he was on the brink not only of his teenage years but also of full-blown delinquency.

Mr Horner decided to take him in hand. He also, for some reason, saw potential in Alan, Mervyn and me, and the four of us, with several others, were invited to join the school's Dramatic Society, which he ran. We agreed. I don't know why. Maybe it was to cocoon ourselves from the gritty reality of 'intermediate' education – though, in my case, it might have been something to do with avoiding sport.

I ended up that first Christmas playing the lead role of an astrologer in *The Invisible Duke*, by F. Sladen Smith. The production, for which I won an award at the 1961 Festival of Plays in Portadown, also starred Robert Freeburn, from the year above us, as the Lady Anya Alexandrovna, Alan Kirker as Count Nicholas and the burly and affable Sam Bracken as the Archduke. Robert was a brave and adoring clone of Mr Horner, who, in his determination not to compromise on his ideals, ended up respected by all who knew him. He went on to become head of drama at, of all places, Eton College – as unlike Orangefield as Baluga caviar is unlike a Scotch egg – where his dramatis personae included Prince William, second in line to the throne of England. The Wee Man, more earthy but equally true to himself, played a girl, which suited his coquettish nature. He fell for himself straight away. Ronnie was, I think, some kind of servant, a role he was to reprise with relish two years later when we attempted Molière's *The Miser*. For this, as though offering a chapter heading to some future biographer, he wore a butcher's apron and carried a cleaver.

Orangefield's Molière sequence, which also ran to *The Would-Be Gentleman* and *Tartuffe*, was a triumph of ambition over experience. Mr Horner, a gifted producer with an astonishing eye for detail, inspired colleagues in the school to assist him with his project and the result was sets of an almost professional standard and costumes so lavish that, on one occasion, during a performance of *Tartuffe*, we attracted the attention of not only the French consul but also a leading Parisian fashion house, one of whose designers was across on a rare visit to Ireland.

Rehearsals were painstaking and lasted months. We were coached in our accents (for the most part, BBC and cockney). We were given fencing lessons, employing épée and foil. We even made visits to the home of an elderly seamstress, Mrs Kennedy, to discuss our costumes. At every stage, we were brought into the creative process and the result was a series of plays of the highest possible quality.

The fact that we were a single-sex school caused obvious problems: Arthur Murdock, squinting into the houselights to compensate for his missing spectacles, would not have been Peter Hall's choice to play Orgon's daughter in *Tartuffe*; likewise Wilfred Pyper, with his Gérard Depardieu schnozzle, made an alarming lady's maid. But, as Mr Horner reminded us, classical Greek drama had been an all-male affair, and Juliet and Ophelia were originally played by teenage boys. So we were part of a honourable tradition. That, at least, is what we told ourselves.

Music was provided by Mr J.S. Mercer, known as 'Minnie', head of the two-man music department, another of those who encouraged their pupils to rise above their apparent station and seek out better lives. It was John Mercer — later to form the Belfast Operatic Society — who introduced me to classical music. Wisely, I think, he made little attempt to instruct us in the actual practice of music. (I was as adept with a recorder's finger stops as I was with a tennis ball.) Instead, he played records to us and talked afterwards about the composer and the context in which the music had been written. Even now, I cannot listen to the *Lieutenant Kijé* suite without thinking of the view outside Mr Mercer's classroom, extending across a small yard (where the Late Prefects lurked) to a path that led up to the side gate and freedom. Normally, that was the path I wished to tread, but as Prokofiev's mournful drama, based on its non-existential theme, drifted by on the departmental record player, for once I was happy to stay.

I never thought Mr Mercer noticed me (and I gave him little cause to do so), but I must have been wrong, for one afternoon, as I was about to leave for home, he gave me a handful of LPs on the old Ace of Clubs label – Rachmaninov, Tchaikovsky, Brahms, Beethoven, Holst – which he was replacing with superior products from the Deutsche Grammophon company. I took them eagerly. For years, they were the core of my classical collection.

Mr Horner, disguised as a conservative martinet, was, in fact, a closet radical. He enjoyed the *form* of conservatism all right; it was evident that he wished to look the part. But he was at heart a libertarian. At one point, out of his own wages, he bought the entire class a guide to sexuality and 'growing up', which, while they were the cause of much sniggering and a frantic search for the 'dirty bits', were widely appreciated. He took us to the cinema to see *Tom Jones!*, James Bond, *The Pink Panther* and *The Longest Day*. He read us risqué poetry ('"Her dumplings were boiling over." Boys, what do you suppose that means?'). He deciphered Shakespeare for us ('Reilly, what's a "leaping house"?' – Reilly [in a snap]: 'Leap in, leap on, leap off, leap out.' – Mr Horner: 'Very good, but let's keep that to ourselves, shall we?'). And it was with Mr Horner in 1964 that we first went to see The Beatles at the King's Hall, the screams of the girls echoing afterwards like tinnitus.

After our outings, we invariably ended up at the Chalet d'Or, a slightly down-at-heel would-be bistro next to the Linen Hall

Library, where, over prawn cocktail and beef stroganoff, we would talk about music and books and drama and the whole ghastly business of adolescent fancy.

Inevitably, the school establishment was suspicious of such a hands-on approach. Some of the senior staff, mired in their ordinariness, probably wondered at times if hands-on was not what it was all about. The tragedy of Orangefield was that it was less than the sum of its parts. Of course, the headmaster thought the opposite.

Mr Malone, a decent man and a visionary of sorts, was highly intelligent and motivated by a genuine desire to improve Ulster society. But he didn't like Mr Horner much and – whisper it softly – his vision was not exactly in William Blake's league. He was a Cambridge graduate from a wealthy farming family who opposed the 11-plus on class grounds and was an early exponent of the comprehensive system that would do so much to damage secondary education in Britain. What he didn't realise was that, with most of his attention focused on us, and the likes of us, at the school's top table, the revolution he led was no less selective than the status quo it was trying to subvert. It was as if there was a tiny grammar school inside the main school that, sport aside, just happened to mop up most of the available resources.

Malone would no doubt have countered that he was giving 'failures' like us a second chance (which he was), but for the 'no-hopers' who continued to make up the bulk of his pupils, the relentless diet of woodwork, metalwork and football – alleviated by self-help projects and occasional weekends at the school's country cottage – continued much as ever. Did the majority in the A–D streams resent the grammar stream and its peculiar privileges? I doubt it. In my experience, misery is evoked either by horror or else (more usually) by envy or disappointment. There wasn't a lot of horror in Protestant east Belfast when I was 15. Nor was there an unusual weight of envy or disappointment. Working-class boys expected to lead working-class lives, which meant getting a job in the shipyard, or the aircraft factory, or in one of the many engineering works strung around the city. Envy was what a fitter felt if someone no better than him ended up as foreman. Disappointment was the response if you were rejected for an apprenticeship and ended up as a bus conductor or road sweeper. These were not the sort who dreamed of going to the barricades.

For the nationalists, the perspective was radically different. It was raised expectations that led to the civil-rights movement at the end of the '60s, and when Catholics didn't get what they wanted out of the reform business, they weren't just disappointed, they were *livid*.

In my time at Orangefield, the old order was barely disturbed. The reality of the school's more representative life hit me like a fist on the first day. A group of us were being shown round by a prefect when the door to one of the first-floor classrooms burst open and a teacher emerged, in fighting retreat, pursued by a huge boy who could not have been more than 15. The teacher turned towards us, glaring, then, employing a nifty piece of footwork, danced forwards, catching his opponent with a sharp jab to the stomach. The pair of them then disappeared once more into the classroom and the door slammed shut behind them.

We stared, horrified.

'That was Mr Holland,' we were informed. 'He'll be teaching you French.'

In fact, Holland – known as 'Dutchy' – was a lot more than a street-fighter. He was a flamboyant, hard-living son of a bitch, a lover of literature and pretty well fluent in French. For him, teaching was performance art. He admired high literature but was prepared to sink as low as any of us if it meant scoring a point in class. If only I had managed to convince him that I was worthy of his talent, I might even have learned something worth knowing.

One of Dutchy's pals at the school was David Hammond, generally a soft-spoken, tousle-haired teacher of English and general studies, who would go on to achieve local fame as a maker of television documentaries, the best-known of which was *Dusty Bluebells*, about Belfast street songs. Hammond, a friend of the poet Seamus Heaney, was a talented man, who both sang and collected Irish ballads and would play his guitar at the drop of the floppy hat he habitually wore. But 'Davie' was not all sweetness and light verse. There was a dark side to him as well. His favoured method of punishment, concealed amid the mayhem of his classroom, was 'the block', the exact nature of which I never discovered but which raised in my head the spectre of medieval torture. To be fair, his pupils – a rowdy lot – all appeared to survive the experience. There were no known fatalities. But every time I saw him on TV singing 'I'll Tell My Ma When I Go Home, the Boys Won't Leave the Girls Alone', I heard him in my head roaring behind closed doors, 'You're goin' to the block for that, son!'

Canes were constantly swishing at Orangefield. Ernie Cave, our maths teacher, could be sweet-natured one day, venomous the next. When he drew a perfect circle on the blackboard one afternoon, he was so pleased with himself that he spent the rest of the lesson admiring his handiwork. But when the black dog overtook him, it was different. One afternoon as he was teaching some theorem or other, I was miles away. He then wiped the board and, having demanded our attention, re-drew what had just been there. He glowered at me, pleased by the prospect of what would now unfold. 'Master Ellis!' he began, 'maybe you'd like to enlighten us and tell the class where you saw this before.' He pointed to the squiggle on the board.

My mind blanked. 'I don't know, sir. I don't think I ever saw it before.'

'Ah! And friend Bunting! What about you? Where did you see it, boy?'

Ronnie looked bemused. He, too, had not been in the room. 'I dunno. Primary school?'

Less than a minute later, the welts were rising on our palms like eels.

Dear old Ernie.

More truly than university or the workplace, school is the place that finds you out. I suspect that the Army is similar. I felt threatened and exposed throughout my school life. In some subjects I was fine, even top of the class. I could write and spell, and I enjoyed books of all kinds. I could memorise dates and events and make sense of them so that, even now, I would be able to produce a cogent account of the themes of British, Irish, European and world history. Geography and biology were a breeze; art history, when it came along, was a pleasure.

But maths in those crucial early years, so tied into self-worth, evoked both fear and dread in me. Algebra, geometry and arithmetic: I might as well have been reading the runes. Algebra was a mystery, like magic. I could make no sense of it – all those xs and ys. My dictionary, which I have just consulted, tells me that a quadratic equation is 'an algebraic equation that involves the square, but no higher power, of an unknown quantity or variable'. I can't understand that now, when it doesn't matter and no one cares. Then, I might as well have been arguing the toss with Wittgenstein.

Geometry seemed, on the face of it, more straightforward. Its definition reads: 'the branch of mathematics dealing with lines, angles and shapes and their relationship with each other'. I can grasp that. Theorems, too, present no conceptual difficulty: 'mathematical statements which make certain assumptions in order to explain observed phenomena and which have been proved to be correct'. Yes, but you see it's the *proving* that's the hard part. The talk bit I could do till the cows came home – I have always been glib. But the *proving*; that is a different story. Neither Mr Cave nor his lanky sum-time successor, Mr McKeown, could do anything with me. I stared at the squiggles in the books. I struggled with the examples and tried to apply them to the test questions. But it was no use. I was a lost cause.

Forty years on, I can't help noticing that I have never once in real life been required to solve a simultaneous equation. Nor has anyone I know. My son, who is 23, is in much the same position. As lead guitarist with the rock band Battle, touring Britain and Europe to widespread popular acclaim, he has an intuitive grasp of computer-based sound engineering but has forgotten nearly everything he was taught about maths in 15 years of private schooling. It makes you wonder about the efficacy of a broad-based education, which is terrific in theory but for most people means merely going through the motions. The time it hurts, and the only time it's important (unless you have a special aptitude), is when you're in the middle of it and it's going badly. When you are 13 years old and you can't get it right and the teachers are standing over you telling you that your whole future could stand or fall by the answers you give to half-a-dozen riddles on a page, you feel like the most miserable creature on earth. Surely, there has to be a means of making young people numerate and scientifically aware in a way that assists them to understand the world they live in (and fill in their tax returns) without the pretence that we are all proto-mathematicians or scientists. We're not.

But if maths was bad, sport was worse. For me, you will not be surprised to learn, sport was the physical expression of mathematics. Lines, variables, angles: I just didn't get it. I couldn't catch or kick a ball. I had no hand–eye coordination. I saw only mayhem in a rugby scrum and artillery fire in an indirect free-kick. I couldn't score a basket in a month of Sundays. I couldn't even swim.

Rodney Usher, head of Orangefield's sports department, was the living antithesis of Mr Horner. He had no time for 'play actors'. He believed with every wholewheat fibre of his being that a school's worth was measured by its performance on the field, and he couldn't abide fainthearts. It was obvious to me (the faintest of hearts) that he despised me, and I like to think that he knew how warmly I returned his sentiment. A big, broad-shouldered man with a Desperate Dan chin, who had once nearly played rugby for Ulster, he lived his life among damp towels and sweat, muscling fat boys and skinny boys naked into the showers and turning away disgusted if they began to cry. I know that sports masters tend to get a raw deal from those pupils who do not share their enthusiasm for athlete's foot and muddy shorts, but maybe there is a reason for this. However unfairly, if I had ever held on to the gun that I used to mentally despatch Mr Moffet, 'Rodders' would have been next.

The remaining masters were a mixed bunch. There was Duncan Scarlet, who walked up and down our rows of desks firing off questions about geography and flicking us with the sleeve of his gown when we got the answers wrong; Sam Preston, a pocket-sized weightlifter with shoulders out to here and arms like legs ('Stand up, Sam,' someone once said to him – 'I am standing up,' he replied); and Mr Francis, the school librarian, who was Welsh and tried to imbue in us a love of cricket ('You are all *heathens!*'). Then there was Sam McCready, Mr Horner's gnomic successor as a teacher of drama, a scholar of Yeats, later to be Professor of Theatre at the University of Maryland; and the Sinnerton brothers, one of whom became an author, the other a scriptwriter with his own production company. They were a varied and talented bunch – no doubt about that – but the best of them tended to move on as soon as they could find something better. Of the long-term staff, the two who stand out in my memory are Jim Craig and Ken Stanley.

Mr Craig, small and bespectacled, with a cynical bearing that came into its own with the astutely observed put-down, was a painter who had recently persuaded the headmaster to let him teach history of art. This looked like a soft subject to us, and we signed up at once. Serendipitously, all of us did well. I achieved top grades at both O level and A level (for the latter, I even scored the highest mark for my year in Northern Ireland), and I still regret that I didn't follow up on the experience. None of this would have been possible without Mr Craig and his Observer books on art and architecture. He had no budget and there was no art gallery worthy of the name in Belfast at that time. Everything he achieved he did with books, an overhead projector and his own matchless enthusiasm.

Mr Stanley was a delightful man. He hardly spoke a word of French – and ensured after a year of his tutelage that we were equally fluent – but as a history teacher, he didn't miss a trick. He worked achingly hard, cyclostyling hundreds of pages each month of notes he had written out in his big loopy handwriting. Like Mr Mercer, he tried hard to be gruff, but his heart wasn't in it. The fact of the matter was that he was a kind, well-intentioned man and a born teacher, and I was glad to learn, some years after we left, that he had been appointed deputy headmaster. Sometimes, there is justice in the world.

But not often.

Carpe diem. When Mr Horner and his generation of teachers left, decline quickly set in. Today, Orangefield, having long since merged with the neighbouring girls' school, is just another east Belfast comprehensive. Even its playing fields have been depleted, sold off to developers to make a fast buck. Yet, for a while, the light of learning did indeed shine down Cameronian Drive. What the local education authority had intended should be no more than an enlightened version of Dotheboys Hall had ended up, by a mixture of accident and design, as a forcing house for young talent. The singer-composer Van Morrison left Orangefield the year I arrived. Retrospectively, he made quite an impression on the staff. Yet, with the possible exception of David Hammond (whom he remembered singing 'The Ballad of Casey Jones'), he had nothing good – indeed nothing at all – to say about his teachers. In an interview with Gerald Dawe for his book *The Rest is History*, he commented:

There was no school for people like me. I mean, we were
freaks in the full sense of the word because either we didn't
have the bread to go to the sort of school where we could
sit down and do our thing, or that type of school didn't
exist. Most of what was fed me didn't help me that much
later.

Others were more positive. The author and academic Brian
Keenan recalls his schooldays at Orangefield with pleasure and
gratitude. Keenan became something of a celebrity during the
Lebanese civil war when he spent four and a half years as a hostage
in Beirut alongside journalist John McCarthy and the Archbishop
of Canterbury's envoy Terry Waite. His autobiography, *An Evil
Cradling*, sold well and he went on to write travel books and novels
and teach literature at Trinity College, Dublin. I didn't know Brian
at school, though we were almost exact contemporaries. Schools
are like that: cross-pollination is rare. But many years later, when I
met him in Dublin, he was full of reminiscence about the old
place. His experience was different to mine; he hadn't made the
'grammar' stream. He was placed, as if by the Sorting Hat in Harry
Potter, in the 'technical' stream. But he knew most of the same
teachers and recalled several of them with great fondness. I asked
him what he remembered about us, the celebrated Horner Boys.
Disconcertingly, he hardly remembered us at all – no more than I
remembered him. He had avoided the Dramatic Society like the
plague. But he remembered Ronnie Bunting.

Oh, dear. Ronnie Bunting. How much longer can I avoid talking
about the Baddest Boy in School? For the next seven years, he
would be the Godfather and I the *consiglieri* of our two-man 'mob'.
In our first couple of years at Orangefield, I sat beside Alan Kirker,
a true friend, who turned out, somewhat alarmingly from my point
of view, to be good at sums and rugby. Mr Horner said Alan had
'O' qualities and always cast him in 'sensible' roles in our school
productions. But as the years passed, the seat next to me was more

and more occupied by Ronnie: a malign version of myself, more outrageous, less restrained, yet at the same time more cunning. If he was Caliban, he was also McCavity:

> *McCavity, McCavity, there's no one like McCavity.*
> *There never was a Cat of such deceitfulness and suavity.*
> *He always has an alibi, and one or two to spare:*
> *At whatever time the deed took place – McCavity wasn't there!*

Ronnie's monstrosity grew year by year. When we first started out, he was just a bit rowdier than the rest of us. He was good at English and from the earliest days a lover of the sound of his own voice. He liked to argue and dispute. Playing football in the playground, he was like a machine, scything through the opposition, willing the ball into the goal and, if that didn't work, bundling the goalie out of the way. I didn't like that side of him: the bully and the braggart. But the other side – the dreamer, the thinker, the fool – was attractive to me. He helped take me out of myself and introduced me into the wider school community.

There was also the fact that he was my second cousin once removed (a concept that, if you are not careful, embraces just about everyone in a small community like Northern Ireland). Ronnie's grandfather on his father's side was first cousin to my granda and had once, I was told, been lighthouse keeper at Donaghadee. His dad, the Major, was one of those who tried to help my Great Aunt Sissy when she grew old and started opening up her home to looters. On one occasion, he called my mother to say that he had met a tradesman outside her aunt's front door carrying a selection of Sissy's best china. He had ordered him to return it, which he had done with alacrity. So, there was a blood bond there as well.

But by the time we were into our teens, our relationship had begun to go seriously wrong. Ronnie had taken against the school and the system that underpinned it. He began talking about revolutionary socialism – Maoism, really – and was thrilled by the potential of the Cuban Missile Crisis to unleash a nuclear holocaust on the West. But at the same time, he wanted to pass his exams and go to university. What he needed was an instrument with which to upset the equilibrium of the school, and I was to be that instrument.

It wasn't that I wasn't willing – at least to begin with. I had my own 'issues' with the school: I was failing disastrously at maths and my French wasn't much better. To make things worse, Mr Horner announced that he was leaving once we had completed our O levels. He had won a place lecturing drama at Neville's Cross College, part of the University of Durham, and had already packed up the Dramatic Society. It was time for paranoia to do its work. Looking around me, I had the sense of a world beginning to fall apart, with me as its principal victim. When Ronnie outlined a programme of rebellion, I was all for it.

It began as farce and ended as history. We made phone calls from a local telephone box ordering up all kinds of goods and services for Dutchy Holland, who, incidentally, Ronnie had renamed Gunther Toody after an ineffective policeman, played by Joe E. Ross, in the American sitcom *Car 54, Where Are You?* Flowers, chocolates and, in one famous case, a set of outsized corsets duly arrived at the school to be delivered to a Mr Holland. Dutchy – Toody – was livid. He knew it was us, but he couldn't prove it.

Even as I made the calls, I was in two minds about what we were doing. Mr Holland wasn't so bad. He was just the wrong man in the wrong place at the wrong time. But that didn't stop me. The weaker half of me was what drove me; my better half merely took notes. Rules were only there to be broken, Ronnie told me. That was the one unbreakable rule.

Ronnie made up obscene songs for us to sing. He encouraged me, for some unexplained reason, to shatter milk bottles against walls. 'Go on there, Smokey [he called me Smokey – I never knew why, though there was a maths teacher with ginger hair whom he blessed with the same sobriquet]. Here's a couple more. We'll show the bastards they can't tell us what to do.' *We*?, I thought, seizing the bottle rather than the day. Who is *we*?

Ronnie also felt that I should be asserting myself more in the life of the school. I should square my shoulders and stand up for myself, he said. That was the only way to gain respect. I experimented with this. When a smaller boy 'cheeked' me one day in the library, I picked him up, holding him at arm's length, and warned him not to fuck with me. What I didn't realise was that my new-found aggression – beaten into me by Bunting – was the worst thing that could have happened to me. Walking towards the caretaker's room one lunchtime with an empty bottle of milk in my hand (one that I didn't intend to break), I suddenly found myself in the OK Corral. Ahead of me, filling the full width of the corridor, were several known ruffians led by Herbie Mercer, looking like a cut-down version of James Dean in *Rebel Without a Cause*. Herbie wasn't looking for a fight; he just wanted to get to the other end of the corridor. But, in school terms, he was a 'made' man and there was no way he was going to back down from a confrontation. All it took was an implied challenge. From that point, it was lights out for Smokey.

Ordinarily, unless actually struck, my preferred course of action would have been to duck into the cloakroom section to the right of the main passage and wait until Herbie and his lieutenants went by. But remembering Ronnie's injunction to live more dangerously, I stood my ground. As Herbie and I met, I glared down at him with just a hint of a sneer. My opponent was not amused. Faster than I could blink, he struck out, catching me full on the mouth with a short-arm punch. As he was wearing a large signet ring on his second finger, this proved spectacularly painful and I fell backwards, striking my head on the stone floor. I bear the scar to this day: a tiny X just above my upper lip.

Blood gushed from my wound. I was not just out of the fight, I was roadkill. Herbie was, however, a gentleman thug. This was not what he had intended and he was genuinely concerned. He extended a hand. 'You all right there, big fella?'

'I, I don't know,' I said, gulping in air. I was holding my hand to my face, and when I reached up to him I watched it run scarlet. I was both dazed and frightened. Herbie, who meant me no harm, helped me to my feet and escorted me to the medical room. After I was repaired – I should have had stitches but that was for babies – we were summoned to the headmaster's study. Mr Malone was more Dr Arnold-ish than ever. I told him that the altercation was as much my fault as Herbie's, which he appeared to have no difficulty believing. We had behaved disgracefully, he said, and in future we would have to be on our best behaviour or else face the consequences. Herbie and I looked at each other. We had been sworn enemies but from that day on were the best of friends.

I think, by then, it was already too late for me. My personality, which once went its own way, was held captive. I would rebel from time to time. On one occasion, I even gave Ronnie a good kicking. I read books and listened to music. I dreamed of what might have been. But though I wriggled and squirmed, I could not break free.

Out of school, the situation took an unexpected turn. Ronnie announced one afternoon that he and I should become football fans. It would be good for me, he said. I'd get respect. I groaned. The problem (apart from my obvious lack of interest) was that it meant following the fortunes of the Irish League, then and now the least glamorous collection of teams in European competition. Our local side was Glentoran – they played at The Oval near Harland & Wolff's – but the Glens weren't going through an especially good phase at the time, so Ronnie opted instead for Linfield, the big-time outfit from Windsor Park, whose ground was also used for Northern Ireland internationals. The Blues, as they were known, were closely modelled on Glasgow Rangers and their supporters were equally sectarian. In spite of his incipient republicanism,

Ronnie didn't seem to mind this. It brought him closer to the working class and had an authenticity he craved. Or perhaps he was getting to know the enemy. At any rate, he regarded our fortnightly expeditions across town as a kind of rough social experiment. He and I would stand in the Kop at Windsor Park every other Saturday among supporters so tightly packed that you just let go where you stood if you needed to go to the toilet, doing your best to avoid the man in front of you. Ronnie liked to lead those around him in raucous versions of familiar anthems. 'The bells of hell go ting-a-ling-a-ling for you, you Fenian bastard!' we sang; or if we were feeling more whimsical:

> *Holy Mary, I am dying,*
> *Just a word before I go.*
> *Lay the Pope upon a table,*
> *Stick a poker up his*
> *Ho-ly Mary, I am dying . . .*

And then we'd all laugh and jeer. The football was entirely peripheral to the 'experience'. But after the Blues won all seven trophies one year (the league was so small new competitions had to be devised to keep things going beyond Christmas), Ronnie decided there were no more heights to scale – or depths to probe. To my relief, he dropped Linfield and, with it, bigotry, and took up girls instead.

Being a year older, he had discovered sex earlier than the rest of us – except possibly the Wee Man, whose after-school activities were legendary. While we spent increasing amounts of time in our bedrooms whacking off, Ronnie had a girlfriend called Pat. He was besotted by her. Unfortunately for their relationship, Pat's father did not share his enthusiasm. This led to the episode known afterwards as Le Déluge. I was 15; he was 16.

★

Ronnie moved swiftly, as befitted someone bent on revenge. My progress was considerably more jerky. But then I was carrying the bucket.

'You should have brought the belt,' he said. 'What are you going to do if he turns nasty?'

'Well, I'm not going to hit him with my belt, that's for sure. We're supposed to be showing him he can't make a fool of you, not crippling the man.'

Ronnie tended to get carried away. So did some of his victims.

Halfway up Braniel Hill, the pain in my right arm and shoulder became acute. A full bucket of water was no joke, even if the top quarter of the slopping liquid was by now over my trousers so that my knees were held in an elastic grip. It was late on an August evening, and the birds were staking their claim to the trees as we proceeded up that long hill. But the tranquillity of our surroundings only served to highlight the absurdity of the enterprise. In any case, I was exhausted.

'Any chance of you carrying the bucket for a while?' I asked him. 'The way things are going, I'd be lucky to hit him with a duster, let alone a belt.'

'Fuck off!' he said. 'I've told you, I've got to be ready to take a swing at him.'

On your own head be it, I thought.

We continued our uncertain ascent of the Braniel with Ronnie darting forward and back, alternately needing to speed things up and make sure that I kept going. Not that I couldn't understand his concerns.

Pat was 16. I think it was her permanently half-closed eyes that first attracted Ronnie: she looked like she was already *in* bed, let alone heading that way. She was of average height, I suppose, slim, with black hair, and she had what were always known at school as 'thrusting' breasts. Quite what Ronnie and Pat got up to when they were alone – which was surprisingly often considering they were both living with their parents – was a mystery. Had they 'done it' or hadn't they? The consensus view was that they had, which would have been a first for any of us (except maybe Mervyn). But Ronnie never said. In fact, his whole relationship with Pat was like a junior version of what Heathcliff and Catherine Earnshaw might have got up to if they had got things together in east Belfast in 1963 instead of being kept apart in the Yorkshire moors a century before. There were lots of secret trysts after school, which we were forbidden to witness on pain of pain. Ronnie stared out of the windows a lot, and there were even dark mutterings. All a bit strange. Strong stuff.

Now, it had all come to an end. Pat's dad – a postman, I think, or a salesman of some kind – had put his foot down. He hadn't taken to Ronnie. He found him a bit dishevelled (he should have seen his underpants!) and thought he was morbidly obsessed with his daughter, and like any concerned parent had warned the young vermin off. Pat had accepted it. She was an active girl and no doubt was ready to flutter her eyelids elsewhere.

But Ronnie took a different view. He had come round to my house earlier that evening like a raging bull, talking of the need to teach her father a lesson he wouldn't forget in a hurry. And so here we were, two rough beasts slouching round to her place, him with a straw cross and me with my mother's zinc bucket and what was left of two gallons of water.

With that touch of melodrama that was to colour the rest of his short life, Ronnie had decided to fix the straw cross to the front door of the father's house and set fire to it. A loud knock at the door would announce to those inside that the curtain was going up on their tragedy. The symbolism of the cross was largely lost on me. I could only think of the Ku Klux Klan. But for Ronnie, the flaming emblem was clearly important.

The idea was that Pat's father would answer the door and gaze in dumbstruck horror at the blazing cross, then, as recognition dawned (apparently, he would see it as his just punishment for breaking up young love), he would find himself drenched from head to foot in water. *Après* Ronnie, *le déluge*. I was there as chief witness and loyal bearer. Ronnie would do the actual work himself. My one reserve function was to wade in with my belt if the going got rough.

We reached Pat's street: neat 1950s terraced housing with tiny square front lawns, no fences and trees along the roadside. Ronnie put out his arm to my already stuttering progress. 'Right, Smokey, don't forget, if he looks like he's got the drop on me, use your boot. Now, hand us the bucket.'

I was going to ask if he wouldn't reconsider. But I reconsidered. 'OK, Ronnie, just go easy.'

Clutching the bucket in one hand and his eighteen-inch straw cross in the other, Ronnie made his way stealthily to the front door. The pail, by contrast, was set down on the porch with a discernible clank. We both grimaced, but no one came. Now he delved in his jacket pocket and pulled out drawing pins and a box of matches. The cross was attached to the middle of the door and a match was struck. I watched, heart thumping, from behind some bushes. Christ! Is he mad?

The evening breeze quickly blew out the first match – Ronnie was not a smoker and lacked experience in these matters. After two or more had sputtered out, he finally got the fourth to set light to one arm of the cross. There was more smoke than fire. He applied a fifth, then a sixth match to the middle of the thing and, as a pitiful flame arose, slid back to the bucket.

'*The door!*' I hissed from the bushes. '*You forgot to knock on the door!*'

'*Shit!*' Ronnie advanced again. But he didn't knock; instead, he kicked the door roughly and drew back a second time. Safely hidden, I watched with appalled fascination.

The door opened swiftly. It was her father. What if it had been her mother?, I suddenly thought. He was not a particularly big man, but he was only in his early 40s and he looked mean.

'Who the hell is that?' he called out. 'What's goin' on here?' Then he caught sight of the cross, which was at this stage smouldering feebly, and gazed at it in understandable astonishment.

Seizing his chance, Ronnie roared out from the side of the porch where he been waiting and hurled the contents of the bucket at his enemy. But the father was no slouch. He at once backed in behind the door. Ronnie's momentum, meanwhile, was such that he failed entirely to halt his progress. The water described a high arc in the air, and as it descended, Ronnie ran into it. His hair, his face and his clothes were soaked in an instant. He bellowed with rage and surprise, and as he did so Pat's father re-emerged onto the porch, this time carrying a blackthorn walking stick. It looked like he was ready to do vicious battle. Instead, when he looked at Ronnie – sodden and red-faced, the veins bulging in his neck – he began to laugh.

Half-blinded, Ronnie lashed out at him. Before he could land a blow and, more importantly, before Pat's dad could get going with his stick, I dashed out and grabbed him round the waist. 'Come on, Ronnie, for fuck's sake. Let's get out of here. The police'll be round any minute.'

For a moment, Ronnie seemed incapable of movement. His humiliation was complete. Then his nerve returned. 'I'll fuckin' get you, you bastard!' he shouted. The father's mocking laughter followed our wet, retreating footsteps as we ran.

★

School wasn't only fun and games, of course. There was the serious stuff, too. I got through my O levels more or less intact, with top marks in English and art history. But I only just passed in French and failed abysmally in maths, with a grade nine (out of nine). The French fiasco annoyed me. I knew that somewhere inside me there was the ability to speak a foreign language, but the quality of the teaching just wasn't there . . . or maybe it was the lack of facilities, I don't know. All I knew was that, whoever was to blame, it wasn't *moi*. Not that anyone gave a stuff – even those who had done a lot better than me. Britain and Ireland would not join the Common Market for another seven years, and if anyone from Belfast ever took a holiday abroad, it was not to France they went but Spain – for the sun and the fish and chips. But I felt the loss. Perhaps I had a premonition that I would spend years of my life among French speakers and needed to be prepared. My father took no notice of my linguistic frailty, which was not a surprise. He had difficulty accepting there was a world outside Belfast, let alone Ireland or the UK. But he was disturbed that I couldn't do sums. This was a serious deficiency that would make it difficult for me to embark on the career he had chosen for me, as an accountant. He arranged for me to be given special tuition by, of all people, Ronnie's father, the Major, who taught maths for a living. This was the blood link again. I remember the dining room table *chez* Bunting, where we sat for two hours every Saturday morning. It was oval, made of dark burnished wood, with an embroidered doily in the middle. Other than the Major droning on, I remember nothing. A year later, I re-sat the paper. This time I got an eight.

Oh, dear. When I think of what might have been.

The next school year began on a hopeful note. Studying for A levels, I found myself confused by *Gulliver's Travels*, which I had previously thought of as a children's story about giants and midgets. Suddenly, it was dead serious and we were expected to analyse it to death. I didn't get it. On an impulse, I wrote to the great critic F.R. Leavis at Cambridge, asking for his help. He replied at length, putting me straight. More to the point, he impressed the hell out of Toody, who advised me to have the letter framed. I said I would. I've no idea what happened to it.

Soon after, at Toody's invitation, Seamus Heaney turned up to teach us poetry. His first collection, *Death of a Naturalist*, which started him out along the road that would eventually lead to the

Nobel Prize for Literature, had yet to be published and we were given a privileged preview of several of his poems, including 'Scaffolding', which ended:

> So if, my dear, there sometimes seem to be
> Old bridges breaking between you and me
>
> Never fear. We may let the scaffolds fall
> Confident that we have built our wall.

That made sense to me. Heaney, with his twinkly eyes and his Derry accent, was a revelation. It would be another ten years or so before he became Famous Seamus, Ireland's foremost Man of Letters, but that wasn't the point. He made it seem, just for a moment, as if a poet could be one of us. I never would have guessed that, years later, he would be guest of honour at my wedding. When he read to us another of his new poems, 'Elegy for an Unborn Child', and explained how it was that he had come to write it, I felt in at the start of something, as if the child had died but the words would live.

All the time, Ronnie was egging me on to greater and greater excess. Most of what I actually did was like something out of *The Dandy* – and touched with the same desperate madness. Typical of my elevated behaviour at the time was my afternoon excursion from one side of the school to the other, across the *outside* of a first-floor central classroom, holding on to window frames with nothing but empty air below. This foolishness caused the headmaster to remark that when he wanted to make the same journey he didn't put on climbing boots, he used the doors and passageways provided. On another occasion, after it was thought – correctly – that I had written a series of radical slogans on a classroom blackboard, I was called in to the vice-principal's office, where the VP – a man of limited sympathy, who had rowed for his university

– tore into me to the extent that we ended up exchanging blows and I had to defend myself with a chair.

As I relate this sorry tale of academic intifada, I am forced to ask what on earth was going on. Why did I not just stay away from Ronnie? And why did he not stay away from me? If only it was that simple. Events in the wider world would establish soon enough the strength of Ronnie's personality and his peculiar ability to bend others to his will. As for my own weakness, I have no explanation to offer that makes sense or allows me any dignity. I tried to break free of him several times during our long friendship. But he always drew me back. Not until I left Ireland in 1974 was I able, finally, to put him out of my life. Even then, from hell's heart, he continued to stab at me.

Mr Malone, who may have seen the darkness closing in, tried to save me from myself (and Ronnie) by persuading me to take part in the school's upcoming mock elections, which were intended as a lesson in civics for the greater student body. He wanted me, he said, to represent the unionist position, but without the slogans and shibboleths that had so soured politics in the real world. Ronnie, as he must have foreseen, promptly stood as a communist, sporting the emblem of the Connolly Society, which he had recently joined (Connolly being James Connolly, the Irish socialist leader shot by the British after the Easter Rising of 1916). Crowds came to listen to both our harangues, but though Ronnie may have won the argument, I, clutching my Union flag and ending each rally with a rendition of 'God Save the Queen', won the vote.

Malone was not amused. He couldn't see that I was fighting for my life. Drifting around the school's front lawns one afternoon, he outlined to us the challenge of what he described as a 'quarterly review of the arts', while we, like recidivists in conversation with the prison chaplain, trailed listlessly in his wake. It was only when he mentioned the possibility that we might like to represent the school at a three-day seminar in London called Race Against Time, covering problems of race relations and the developing world, that he finally got our attention.

Ronnie and I looked at each other. This was more like it. Three days in London at someone else's expense? Fantastic!

Four weeks later, in the middle of the second day of the conference, we were bored and listless. 'Let's see if we can't pick up a bit of action,' Ronnie suggested. 'Sure you know what the English girls are like – gaggin' for it.'

Out in the foyer, next to the tea stall, were a group of girls from Reading. Two of them were called Alison and Laura. They were attractive and aged 16, and they found our Ulster accents bizarre but endearing.

'Fancy a Wimpy?' Ronnie said.

'Yeah, awright. You paying, are you?'

'Sure, why not?'

It wasn't long before we were laughing and joking, and showing off at the back of the Wimpy, somewhere off Piccadilly Circus. But it was a public place and we had nowhere else to go. The girls were staying in a youth hostel and there was no question of taking them back there. Much the same applied to our cheap hotel. At my suggestion, we went to the Planetarium on Marylebone Street. It was late afternoon and so the place was practically deserted, but it was also pitch black. I tried not to pay attention to what Ronnie was up to and turned my attention to the long body of Laura sprawled accommodatingly beside me. The audience, such as it was, concentrated its gaze upwards at the stars, and the seats were low as deckchairs. She was wearing a short skirt and as she clung to me, I felt her legs open. I whimpered. The universe was born and died as I groped with adolescent passion at the elastic of her knickers.

But hold on. There's something wrong with that story. It's not true. It never happened. Oh, it *could* have happened. It *might* have happened. You could even say it *nearly* happened – the girls existed; we bought them lunch in the Wimpy; they almost agreed to skip the afternoon session at the conference and come to the Planetarium. But that was all. The reason teenage fantasy is so intense – that curious blend of pornography and romance – is that reality is so relentlessly mundane. Frustration is the driving force behind the actions of teenage boys. They are young males whose reach far exceeds their grasp.

When I first tried to recall what happened in London that summer, I actually believed for a moment that the action described above truly happened. It was only when I began to piece the story together that I realised I had made it up – made it up decades ago, then come to accept it as a bittersweet memory. I think we do this all the time, slowly turning our lives into fiction – which is what they are, really. We don't live in novels, within an imposed artistic structure, where every action, every incident, every observation has a purpose. We live at random, with a series of plot lines, many of which peter out or lead nowhere in particular. Most lives have no *theme* at all. If anything, they are proof of the fact that randomness and chaos are what rule the universe. But if we are hapless characters in our own kitchen-sink dramas, we are also the authors of our story, editing out the tedious and the meek, inserting the bold and the dashing. All reminiscence is coloured by this fact.

The only truly interesting thing that happened to us when we were in London was that Ronnie and I joined the Young Communists League, which had a stall outside the conference centre. We did it for a laugh and it never came to anything. We never attended a meeting or bought a book. Yet years later, when I was questioned by the police about my 'terrorist' past, this was one of the issues raised.

Back in Belfast, nothing had changed. Since leaving Holland Crescent in 1960, my parents and my sister and I had lived at 59 Abbey Park, a newer and somewhat grander street, between Knock, where the RUC had their headquarters, and Dundonald, where

Granny lived. The house was four-square and solid. It had coal-fired central heating and in the kitchen my mother not only had a Hotpoint twin-tub washing machine but also an electric mixer. Talk about moving up in the world!

I could see Stormont from my bedroom window. It was enormous; as big as the Palace of Westminster, even though there were fewer people in Northern Ireland than in London's East End. Directly across the road was the wall that Dad demolished one day in the car when he reversed, as usual, down the steep driveway, then stepped on the accelerator instead of the brake. Mum enjoyed that. It made her laugh out loud. But Dad was furious. He couldn't blame anyone except himself, and that was unacceptable.

Sex, meanwhile, continued to raise its horny head. When I turned 17, I started going out with a girl from down the road who had a low voice and large breasts. At parties, we would head off to dark corners, where I would spend the entire time trying to unfasten her bra. 'Stop it,' she would say, pulling her hand away, 'I love it.' I gave up in the end; it was just too maddening. I was dry-throated with lust. What was particularly galling was that after I dumped her she started going out with an older boy and abruptly lost her inhibitions. Sitting on a sofa at a party one night, feeling sorry for myself, I became aware of movement and heavy breathing from the floor behind. I stretched up, the way you do, and peered over the top of the sofa. My ex-girlfriend's skirt was up round her waist. Her blouse was open and one breast stuck out between her lover's elbow and the side of his head. His trousers were halfway down his thighs and his rump clenched and unclenched as he drove himself into her with the urgency of a thief. Her legs clung to his, the back of her heels reinforcing every stroke of his hips, and I could see her suspenders drawing tight and then relaxing with each thrust.

That one's true. That's the worst of it. Talk about unfair! After all the work I'd put in. But sexy, too. I was compelled to watch. I was simultaneously revolted and excited, not knowing where one sensation ended and the other began. These are the images that stay with you.

Among the images that have *not* stayed with me down the years were those produced by some of France's greatest post-war film directors. There is a reason for this. My friend, Jim Palmer, who lived down the road (but had passed the 11-plus and gone on to grammar school), was persuaded by his brother, Wilbur, that some of the raunchiest X-certificate films ever made were being shown at the Willowfield Cinema on the Woodstock Road, near my Aunt Sadie's. So off we went on the number 16 bus, dressed up in long coats, trying to look like we were 18. The Willowfield, known locally as the Winkie (but more properly 'wankie'), was an authentic flea-pit that by the mid-1960s struggled by on a diet of foreign cinema masquerading as porn. The stench hit you as soon as you entered the auditorium. No one bothered with ice cream or lemonade; the distraction would have been too great. Scores of single men, most of them well into middle age, occupied the seats, putting as much space as they could between themselves and other customers, while up on the screen, without benefit of subtitles, ran such classics as *Jules et Jim*, *Cléo de 5 à 7* and *Antoine et Colette*. The irony was that there was very little on view that wasn't available in a typical Hollywood movie: the censor had seen to that. But so powerful was the perception of French films that the same hardcore audience turned up week after week, praying for the unexpected. In our case, twice was enough. Wilbur had got it wrong. Jim and I derived more satisfaction from eating pasties and peas in the local chipper than we ever did at the Winkie.

Back in the real world, the obstacle course of true love continued as before. One of the girls I went out with around this time lived in a huge detached red-brick house in Cyprus Avenue, close to where I caught my bus home from school. I can't remember how we met, though it may have been at a Methodist youth club that we used to raid for girls from time to time when we were desperate. Talking to her one night in her bedroom (her parents must have been out), with the light from a streetlamp shining in through the window next to a Monkey Puzzle tree, she told me about this other boy she knew who had been crazy about her. She remembered him sitting outside in the street in his car, staring up at her window. She liked him, she said, only her parents didn't think he was good enough for her. He was too old for a start. And he was the wrong sort. He had wild hair and long fingernails and he'd left Orangefield when he was no more than 15. He was obviously going nowhere. What was his name? I asked her. It occurred to me that I might have met him. Van Morrison, she said.

I hadn't, in fact, ever spoken to the then Them singer. But on one of the most famous tracks from his magical *Astral Weeks* LP, released in 1968, Morrison talks of being caught one more time up on Cyprus Avenue. He may go crazy, he laments, before that mansion on the hill. Every time he tries to speak, his insides shake just like a leaf of a tree.

If it was indeed the singer at the window, he did not have to worry. His world – and his sexual marketability – were about to change dramatically.

The bugger of it was that while the girl in the window fancied me, I didn't really fancy her. Life was like that. It was a mug's game. You couldn't have the one you wanted, while the one you didn't want stretched out her arms to you. But at least I wasn't the only one suffering. We were all suffering.

One day, Ronnie told me there was this girl who would take me out of myself (well, *Jesus*, someone had to). Her name was Avril. Yeah, but hold on, I said. I'd *seen* her. Wasn't she too old for me? I mean, she must have been 19 and I was a young-looking 17. It would never work and I knew it.

'Don't be too sure,' Ronnie counselled, tapping the side of his nose. 'Leave it to me.'

A couple of days later, he came back to me. 'She knows you, all right,' he said. 'Thinks you're OK. I've fixed up for you to meet her outside the Astoria, Friday night, half-seven. Don't be late.'

I didn't know what to think. The Astoria was our local picture house. It was where Uncle Norman and Aunt Nancy used to go. But I wasn't going to say no, was I?

Thank you, Godfather.

The deal was that I should wear my white shortie raincoat, with its red lining ('Just in case she confuses you with someone else') and wait outside for her to turn up. When she did, and tapped me on the shoulder, she was all too obviously disappointed. I was just a kid. Was this some kind of joke?

'What age are you, anyway?' she wanted to know.

'I'll be, er, 18 in September,' I stammered. She was beautiful – heart-stoppingly beautiful. It was ridiculous, impossible, absurd.

Fuck Bunting!, I thought. Damn him to hell! But I didn't give up. Not this time. Avril was wonderful. *I'd* show him! So I sweated through the next five minutes, trying to persuade her to go ahead with the date, as people pushed past us. It was a good picture, I said. I'd bought the tickets, I said – balcony, not back stalls. And I wanted her to know that she looked terrific. Stunning, I said. Beautiful. I looked at her, my heart in my mouth. Maybe this touched something in her. Maybe she just felt sorry for me. But after a moment's further hesitation, she smiled, shrugged her shoulders and swept ahead of me into the foyer.

I made a half-hearted offer of an ice cream or a Kia-Ora orange. I wanted her to know that my intentions were pure.

'No, thanks,' she said. 'Let's just find our seats.'

We climbed the grand staircase to the balcony, passed the roped-off café counter with its huge silver dispensers for coffee and hot milk. I showed the tickets to the uniformed girl at the double doors, who directed us to a pair of seats near the back with herding-like movements of her torch. We sat down, with our coats on our laps. For half an hour, as a black-and-white film set somewhere in Cornwall unwound its tedium on the screen in front of us, I writhed and fretted, yearning to reach out and kiss Avril, unable to make the necessary move. Finally, I allowed my arm, like a snake under the charmer's spell, to drift in waves towards the nape of her neck, and when contact was made and she did not cry out, with a cobra's stealth I drew her mouth to mine.

The kiss, against all the odds, was a success, causing me to have an immediate and overpowering erection. It was a good 30 seconds before Avril drew back her head. She looked faintly surprised, but not as surprised as I did when, suddenly, out of the corner of my eye, I found myself peering at an appallingly familiar face less than a foot from my own.

It was Ronnie, leaning forward in the row behind. Dressed in a long coat and flat cap, he had come to enjoy the show and now, as grin met grimace, he began to giggle like an idiot. 'Very good, big lad,' he said, removing his cap with a flourish. 'You looked almost competent there . . . nearly human.' He laughed again.

Avril spun round. 'Ronnie Bunting! What the—?'

She turned back to me, ignoring the shadowy figures hissing at us in the darkness. 'I should have known. Do you think I'm some kind of eejit? First, I end up with a kid who spends half the night trying to work up the courage to kiss me; then I find he's brought you along to hold his hand. I mean, for *God's* sake!'

Shit! Fuck! 'But Avril,' I began.

It was no use. She rose abruptly to her full, and considerable, height, straight into the smoke-wreathed beam of the projector. Her shadow, magnified to giant proportions, passed menacingly over the screen and then she was gone.

Winter gave way to the spring of my discontent. It was in March 1967, just before Saint Patrick's Day, that I committed one of the cardinal errors of my life. In a fit of madness that may or may not have been related to my sexual-deficit status, I allowed myself to be persuaded one afternoon to set fire to the prefects' room. If I had any doubts about the wisdom of this enterprise, I soon overcame them and promptly put a match (provided by Ronnie) to a series of posters on the wall. Everybody cheered. *Burn, baby, burn!* I was the hero of the hour. For a couple of minutes, the posters flickered feebly, scorching the walls and ceiling. Then they went out, causing no lasting damage – which is what you would expect. If the situation had got out of hand, I would have fetched a fire extinguisher. That's what I told myself. Unfortunately for me, the smoke set off the fire alarm and the deputy head – my sparring partner from a few months previously – came rushing up to investigate.

A fateful episode. One of those that comes out of nowhere and changes everything. You think to yourself, I didn't have to do that. I didn't even *want* to do it. It just happened. You see that, don't you? I mean, it's obvious. And sure what does it matter anyway? It's not like anyone was hurt, just a few old posters smouldering. But the room is emptying. Nobody's cheering now. Not any more. Suddenly it's a serious business, no joke, and all your friends who, a few minutes before, thought you were so daring and so cool – and so *stupid!* – they're not around any more. They're gone. They've turned away. They've remembered they've got other things to do and they don't want to look you in the eye. But for you, the consequences of this daft thing that doesn't matter and harmed no one are immediate and enduring. It's as if you really *had* done something terrible. As if you were an *arsonist!* You wonder if the police have been called and if this thing that you never planned and wouldn't have happened if Ronnie hadn't been there will hang around your neck for the rest of your life.

Someone peached on me; maybe more than one, I never found out. But it was the final straw. Malone, at his most unctuous, expelled me (with great regret, he said). In anticipation of his verdict, I was more fearful than I had been in years. I was shaking, drenched in sweat. But I wasn't going to give him the satisfaction of a full confession. There would be no plea bargaining. Under close questioning, I admitted nothing about Ronnie, who was well known as my Svengali, and he was not formally indicted. Nor did he step forward to take his share of the blame. He went on instead to take his A levels and win a place at Queen's University, Belfast, to study ancient history, with the vague intention of going into teaching.

Expulsion is a serious matter. Put out of school, you quickly acquire the dull patina of failure, lacking state protection and investment. It's a form of excommunication. It's like your clothes don't fit any more. My father despaired of me; my mother, embarrassed, pretended to herself that I would settle down and find a job. They had no idea what was going on. I took to lying in bed all morning, but then Dad said if I wasn't going to study, then I'd have to go to work with him at the shop. This alarmed me. Expulsion was one thing, but I was bloody sure I wasn't going to be a grocer. So I got out my books, sat down at the table in the living room and made some kind of an effort.

I couldn't do it. School is a communal activity. You learn by rote. Even if you think you're not listening to the teacher, something gets through, and there is always the tedium of homework to reinforce your ignorance. Sometimes, stuck at home, I would read a few pages of history or a snatch of poetry, or leaf through my art books, but more often I was so overcome with rage that my principal focus became the construction of elaborate, hate-filled cartoons of my tormentors, in which I depicted them as Nazis and criminals determined to destroy me.

Martin Amis, in his memoir *Experience*, writes about how his school career lurched into crisis following the break-up of his father's first marriage. He switched from school to school, rarely staying anywhere more than a few weeks or months, and eventually secured a place at Oxford only after attending a 'crammer' in Brighton. Well, that was nothing. Amis had tutors. He had also throughout his life been comprehensively schooled (though not in a comprehensive). An aura of expectation surrounded him, and even at his lowest ebb he never seriously doubted that he would win a university place.

I had no idea what I was doing. I drifted through each day, staring out the window, grinding my teeth, wishing there was some way I could get back at the world that had so cruelly turned its back on me. I read books all right. But they weren't the right books. I couldn't stand *Nostromo*; I never wanted to see another fucking couplet by Alexander fucking Pope. Instead, I ploughed through Thomas Mann, Heinrich Böll, Arthur Koestler and Franz Kafka, only half understanding them. My light reading, when I felt in need of a chuckle, was Bernard Malamud's *The Fixer*.

Poetry also made an appearance. I bought a slim volume by Apollinaire. How many young men, disappointed by love and life, must have thought 'Le Pont Mirabeau' was written just for them.

L'amour s'en va comme
Cette eau courante
L'amour s'en va
Comme la vie est lente
Et comme l'Espérance est violente

Vienne la nuit sonne l'heure
Les jours s'en vont je demeure

Love goes by like water flows
Love goes by
As life is slow
Held hard by Hope

Night falls, the hours declaim
The days pass by, I remain

In art, Goya seemed suddenly to be the painter who most closely mirrored my mood. His *Saturn Devouring One of His Children* became a firm favourite and remains so to this day.

If my parents ever guessed what was going on in their son's life, they said nothing about it. But then most parents raise their children in ignorance. When Ronnie came round in the evenings to bring me up to speed with the gossip, my father and he would exchange hearty words and Mum would bring us mugs of tea. Ronnie could see I was depressed. This cheered him up considerably. He suggested that if I didn't like the way things were going and could see no clear way ahead, then maybe I should think seriously about suicide. Pills, he thought, would be the best approach, or maybe I could just throw myself into the Lagan. 'Sure you can't swim, it'd all be over in a minute.' Was he serious? I have no idea. At any rate, though it was a tempting line of thought, I declined to take up his suggestion.

At some point or other in the middle of all this, I was given an appointment to see a psychiatrist. I don't know how it happened, but I think it may have been a referral by Mr Malone at Orangefield, which would have been entirely typical of him. The thought of it irritates me even now. I wasn't mad; I was *angry*. But my parents went along with it. For them, it was a better answer than no answer at all.

The shrink in question was a rather dull, workaday woman (I had expected a man) who sat on her side of a regulation NHS desk and asked me a load of daft questions, mostly about sex. We did the word-association thing; we did the ink-blot test; we talked about my earliest memories. Mainly, though, she wanted to know about my relationship with girls and how often I masturbated. I lied to her, point-blank. If she saw through my deceit, she didn't say so. At the end of our session, she simply advised me to pull myself together (as distinct from 'off') and make the best of my opportunities. Ever since that day, I've had no time for psychiatrists. As far as I'm concerned, they're off their tiny shrunken heads.

Family life continues, no matter what. My sister Elaine was 21 now and had broken up a year or so earlier with her long-time boyfriend, Ricky, whom I'd always liked. The new love of her life was a young textile chemist, Leslie Blackburne, who drove a red MG sports car and played football with Ronnie at weekends. Leslie and she were married, amid some splendour, in the spring of 1968 and went on to have three children: Nick, Mark and Christina. The marriage was ultimately not a happy one, ending in divorce some 15 years later. But Leslie, in the meantime, had set up his own inks and dyestuffs consultancy and become one of the richest men in Northern Ireland. Elaine's second husband, Bryan Somers, was no slouch either. After splitting up from his first wife and winning custody of his sons, Robin and Steven, he married Elaine and set about building up a successful travel and holiday business. If I ever thought, as a journalist, that I was the one making the smart decisions, the examples of Leslie and Bryan (and Elaine, a respected art consultant) are there to prove me wrong.

Exam time rolled round in the early summer, and I was allowed back to Orangefield to take my A levels. Mr Malone did not speak to me, and each day after I had put down my pen, I was escorted off the premises. Fuck them, I thought. And considering the circumstances, I did OK: I got an A in art history, a B in history and, not surprisingly, a C in English.

But I had given no serious thought to what I should do next and ended up rejecting a couple of offers from English universities in favour of one from Queen's. This was a mistake. Another road not taken. Again, it was frustration that drove me. Where I really wanted to go was Trinity College, Dublin, the alma mater of more famous Irishmen than you could shake a stick at, including Swift, Wilde and Beckett, the philosopher George Berkeley, Nobel Prize-winning physicist Ernest Walton, and Bram Stoker, the creator of *Dracula*. More to the point, it was where both J.P. Donleavy and his archetypal anti-hero Sebastian Dangerfield (aka *The Ginger Man*) had studied, and if it was bad enough for them, it was good enough for me. Trouble was, I didn't have maths and had never even studied Latin. My application simply didn't add up. *Ipso facto*, they turned me down. It was a bitter blow, though surely not unexpected.

Now what? England didn't appeal to me at the time; I hardly even thought of it as an option. The red-brick Victorian pinnacles of Queen's University rose up in my mind like figures out of an alcoholic mist. At least, I told myself, I would be among my own. Including, of course, cousin Ronnie.

During the long summer of 1967, the Summer of Love, marijuana and psychedelia were supposed to be the big thing, but, as I have indicated, drugs left me cold. I don't know why. It wasn't that I wasn't susceptible. Coming out of my depression, I read Rimbaud and Verlaine. I had the same Beatles and Stones albums everybody else had and was an early fan of Stevie Winwood while he was singing blues in the Spencer Davis Group. I wore my hair long and my trousers preposterously flared. On television, I watched *Late Night Line-Up* and Monty Python. But that was about it. Allen Ginsberg did not 'speak to my condition'. I wasn't interested in his sort of wordy, self-regarding 'alternative' lifestyle. Maybe it was simply that I was Irish and a pint of plain was my only man.

At the heart of the summer should have been six weeks of hard labour in the bulb fields of Hillegom, south of Amsterdam. My parents had spent their first-ever holiday abroad in Majorca in the spring, where Dad had made friends with a Dutch flower grower who promised me a roof over my head and money in my pocket in return for six weeks' picking and packing. I didn't want to go on my own, but I didn't want to go with Ronnie either.

Mervyn Watson drew the short straw. He had heard that Dutch girls were particularly free with their favours and was in no doubt they would succumb to his Latin charms. For myself, I just hoped that one of them might give me a hand job.

No one flew to the Continent in those days – certainly not if they were starting from Belfast. You took the night ferry to England, then caught a train to the appropriate point of departure. Thus it was that, 24 hours after setting out from Belfast, we stood on the deck of the Harwich ferry, watching the dunes and fields of the Hook of Holland emerge from a cloudscape by Jacob van Ruysdael. I was really looking forward to my first overseas adventure.

But it was not to be.

Upon landing, we were immediately taken into custody by immigration officers, who searched us for drugs and, having discovered that we were 'clean', declared us, unaccountably, to be undesirable aliens. I have no idea why they did this. I have never used drugs and hadn't drunk so much as a bottle of Guinness for the previous two days. Could it have been because Ronnie and I had joined the Young Communists League a year earlier? Perhaps. But what about the famed Dutch tolerance? What about the liberalism – especially towards drug users – that was supposed to define Dutch culture? Years later, as the *Financial Times* correspondent in Amsterdam, I would come to realise that there were two street cultures in the Netherlands: that of the capital – liberal, drug-induced and coarse; and that of the rest of the country – traditionalist, provincial . . . and coarse. Neither of them appealed to me.

We were not permitted to make a phone call to our prospective employer. Nor were we able to call home. Instead, having been held for the night in a windowless cell, we were escorted onto the morning boat and deported. I shouted abuse at the officials who handed us across, making specific reference (with the wit that has since marked me out) to their ubiquitous 'Dutch caps'. When we docked back at Harwich, Mervyn decided to do a Dick Whittington and go for broke in London, where he cut a swathe through the female population. I headed back to Belfast, vowing to drink myself to death if that's what it took to have a good time.

At least on this point I was on firm ground. Going to the pub had begun for the Horner boys when we were 16. Sometimes we were successful and got a drink; sometimes we weren't. One afternoon, early in our drinking careers, Alan Kirker and I sauntered into the Elk Inn in Dundonald trying to look as if we were shipyard apprentices or something grown-up like that. The real drinkers were silhouetted against the windows, their cigarettes stuck to their lower lips. 'What'll you have?' the barman asked.

'Pint a' Guinness,' I said, gruffly.

'Uh-huh.' He turned to Alan. 'What about you?'

'Em . . . you wouldn't have a Tia Maria, would you?'

That was it. Seconds later, we were back out on the street.

'Stupid gonch! What did you have to order that for?'

'Fuck off!'

At weekends, it was different. Belfast was a hard-drinking city and it was expected of its young people that they should partake of the prevailing culture as soon as possible. The minute we hit 18, we started drinking in Kelly's Cellars, where Wolfe Tone and a group of northern Presbyterians had discussed the formation of the United Irishmen back in the late 1780s. There was also Mooney's, in Cornmarket, overlooking the spot where Tone's northern lieutenant, Henry Joy McCracken, was hanged after the failure of the '98 Rebellion. In the early days, we tanked up on vodka and orange and Green Chartreuse (said to be drunk by the Pope), or maybe a wee rum and blackcurrant. Later, when we had weaned ourselves off our high-fructose diet, it was Carlsberg Special and then, finally, the black stuff, Guinness XX.

Double X, so-called to distinguish it from Porter, was the standard drink of the working man, Catholic and Protestant – though, even then, lager was starting to make inroads.

'Four pints of Double,' we said.

'Four pints of trouble comin' up,' the barman replied, wiping his hands on his apron.

Ronnie was a determined student of drink but had no 'swallow'. He drank Harp lager – never Guinness – in the manner of those wooden birds in the rear windows of cars that dip and nod their beaks into miniature bowls. I, on the other hand, was well on my way to obtaining my Masters. On a good night – i.e. a very bad night indeed – I would down as many as 14 pints, sometimes chasing them with a Wee Bush or a hot Powers. It was just one of those things.

By closing time, we were 'stocious' – so drunk that we would often throw up on the street outside before making our way unsteadily to the nearest dance hall. Sometimes we couldn't go on. After one particularly heavy session, Alan staggered off into the night. He didn't know where he was going and ended up asleep in a public park. When he stumbled to his feet hours later, his backside soaked with dew, he caught an early bus home. There, he threw up in a dignified manner into a drawer full of shirts, closed the drawer and retired to his bed. Fortunately for Alan, his mother was immensely tolerant, as well as infinitely nice. Well, she had to be. Her husband, Alec, was a drinks' trade executive with a fondness for fine cognac, who, on more than one occasion, invited me to join him below the dining-room table to continue our conversation.

These were pre-disco days and in Ireland, North and South, the pattern was huge venues – 'ballrooms of romance' – with a seven- or eight-piece showband up on the stage, blaring out its version of the latest hits. Irish tribute bands were the real thing, wowing audiences decades before they appeared in England. The more 'authentic' the sound, the greater the appreciation. Originality was not an issue. The big names were Dickie Rock and Brendan Bowyer, lead singers of the Miami and Royal showbands, but there were dozens of them. Usually, they wore uniforms, sometimes even military-style, like Eileen and the Cadets, and their legs would move in time with the music, like the Tiller Girls. The pattern never altered. First, though, you had to get in. Outside, in the snaking queue, Ronnie and Alan and Mervyn and I crunched our Polo mints, buttoned up our jackets and straightened our ties. We had to appear reasonably sober to get past the door, and any slip-ups could be disastrous. It wasn't wise to question the bouncers' decisions. More than one recalcitrant, rejected at the door, had flown back down the steps onto the pavement, their faces streaming with blood, as the men in the big suits made their point.

The King George VI Youth Centre, where we went on Saturdays, reminded me of our school assembly hall, and even had wall bars and ropes and the accompanying aroma of athletes' sweat. Our tactics in the subsequent proceedings were entirely typical. We joined the straggle of drunken, sexually anxious youths slowly circling the hall. In the middle, girls aged between 15 and 25 danced with each other or round their handbags: the pretty ones flaunting themselves with flicks of their skirts; the fat, spotty ones desperate that someone – anyone – would catch their eye and ask them to dance. Not me.

Gradually, we moved in, affecting a casual maturity beneath our beery belching.

'You wanna dance?'

'All right.'

And that was it. The wheel was in spin. Should the ungrateful wee bag have said no, which was far from uncommon, the standard reply was, 'Good, neither do I.' But this rejoinder, though intended as confirmation of our lofty indifference, became feeble after the third usage, so that the actual feeling, cumulatively, was of intense rejection. In the ballrooms of romance, heartache was on a loop.

But there were successes, too. In the event of a more positive response, the ensuing conversation followed a well-worn script.

'D'you like the band?'

'They're OK.'

And after a bit: 'Do you want a mineral?'

'No. Have you been drinkin'?'

'No . . . maybe one.'

The art was to ask a girl up when it looked like a slow set was on the way. As the band performed its impersonations of Elvis, Gerry Marsden or the Walker Brothers, down below, hands would slip up the backs of blouses and passionate kisses would be exchanged between strangers.

Competition was brutal. It was shit or bust. 'OK, ladies and gents, that's all for now. Next dance, please.' These were the words, uttered by the singer, that nipped many a sordid little affair in the bud. Arms would slide away from around necks, lips would return to their owners and be wiped with the back of a cheaply perfumed hand. Many nights I went home with my entire abdominal area frozen solid, like an ice-pack straight from the fridge.

University, when it came along at the end of the summer, brought no immediate relief. In spite of the fact that he lived less than five miles away, Ronnie had somehow managed to wangle his way into one of the halls of residence. I, on the other hand, was still living at my parents' place. I couldn't have been more jaded if I had been back in the Major's front room studying maths.

But it wasn't all bad. At the time I was awarded my place at Queen's, my dad owned two shops and was doing better than he had in years – yet I received a full grant. Don't ask me to explain. What it meant was that I didn't have to worry where the next pint was coming from, or the next pair of high-waisted trousers. Everything was paid for. To celebrate, I spent virtually an entire afternoon in John Patrick's, then the trendiest boutique in town. I even bought Ronnie a pair of white bell-bottoms with pink candy stripes.

Irish universities offer four-year degree courses, with a foundation year that leads on to an honours course. I had selected English literature, medieval history and archeology as my three foundation subjects, but, though I found aspects of each interesting,

I found it impossible to take the whole business of learning seriously. There was, to me, an air of unreality about it. I had everything I needed except for motivation. Perhaps it was the times I lived in. Dropping out had become fashionable. With protest in Prague, civil rights in America, war in Mozambique, and Angola moving to the top of the liberal agenda, it seemed to me sheer indulgence to be studying Old Norse, the agricultural development of prehistoric Mohenjo-Daro and the ambitions of Clovis, King of the Franks, instead of the efforts of ordinary people around the world to live in freedom.

It's possible, of course, that I'd have been a lazy bugger in any circumstances. But I've thought about this and lack of movement towards the goal of world peace is my justification of choice.

I wasn't, in fact, completely idle. I attended lectures from time to time and even turned up for the odd seminar in history or English – especially if Marion Rowan was going to be there (Marion Rowan! Good grief, I haven't thought about her in years). I turned in occasional essays, some of them well received, some of them not. But it all seemed like a bit of a slog, aimed at nothing in particular. Surely there had to be more to life than this?

Alan was already studying maths at Durham; Mervyn, whose parents had both died suddenly, within months of each other, disappeared to London and, after some confusion, went into the museum business; Robert Freeburn, complete with shiny shoes, followed Mr Horner to Neville's Cross College. Time, I realised, for me to make new friends.

Fortunately, these were not in short supply. There was Derek Flack, gentle and diabolic by nature, the spitting image of the late Luke Kelly of the Dubliners. Derek was a wild man in those days, a card-sharp, who liked to snap aerials off cars and would sometimes go rigid with drink. Today, he's a librarian. Then there was Moore Little, big as a bear, with a beard large enough for a bird to nest in. There were lots of stories about Moore. Late one night, when driving from Belfast to Bangor, he and a friend were pulled over by the police, who said the car was swerving all over the road. Moore's pal, who was doing the driving, put on a creditable display of self-control and the issue, in these pre-breathalyser days, remained undecided until Moore began to piss down the constable's leg. From that point on, he would recall, things went from bad to worse.

I can't leave the subject of Big Bear without reporting a celebrated exchange between two of his acquaintances.

Drunk A: What's Moore's second name?

Drunk B: Moore who?

Drunk A: Moore Little.

Such were the 'master race'. But many of my new pals were Catholic – the first representatives of the 'other side' I had known socially in 19 years of living in Ireland. There was no doubt in my mind that this was the important part of life at Queen's. Here they were, representatives of 40 per cent of the population – 75 per cent if you counted the whole island of Ireland. They were my age and they'd lived in the same Six Counties – even the same city – all the time I'd been alive. And I didn't know one of them. Not one. They might as well have come from Mars.

There was Brian McClarnon, a keen footballer, part-time manic depressive and full-time Van Morrison fanatic; Dominic Keary and Colm Delaney, both from St Malachy's College, one camp, the other sporty; and Declan Breen, who seemed to me to have been born for no other purpose in life than to be an arts producer for the BBC. I liked all of them very much. They made me laugh and they made me realise how much I was missing in an all-Protestant environment. I felt second-rate and underprivileged. What about *my* civil rights?

For a time, it must have been embarrassing – for them. I spoke to Catholics in the way that I imagine white liberals in Virginia must have spoken to blacks in the 1960s. I was from the ruling tribe, still in charge – just – and fearful of the effects of change. But I wanted them to know that I admired them and felt for their predicament. I wanted them to accept me as a card-carrying member of the human race who meant well and, whatever else, wasn't one of *them*: the unionist Establishment. I even wanted them to know that, deep down, I recognised the superiority of their culture and my own supplicant status. If they found me naive, or condescending, they didn't say so. Instead, they made me welcome.

Looking back on the way in which my generation took Ulster apart, without ever properly reassembling it, two thoughts occur. The first is that the Catholic/nationalist position was not only rooted in genuine injustice, it also had an intellectual coherence and (at least, in theory) some generosity of spirit towards the other side. The second is that Protestants/unionists – my people – never did or said an honourable thing before 1968. We believed ourselves to be a subset, or dependent tribe, of the English, who had created a great empire and won just about every war they had ever fought. At the same time, we identified closely with the Boers of South Africa, another proud people swamped by natives. There was an irony here, but we didn't see it. Afrikaners never thought of themselves as British: quite the opposite. They fought bitterly and effectively against the empire in pursuit of freedom and independence, earning the respect of the old IRA. What Protestants actually identified with was the Boers' suppression of blacks, whom, with a familiar old-style religiosity, they saw as hewers of wood and drawers of water.

We couldn't even allow that. There have always been hooligans and bad bastards on both sides of the Irish struggle. Some of the worst bigots were true sons and daughters of Rome, who felt that Protestants didn't deserve to live: witness the massacre of Protestants in Wexford during the 1798 Rebellion, or the Kingsmills Massacre of 5 January 1976, when the IRA in South Armagh separated Catholics from Protestants on a bus full of workers, then shot dead all ten of the Protestants. But I'm not talking about extremists here. During my childhood, even the more enlightened Protestants didn't want Catholics to hew wood for them, or draw water; they wanted them to go away. They wanted them to disappear over the border or else emigrate to England or America.

Fuck them all,
Fuck them all,
As over the Border they crawl.
We're not gonna be mastered by no Fenian bastards,
So cheer up, my lads, fuck them all.

As Lord Brookeborough, Prime Minister at Stormont for 20 years, made clear, those papists who remained would, regrettably, for reasons of state, have to accept high unemployment and relentless discrimination. There could be no equality for Taigs, who 'bred like rabbits'. If we gave them an inch, they'd only take on airs and graces and start demanding a share of government – and we weren't having that. 'Croppies lie down!' was the official line from the Big Houses of the Ascendancy all the way through to the mean terraced homes of the Protestant poor.

Today, with the Republic of Ireland one of the wealthiest members per capita of the European Union, it has become obvious to all, even the loyalist diehards, that Catholics are in no way inferior to Protestants. What we are beginning to see, in fact, is a concealed cultural cringe in which Prods have moved, as they say in America, from *off*ence to *def*ence. 'Fair enough, so the Free State has done OK ... well, what do we care? What's that got to do with us? Just leave us alone, would you!' But the day has already dawned when thoughtful, educated Protestants are starting to whisper their support for Irish unity, not as an expression of any form of cultural identity but because it makes sense and allows us all, Britain included, to go forward in a spirit of amity. A United Ireland next to a United Kingdom within a United Europe, friends with the United States: now there's a goal that James Connolly would have thought it worth dying for.

The process takes time. Change, like peace, comes dropping slow – and not every revolutionary is benign. Ronnie Bunting in his student days was hugging his destiny. After a couple of terms at Hamilton Hall, he moved with his new girlfriend, Suzanne, into a flat on the first floor of a period home next to the Ulster Museum. Suzanne Murphy came from the housing estate just down the road from my parents' house. Her real name was Ena and I think she only changed it to Suzanne because Ronnie insisted. She was, you'd have to say, an unlikely choice. She was non-academic and came from a Protestant background that had no truck with republicanism, or even liberal unionism. Nor did she like Big Bill Broonzy or Mississippi John Hurt or support the armed struggle in Angola. How they ever got together in the first place is a mystery. Ronnie's view was that the only solution to Northern Ireland's problems was a socialist system within a united Republic achieved through violence. She, by contrast, liked to keep the house tidy and wanted Ronnie to become a teacher so that he could provide for the children she was sure would come along.

Me? I was a mess. But, if nothing else, I was comfortable with a sense of where I came from. At 15, my choice of book when I won a school prize for English was Frank O'Connor's *Book of Ireland*. Prominent in my music collection were LPs by The Clancy Brothers, the Dubliners, the Wolfe Tones, Na Fíli and Eugene McEldowney (later a colleague at the *Irish Times*). I avidly read Irish history and the short stories of Sean O'Faolain. But, daft though I was, and hapless, I refused to define myself by an accident of birth. In spite of all temptation, I wasn't ready to go over to the Dark Side.

As I searched rather desperately for a future, I had no perspective on events. I lived, so far as I can recall, in a permanent present. I got up each day as late as I could and sought to entertain myself until I could reasonably go to bed again. And then I would repeat the exercise. It sounds like a drug-induced state, but, as I have said, alcohol, not LSD, was my drug of choice.

Much of our binge drinking was done in the then recently built students' union building, otherwise given over to student politics, poker and the Saturday night 'hop'. The real-ale revolution was some years off, so those who didn't drink Guinness were used to going around with their stomachs like churns. Ulster's licensing hours at the time forced pubs, including the union, to close at ten o'clock, and the effect of this was that from nine o'clock onwards orders were placed in multiples. Twelve pints was a typical request, involving a chain of bearers from counter to table. The clamour round the pumps was such that only the most determined got their way.

Ronnie was not a man for half measures (though he might have preferred them). When closing time came, he could sometimes be seen swinging, literally, from the roof beams above the heads of the shifting mass to bellow out his order. Every night, troublemakers were ejected. But not Ronnie. The bar staff, in their blue uniforms, affected to find him a 'bit of a lad' and tolerated his excess.

Of the local pubs, the one I liked best was the Club Bar. For a start, it was just round the corner from a flat I had belatedly moved into, shared with another Orangefield old boy, Jim 'Big Belly' Miskelly, who had been given a hard time at school but was now doing a good job at pulling his life together. I wonder what happened to Jim. The Club (later blown up by loyalists) was run by a trio of brothers vaguely related to Brian McClarnon and attracted a varied clientele. There was a retired major we always spoke to, who drank gin and tonic, and a woman in her 60s who sat on her own in the front snug and was, we were assured, the inspiration for Brian Moore's novel *The Lonely Passion of Miss Judith Hearne*. Whoever she was, she looked sad, as if life had given her a good kicking. When we occasionally bought her a drink, she offered us no more than a watery smile in return.

It was a bar where the unexpected happened. One night, after a lengthy session, I announced (as if it were an achievement in itself) that I was reading the autobiography of Claud Cockburn and that I had been moved by his account of how his son, Patrick, had contracted polio. I felt a tap on my shoulder and turned round to see a young man in thick spectacles extending his hand to me, which I took. 'Maybe I should introduce myself,' he said. 'I'm Patrick Cockburn.'

I like the idea of life in a literary salon. It combines the thin veneer of scholarship with the reality of idleness. I'd have been great as a bit-player in Madrid's Café Gijón, mixing with the likes of Camilo José Cela and César González-Ruano. I'd have hung around Les Deux Magots every day, sucking up to Sartre, Hemingway and de Beauvoir. But in Belfast, where café society meant, at best, a mug of strong tea and a ham sandwich, most of my time wasn't spent talking about books and the world of ideas to a group of my literary peers, it was spent not having sex. I didn't lose my virginity until I turned 19, and then it was in a shop doorway, somewhere off Royal Avenue, with a girl whose name I didn't even know or have long-since forgotten. It was quite erotic, I suppose: her skirt rucked up, her back against the glass of the door, me urging myself on, trying to make sure we didn't come apart before we came together. A grunt . . . a throaty groan. And then afterwards, embarrassment. Her stuffing a handkerchief down her knickers and saying I should call her, and me knowing I never would. Finally, the two of us walking off in opposite directions.

It wasn't much of an introduction to the mystery. It wasn't touched, even remotely, by romance. But at least I had got my key in the lock. I felt relieved (in more ways than one), like I'd been unburdened. What I didn't know was that the lock was about to be changed and I wouldn't be allowed back in for another 18 months.

All this was before the 'Troubles', which finally erupted in the autumn of 1968. The warning signs were already there. The Protestant Ulster Volunteer Force had been banned following the murder of several Catholics; nationalists were starting to demand a better deal on housing; the Northern Ireland Civil Rights Association was about to be formed. But for us, in the Summer of Love, nothing was real. The most daring statement we could make on Irish unity was to get blasted in Dublin one weekend instead of Belfast.

I had recently passed my driving test and my father, in a fit of generosity, bought me a small car, a seven-year-old Ford Popular, in which, one Saturday morning, the four of us – Ronnie, Mervyn, Alan and me – drove the hundred miles south to Dublin. It was the first time that any of us had visited the Republic without our parents. Driving over the Boyne Bridge in Drogheda, we whooped with glee. Halting at a crossroads in Naul, we were stunned by the quiet beauty of the scene. And arriving in Dublin, down the Drumcondra Road, past the North Circular and into Parnell Square, we felt – or at any rate *I* felt – that we were staring into the face of our own future as a people.

But it was in Dublin, too, that we encountered our first example of racism. As we stood at the counter of a bar somewhere off O'Connell Street supping our Guinness, the front door flew open and a young black man ran in, terrified. He looked around desperately, then made his way at full pelt to the back of the bar, disappearing out of the rear entrance. At that point, a group of Irish youths appeared at the front. 'Anyone seen the nigger?' one of them enquired.

'Yeah,' drawled one of the regulars, pint of Porter and cigarette in the same hand, obviously approving. 'Fekker went out the back. If you're quick, you'll catch him.'

I may have been a supplicant, but not everyone in Ireland was my superior. I was reminded of this some years later when I was covering nationalist riots in the Lower Falls. The crowd (or 'mob', depending on your affiliation) carried banners protesting about discrimination against Catholics. When the British troops moved in, black soldiers were singled out for abuse. 'Get the fuck out of Ireland,' the women would shout, 'and take your monkeys with you!'

In Belfast, in the spring and summer of 1968, it was as if our futile little lives had been written on a palimpsest of history and the underlying message was starting to come through. Ronnie and I took to drinking in nationalist areas: first in the Spanish Rooms in the Lower Falls, where they served scrumpy; later in an upstairs shebeen, known as the Old House, in Leeson Street. I relished the experience, especially the rebel songs and the feeling of being, for once, on the right side of the argument. But it didn't make me a hardliner, still less a terrorist. Ronnie was the true revolutionary – a throwback to Wolfe Tone and Henry Joy McCracken. I was simply along for the ride.

Suzanne shared my dilemma (though her personal history, touched by savagery, would eventually transform her into a true believer), but it didn't seem to matter. She and Ronnie had an elemental attachment to each other. Their devotion and loyalty transcended their differences.

Their rows were spectacular. Ronnie was impatient and selfish and possessed of an almost Old Testament jealousy. If he caught her even speaking to another man, let alone having a drink with one, he would fly into an ungovernable rage. One slow-witted fellow student – later to become a warder at Long Kesh internment camp – who persisted in talking to her after he had been warned off was slowly doused with a pint of beer, then told to get the fuck out. He didn't hang around.

One Saturday morning, I climbed the stairs to their flat only to realise as I reached the halfway mark that I was walking into a perfect storm. The angry voices above shook the walls. Better to come back later, I reasoned, proceeding nonetheless.

Something made of glass shattered against the door as I turned the knob. 'Jesus, fuck!' I cried, shielding my face.

'*Walter*!' I looked out, anxiously, through my fingers. It was Suzanne. She was standing on the dining table. 'Would you tell this bastard that if he doesn't stay here and eat the dinner I've cooked for him, I'm going to do something desperate. I'm not going to put up with his shite any longer.'

Then it was Ronnie's turn. 'I've told you, you daft cow. I'm meeting the lads for a couple of drinks in the union – and that's it. Now, get off the fucking table and get Walter a fucking drink.'

I watched in silence as the melodrama played out in front of me. Now, to my astonishment, Suzanne raised her right forefinger and inserted it into the empty light socket above her head. It had been the light bulb that had come crashing into the door. Stretching her other hand behind her, she managed to reach the switch on the wall.

'You go out that door and I'm pullin' this switch,' she said, her eyes wild in an ashen face. 'I swear to God, I'm not bloody jokin'.'

Ronnie was not to be intimidated. 'Aye,' he said, moving over to the sash window and hauling the bottom section up as far as it would go. 'So go ahead. Only, you pull that switch, I'm goin' out this window.'

They stared at each other. The air was thick with deterrence. I let out an involuntary gasp. Suzanne flicked the switch. A blue spark ran down her hand and she moved into a juddering spasm as the electricity coursed through her body.

At the same moment, Ronnie swung his leg to the sill of the window and jumped. A loud cry accompanied his departure.

Suzanne's hair stood on end and her eyes bulged with a maniacal glee. But the effect only lasted a split second. With a pop, her finger shot out of the socket and she collapsed onto the table.

'Are you all right?' I asked her.

'Where's Ronnie?' she pleaded, sucking in air. 'God! God! Is he *dead*?'

I rushed to the stairs. Taking the steps two at a time, I reached the ground floor in a matter of seconds and raced, breathless, into the garden. Ronnie was sitting in a flowerbed, cursing quietly and rubbing his left leg. He had made his impromptu descent by way of the canopy of a tree, which had broken his fall, pitching him into freshly dug soil. His face and hands were bleeding.

'You stupid cunt,' I said. 'Are you OK?'

'Yeah, yeah. But I've twisted my ankle.' He looked up. 'How's Suzanne?'

'I think she's all right. She blew a fuse. But maybe she should see a doctor. So should you, by the looks of it. Jesus Christ, Ronnie, the pair of you are mad. Do you know that?'

By the summer, I came to realise that I couldn't continue like this. My foundation year at Queen's had failed to yield anything of substance. When the scaffolding came down, I was in danger of collapse. I passed some of my exams – doing quite well in history, as I recall – but didn't turn up for others. The consensus among my teachers was that I could probably continue at Queen's, but only if I revised my attitude and sat the missing tests. I thought about it and came to the conclusion that I couldn't be arsed. I was in the wrong country at the wrong time, studying the wrong things at the wrong university. It was time to get the hell out. But where would I go? The answer I settled on would change my life forever.

Or at least till something better came along.

IV

Saint Cuthbert's Way

THE TRAIN THAT set out from the ferry port of Heysham rattled and farted most of the way to York. The trunk I'd struggled with off the boat squatted on the floor next to me; a novel lay unopened on the tiny triangular table that jutted out beneath the window sill. When the conductor came round to check my ticket, I affected an exaggerated Dublin brogue, feeling a need to put some space between myself and the English amongst whom I had come to live.

It was 18 September – late summer or early autumn, depending on your point of view – and the moors and dales through which the train passed were bathed in mellow sunlight. Rainstorms were battering southern England when I left Belfast, but in York, 200 miles to the north, a rainbow so pale you could barely see it hung across the city. It seemed a good omen, maybe. A new beginning, perhaps.

I didn't have long to wait for my connection. A huge diesel locomotive came shuddering to a halt right next to me. It roared like a blast furnace (or how I imagine a blast furnace might roar), and there must have been a dozen carriages behind. I had forgotten how the scale of things increased when you reached England. (The English say the same when they go to America.) We had nothing like this at home.

A conductor stood with his whistle in his mouth, one foot on the step, the other on the platform, the way they did in the movies. He looked like Burl Ives. I called out to him. 'Sure and would this be the *tray-in* to Durham?'

'What?'

'Is this the train to Durham?'

'Aye. And if you're planning to take it, you'd best hurry, for it's about to leave.'

I hauled my trunk on board and found a seat. Half an hour later, after a stop in Darlington, a large rolling escarpment reared up to the right, then out of nowhere, there it was.

Durham must have the most spectacular setting of any town in England. From the station, you can see it all at a glance. The river curls about a rocky promontory, almost meeting itself on the way back. Stone bridges straddle the banks every few hundred yards. Up on the rock sit the cathedral and castle. Durham Cathedral, an epic in stone, was begun in 1093. Twenty years earlier, William the Conqueror himself ordered the construction of Durham Castle, perched on the northern tip of the peninsula. It represented not only his own prestige in the region but also a point of defence against the Scots, who then, as now, liked to kick the crap out of the English when the opportunity arose. I was stunned. Not even the rain, now gathering strength, could dampen that first impression.

'Way-a to, hinny?' the cab driver asked me.

'Eh?'

'Where you goin' to?'

'Oh. College of the Venerable Bede.'

'Bede College. Right you are. Have you there in no time.'

Bede – in those days a strictly single-sex institution – was a

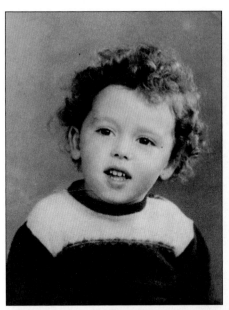

A studio portrait of me, aged two and a half, wearing a jumper that would no longer fit.

Me, aged three, and Elaine, six, sitting in our back garden. I do not look pleased.

Me and Elaine on my tricycle. The boy on the back is Eoin Sinclair, our neighbour's son.

Above: With Dad during a family trip to Donegal.

Right: Me, aged seven, standing outside our garage in Holland Crescent. The almost invisible dog is Nicky, the second of our two Yorkshire terriers.

With my sister, 1953.

Group portrait prior to a fancy dress party. I am the one in the topper. The others, from left, are Gordon Bothwell, Howard Coates, Trevor Lloyd and William Coates (in civvies).

The family in London during a visit by my father to Twining's Tea.

A carefully composed portrait of our little family taken in, I think, 1956, when I was seven. My dad was proud of what he had built; Mother is a study in dignity.

Elaine and me, Christmas 1961.

With Ronnie Bunting during the 1964 dress rehearsal for *The Miser* (thus the make-up). The scarf indicates our new-found love of Linfield Football Club.

Above: A scene from *The Miser*. Ronnie Bunting, as the servant Jacques, is holding a knife to the throat of the Justice of the Peace, played by me. If you look carefully, you can see the blade.

Right: Me, aged 16.

The Horner Boys in the summer of 1966: (left to right, standing) Robert Freeburn, Mervyn Watson, Mr Horner, me; (left to right, seated) Colin Hoskins, Norman Pickles, Alan Kirker, Ronnie Bunting. Alan is holding a comb over his upper lip (Hitler) and I am assisting a sprig of leaves to sprout from his head.

The wall of the prefects' room at Orangefield, 1966. Note the Union flag. This was the wall I set fire to in the lead-up to my expulsion.

Friends from Bede College, Durham, in 1969: (from left) Jonathan Lovell, Chris DiPaolo and Roger Mayo, with Chris's girlfriend of the time.

The Class of '71: I'm the tall one on the right; the woman on the left is Joan Fitzpatrick, head of the journalism department; David McKittrick is in the middle in the back row, next to Gillian Chambers (which is the way he liked it); and Malachi O'Doherty is the one with the beard.

A famous photograph of IRA man Joe McCann taken during the siege of Inglis's bakery. I wonder what my mother would have made of her former weekend guest in his role as armed revolutionary.
(© Victor Patterson/Linen Hall Library)

Alan Kirker after a few drinks
with his future wife, Fiona, taken
during my first trip home from
Brussels in September 1974.

David Blundy with an admirer –
Patricia Kelly, the future Brussels
correspondent for CNN, taken
in Brussels in 1974.

My friend Ronnie was
unimpressed by Airey
Neave's credentials as a
war hero. This is
Neave's car after the
INLA explosion that
killed its owner in the
car park of the House
of Commons on
30 March 1979.
(© EMPICS)

college of the University of Durham, the third oldest university in England, founded in 1832. I had managed to win a place – but only at the last second – studying not for a degree in history but for a B.Ed., or Bachelor of Education, a new qualification geared exclusively to teaching.

It was not how I had seen myself ending up, but after the Queen's fiasco I'd had to do something. Mr Horner had given Durham high marks and moved there two years earlier as a lecturer in drama. And, of course, Alan Kirker was starting the second year of his maths degree just up the road. Given that my academic record was spotty at best, I ought to have been glad that Durham had awarded me any kind of place. The problem was, I didn't want to be a teacher. I wanted to be a writer, or at least a journalist. I wanted to travel the world. I didn't want to be stuck in some classroom.

Be careful what you wish for. The fact that I was awarded a second full grant – almost unheard of – by Down County Education Authority eased the pain. I had a place to go and (once again) money in my pocket.

So, here I was, in a taxi bumping down the hill to God know's what sort of future. It was hard saying goodbye to family and friends. It's true what they say: you only know what you've got when it's gone. But I had been offered a new start, with the slate wiped clean, and I had every reason to be grateful.

Needless to say, I wasn't.

The taxi dropped me off in front of the college's main building, which instantly put me in mind of an insane asylum. I went in and was sent to registration, where I was told I would be sharing a room with another student in a residential hall called Thorp House. 'Sign here,' a woman said, handing me a key and a map of the college. With some trepidation (for I didn't like the idea of sharing), I made my way down the hill, past some tennis courts, in the direction of the river, to restart my life.

Normally, I'm good at remembering people from my past (though hopeless at recalling the names of those I have just met). But in this case I can't bring to mind with whom I was supposed to share. Too brief an acquaintance, I suppose. All I know is that he was a sportsman of some kind, from the Northeast, with fair hair and a heavy, barking voice. He introduced himself ponderously (I remember now, he was a rugby player) and indicated to me with a sweep of his hand which bed was mine and in which half of the wardrobe I should hang my clothes.

I disliked him on sight and could tell at once it wasn't going to work. Dismayed, I sped back to the main building to see what alternatives were on offer. The accommodation officer was not impressed, which was understandable.

'Give it a week or two,' she said, hardly looking up from her paperwork. 'It might not be so bad.'

I sighed. This wasn't the time to make a fuss. 'Is there a bar here?'

'Of course.'

'Where is it?'

'In the main building, downstairs from the JCR.'

'Thank you.' I knew what I had to do. I had to get drunk.

The bar was small and cellar-like but not unpleasant. It sold various draught beers, including Guinness and Newcastle Exhibition, as well as huge pint bottles of Newky Brown. Lots of people were standing around, some of them bearded, others with granny glasses; most had long hair, and one or two wore suits. I wasn't sure what to make of them but ordered a Guinness to assist the process. Thinking of the unpleasant fellow waiting for me back in my room, I decided there and then to see if there wasn't someone more congenial with whom I might cohabit. Amid the hubbub of conversation, one voice stood out from the rest. It was languid, yet had an edge to it, as if used to resisting stupidity. Its owner was tall and slim, with black hair and gold-rimmed spectacles.

I introduced myself. 'Walter Ellis. Pleased to meet you.'

'Chris Dipaolo. Likewise.'

'Dipaolo? What sort of a name's that?'

'Italian. My dad came over from the old country as a boy and set up a restaurant in Darlington.'

'Darlington?' I remembered it from the journey. A dull-looking town. 'So he ignored the blandishments of London, Manchester, Edinburgh . . .?'

'Dead right. Decided the Northeast was where he needed to be, and that was it. Never looked back.'

I had to smile. In Belfast, opposite the Club Bar, there was an Italian café called Smokey Joe's run by 'Poppa' and 'Momma'. Poppa (Guiseppe) had curly hair; Momma wore an apron. The tables had Formica tops. It was where I ate my first-ever bowl of pasta. I wondered at the time, given that Momma and Poppa were in their 60s, what could possibly have caused two such congenial Italians to leave pre-war Italy and relocate to . . . Belfast. Were they victims of a Mussolini purge? Surely, there must have been more tempting prospects! In terms of 'value added', I don't know what they ever got out of it. Italians, for reasons of religious convenience, generally lived in nationalist areas and a surprising number ended up in the IRA, denouncing British rule and demanding equal status for the Irish language. But in the 1950s and '60s, as they watched the movies of Fellini and Antonioni and read about the economic miracle that had sent living standards soaring back home, they must surely have asked themselves what they had ever done to deserve their fate. Much the same thought occurred to me when I drove past a Chinese takeaway in the God-forsaken Irish midlands, somewhere between Dundalk and Mullingar. The rain was lashing down and a dog barked miserably in an adjacent back garden. An overweight girl, one of the family presumably, stood huddled in the rain scraping food scraps from pots into a large aluminium vat – hopefully to be used as pig feed. She looked surly and joyless. To me, it was bizarre: how did her family, with its origins in dynamic metropolitan Hong Kong, end up dispensing second-rate 'chinkies' to ungrateful peasants in . . . *Longford*?

In the bar, Dipaolo took off his glasses and wiped them with a small patent cloth. 'So, what's your accent? Sounds a bit Scottish.'

''Fraid not. It's Irish. From Belfast.'

'Bloody hell! Come to blow us all up, I suppose.'

'Something like that.'

Chris was another new arrival, signed up for a B.Ed. He was also, it turned out, billeted with a sports fanatic.

'Bad luck,' I said, brightening. 'Bother you, does it?'

'Living with a moron? What do *you* think?'

We did the switch that afternoon. I moved into Chris's room, number 16, on the third floor of Thorp, while his erstwhile room-mate moved in with mine. It was a perfect swap. The two 'hearties' became firm friends. So did we. When I learned that Chris had been unable to take up a university place the previous year because of personal issues and trouble over a girl, and that he had only ended up at Bede because he had nowhere else to go, I knew we'd get along just fine.

Other friends materialised in a matter of days. Jonathan Lovell was tall and blond and elegant – a Quaker and a shareholder of some small significance in the family that owned Clarks shoes. He would have reminded me of Sting – a local boy – except that the singer was only 16 at the time and I'd never heard of him. A violinist and (as it seemed to me) frightfully posh, Jonathan was given to long, self-imposed silences and was liable at any moment to fold his legs into the lotus position. Then there was Roger Mayo. Twenty-eight years old, six-foot-four and an old boy of Sedbergh School, Roger was one of the last generation of Britons to do National Service. Following his discharge, he had worked as a tea planter in India and Africa, and then, intriguingly, spent two years as a mercenary in the Congo. He wore tweed sports jackets and handmade Oxford brogues and spoke in a mixture of public-school slang and parade-ground Afrikaans. We liked Roger. We even liked his bristling moustache. If Mr Horner had wandered in from the *Dead Poets Society*, Roger was a refugee from *If . . .*

The fact that I was an Ulster Protestant intrigued everybody. We were a rare breed and nobody really knew what we were about.

'I know what you're thinking,' I told them defensively. 'But we're not all like Paisley. Protestants are people, too.'

All this did was raise expectations. 'Can you do Paisley?' Roger wanted to know.

'You mean talk like him?'

'Yes.'

'Of course.'

'Well, go on, then.'

So I did – which, I have to say, went down a storm around the bar. But then the Big Man was always a crowd-pleaser.

Settling in took a while. Sharing a small space with another man is always difficult. Either you go the alpha male/submissive male route (shades of Ronnie Bunting) or else you try genuine coexistence. Chris and I opted for the latter. It wasn't easy, of course. I am anally retentive. I guard my space jealously. I don't like things to be moved from where I've put them. While my mind is a vagrant, I like my possessions nailed down. Chris, by contrast, was a gloriously baroque figure. He would fling his clothes off at the drop of a hat and stalk around naked, oblivious to the embarrassment he caused. Soon, it seemed like I knew *his* genitals almost as well as my own. 'Look at this,' he'd say, exposing one of his ripe testicles. 'Do you think it hangs lower than the other one?' He was also a smoker, who rolled his own, adding a touch of 'weed' from his stash in the top drawer if the spirit moved him, before leaning back and placing a Bob Dylan album on his record player. Not everyone appreciated 'Diplo', as they called him. The hearties from down the hall often complained about his music and his silly cigarettes, but he always told them to fuck off, which, by and large, they did.

Up to this point, I hadn't given any serious thought to the sort of course I was embarking upon at Bede. I reckoned I was smart and experienced and had learned useful lessons from the Queen's debacle; so long as I turned up at lectures and got my essays in on time, what could possibly go wrong? But, as Uncle Tommy warned me, God never shuts one door but he slams another in your face. Casting an eye down the timetable we had been handed, I was shocked to see inscribed in several of the little squares: 'Phys. Ed' and 'Mathematics'. What the *hell*?

It was my own stupid fault. I should have read the bloody prospectus. The degree course, now scrapped in favour of a traditional degree plus a more focused one-year teaching certificate, combined academic study with professional training. The underlying assumption was that we should be able to function at any level in the state system, which meant knowing not only how to get 18 year olds through A levels but also the best way to organise 'games' for toddlers and teach the binary system to pre-pubescent girls.

I couldn't believe it. Nor could Chris. Over drinks in the Duke of Wellington pub, just across the footbridge from college, we resolved to invent our own curriculum, omitting the kids' stuff and substituting it for courses in politics and creative writing. Roger thought we were mad. 'I say, O bee-bops,' he began, his limbs like the blades of a penknife. 'Bad fucking show. If you don't want to do the training, what did you sign up for?'

'It's not the Army, Rog.'

'More's the pity, *Exay*.'

In fact, it worked out – kind of. I never went to PE. Not even once. I just refused. Chris looked in from time to time, mainly because he wanted to get fit for rowing (a private passion), and it was largely through him that I learned of Matty Tomes, the PE instructor, and how he treated the students like raw recruits, sending them shimmying up ropes or dropping down to give him 20. Roger, sporting long shorts and a white vest, appeared to enjoy it. Jonathan, refusing to be browbeaten, elected instead to play tennis in the college courts.

Maths vanished from my life at Bede with the same dispatch as games. I attended a couple of classes in the binary system, understood not a word (or number) and politely withdrew. No one seemed to mind – or if they did, they didn't say so.

Many years later, out of the blue, I received a letter via the *Sunday Times* from my maths lecturer at Bede, Ernie Shotton, who had long since left the college and gone into industry. He is now retired. 'I lectured to you in a basic maths group on a Monday afternoon,' he wrote, 'my attendance rate much better than yours.'

To my surprise, it turned out that he had protected me from the curriculum police by inflating both my attendance and my scores, getting his sums wrong on both counts. Kindnesses like that often go unnoticed, so let me say now that if my time at Durham was not entirely wasted, part of the reason was Mr Shotton's unsuspected pastoral care. 'Bede helped you to pause, look around and make up your mind about what you wanted to do,' he wrote.

He was right, and I'm sorry I skipped his classes.

One course I did enjoy was linguistics, taken by Ted Prince, a laconic Lancastrian whose practised eye quickly spotted that, lazy and unmotivated though we were, our little group were not stupid. It helped, I suspect, that we liked a beer. Ted, an ex-schools inspector, was something of an authority on Old Norse and the origins of English, and played around with parts of speech as if they were clues in a crossword. I can't remember anything he taught us, but it was great fun. Even more fun was brunch, or Sunday lunch, in his college apartment, where hotpots of all kinds were prepared for us by his wife, Dilys, a flirtatious woman with skin and hair like a gypsy's.

Another of the 'good guys' at Bede was a theologian called

Macmillan, a member, someone said, of the publishing family, distantly related to the former Prime Minister – he of the near-foetal recall. Mr Macmillan was sharp as a knife but blind. We had to read our essays out loud to him and then listen as he patiently corrected both our false assumptions and our naive 1960s philosophy. Like Ted Prince, he was a good listener. When I told him once that I had a problem with my girlfriend – that I fancied her younger sister – he understood entirely.

A less benign figure than Mr Macmillan was a member of a religious order who moved in student circles, looking for impressionable young men to share his calling. He came up to my room one morning, ostensibly to enquire why I had missed some seminar or other. I was barely awake when he materialised at my side. He sat on the edge of the bed while I rubbed the sleep from my eyes and asked me if I was getting along all right. It could be hard for young men, he said, away from home for the first time, and sometimes it helped if they had someone they could confide in. As he spoke, he slipped his hand under the bedclothes and ran it up my leg. I jackknifed in alarm, fearing the worst, and made it clear that I was not that sort of girl. The hand disappeared, as did its owner. I must have threatened to report him to the college authorities for we never spoke again: like the Levite in the parable of the Good Samaritan, when he saw me on the road he passed by on the other side.

Going back to Belfast for the Christmas break was a peculiar experience. My father looked older; my mother complained of her varicose veins. It felt as if I had been gone for years. Ronnie and Suzanne appeared to be getting along well. Inevitably, though, Ronnie made me feel that I had walked out on the situation in Ireland just as it was getting interesting and at the very point when sacrifice was required. He liked to rub it in. 'Screwin' the wee English girls, are you? Havin' a good time? Aye, well, let's see where it fuckin' gets you, you fuckin' eejit.'

You had to love the boy. But he had a point.

The new year began in spectacular fashion. The Reverend Ian Paisley, then leading the unambiguously labelled Protestant Unionist Party, had denounced an 80-mile protest march from Belfast City Hall to the Guildhall in Derry organised by the student-based People's Democracy movement. Addressing a packed meeting inside the same Guildhall, he described the protesters as 'disguised IRA men' and reminded his audience of Derry's ancient tradition of armed defiance. But he did not urge violence. The future MP, MEP and Privy Counsellor was always careful not to be personally associated with what loyalists like to call 'bloodwork'. On this occasion, his 'military' representative was none other than Major Bunting, Ronnie's dad, who had moved from being my maths tutor, with an interest in local government finance, to Protestant fanatic purely – and fortuitously – because Paisley had ministered to his dying mother and, in so doing, revealed himself as a Man of God. Reborn as a loony, with a penchant for stunts (such as laying a wreath in Dublin in memory of British soldiers killed during the 1916 Rising), the Major vowed to 'harrass and hinder' the marchers throughout their journey. Paisley, standing next to him, confined himself to blessing Ulster's cause. What happened next quickly became the stuff of legend. A band of rural thugs, including off-duty members of the police reserve known as the B Specials, was put together to shadow the marchers, disrupt their sleep and threaten their lives. On the fourth day, as the march drew close to Derry, more than 200 of the Major's men descended on the students at Burntollet Bridge, near the village of Killaloo, and beat the living shit out of them, watched over by the RUC. Scores of the unarmed students were injured, some of them seriously. The wounds were inflicted with sharp stones, pickaxe handles and iron bars. A loyalist song, written shortly afterwards, commemorated the heroism of the attackers.

At a place that's called Burntollet, Major Bunting took his stand.
And said 'Men, do your utmost to smash this rebel band.
They're coming down in hundreds and you are 72' –
They answered, 'No Surrender! We're from Killaloo.'

One of those given a bloody nose at Burntollet was Bruce Anderson, now a right-wing columnist for *The Independent* but in those days a '60s radical. Born in Orkney but sent as a boarder to Campbell College, Bruce began his political life somewhat to the left of Paul 'Bonkers' Johnson and has since overtaken him in a two-man race to the furthermost reaches of the respectable right. Quite a trick. For the last five years, he has lived in the peculiar splendour of the Travellers Club in Pall Mall and has been known to turn up on friends' doorsteps with a dead stag over his shoulder and a case of claret at his feet. 'They were quite right to beat me up,' he says of the Boys from Killaloo. 'I was a bloody fool.'

Major Bunting would later go to jail for three months for organising an illegal assembly in Armagh. But the Burntollet ambush was the high point, or low point, of his loyalist career. Ronnie had always respected his dad – who had once been election agent for the Republican Labour MP Gerry Fitt – and the effect on him of this newborn paterfamilias was shattering. He wasn't just embarrassed; he was profoundly ashamed. A metamorphosis began, the first phase of which I witnessed before I headed back to the safety of Durham. No longer was he an onlooker; now he wanted to hit back. He may not yet have crossed the Rubicon, but his toe was in the water and he gazed fondly at the distant bank.

I, of course, had the easy option of getting on the Heysham boat. Ronnie was right about that. I arrived back in Durham at the end of the first week of January and did my best to put the unpleasantness of my homeland behind me. College life may not have had the excitement of Belfast's student scene, but it didn't have clubs with nails driven through them either.

Bede, founded in 1839, was an old-style Anglican foundation with a strong choral tradition, torn between its subfusc past and emergent 1960s radicalism. We were asked to call tutors by their first names, which straight away made me feel uncomfortable, but at the same time, just to show that this was still England and class distinctions were alive and well, once a week we had formal dinner in 'hall', dressing up in suits and being waited on by college servants. The food, served by candlelight, was excellent, the wine abundant. When we listened to the chaplain intone the blessing, *Benedictus benedicat per Jesum Christum Dominum nostrum*, I felt briefly elevated, as if removed from the common herd – a sentiment which Christ, as well as Ronnie Bunting, would have felt made a nonsense of his calling.

A feeling of distinctiveness was one thing – I approved of that – but Bede, like many second-rate imitations of Oxford, was institutionally addicted to the college spirit. Whatever happened to us in the years ahead, wherever life took us and however we ended up, we would always, apparently, be Bedesmen, looking back with infinite fondness at our time on the banks of the Wear.

As part of the bonding process, first-year students were not only required to sing rugby songs in the bar and encouraged to attend Evensong in the 'exceptionally beautiful modern chapel', they were also expected to go camping together in the Easter break. Thus it was that our little quartet of Bedesmen found ourselves sharing a tent on the banks of Ullswater in the Lake District, where we sang jolly camp songs together and rose each morning to go for a dawn run.

Except that *I* didn't. I wasn't having any of that shit. It was bad enough that I was there; the idea that I might, in addition, play at being a Boy Scout was a fantasy to which I took violent exception. My aversion to the common weal was not universally popular. When word got about that I wasn't 'pulling my weight' in camp, an angry mob gathered. I felt like Frankenstein's monster after closing time at the village inn, but I had put on a few pounds since the Herbie Mercer episode and wasn't going to be a pushover for anyone. Chris, who had similarly elected to forego the pleasures of the campfire, stood by me, and together we hurled defiance at our tormentors. Things looked ugly. God knows what might have happened. But then Roger turned up. He had recently beaten up a local thug in a bar and had developed quite a reputation in the fisticuffs department, and it was clear that if a brawl started, someone was going to lose a mouthful of teeth. The two sides growled at each other for several seconds before the mob slunk away, torches lowered, muttering beneath their breaths.

I had survived. The monster *lived*!

Not that our stay in Cumbria was a total washout. After walking the fells west of Patterdale, Chris and I climbed Helvellyn and hiked for several miles along its spinal ridge, high above Thirlmere. That was a memorable day. We also drank a fair bit in the local pubs and sorted out many of the political dilemmas of our time. Chris was much more of a socialist than I was, and infinitely better read. I was not surprised when, some years later, after obtaining a degree at Exeter University, he became, briefly, a salesman for a dodgy range of orthopaedic beds, but you could have knocked me down with a copy of *Hello!* when he entered the Prison Service.

Roger, as our Lake District experience had shown, was not shy about coming forward. His experience as a mercenary had inured him to unpleasantness but also confirmed in him the virtue of loyalty. A South African who had fought with him in Katanga arrived out of nowhere one weekend looking for a bed. He couldn't understand why Roger had given up the good life for a 'girly' job like teaching.

'I tell you something about Roger, *Exay*,' he confided to us one evening. 'He'd never let you down – always stand by you. But he was the coolest killer in the Congo.' Cool he may have been, with a touch of steel, yet there was also a touch of Noel Coward about him.

While a tea planter, he was once visited by Angus Ogilvy, a company executive recently married to Princess Alexandra. Ogilvy asked how the potted plant he had left behind on his last visit was faring. Roger smiled, recalling that he and his colleagues regularly watered the thing by peeing into its pot. 'It's fine, sir,' he said. 'Would you like to see it?' They walked into the main office, where the plant stood next to the window. Ogilvy bent over it and caressed its leaves.

'Oh, yes,' he said. 'It's coming along splendidly. And what a distinctive perfume!'

Roger was an unabashed public performer. Asked one night by a group of rugby players in the college bar to come up with a dirty song, his choice was inspired:

> *Do you remember, dear, the morning after?*
> *I saw your tits and simply roared with laughter,*
> *See how the left one swings,*
> *These foolish things remind me of you.*

Life throughout that first year was full of incident, though entirely uneventful. I went out briefly with an attractive blonde by the name of Karen. She was gentle and decent and I liked her, but – oh! – it had to end. The fact was, she wouldn't have sex with me, which, after all I had been through, seemed like cruel and unnatural punishment. It wasn't that I didn't make the effort and do all the right things. I bought the Leonard Cohen LP, the joss sticks, the red bulb for the bedside lamp . . . everything! There was no justice in this world, and if I was any judge, even less in the next.

Not that I blamed Durham itself for any of this. Ever since my time at Bede, I have had a soft spot for Geordies. I love the accent – said to be derived, in part, from the Norsemen who settled there in the Dark Ages. I admire the way they have held on to their sense of working-class identity without the resentment that makes

Liverpool such a minefield for the unwary. Newcastle is a jewel of a city – even more so today than it was in my time. The riverside area, with its Dickensian steps and alleyways, and the bridges spanning the Tyne are remarkably evocative. And the pubs have the vitality, the sense of community – and the potential for spontaneous violence – that makes Belfast on a Saturday night such a joy.

Durham University was predictably diverse, with students from every corner of the country, if not the world. There were hundreds of clubs and societies and acre upon acre of the most beautiful landscapes in which to walk, or just sit and stare. Most of this was lost on our little circle. Our social life – indeed, our life in general – centred on the Duke of Wellington (now gone), the bar of the Three Tuns hotel and the Shakespeare Tavern, where we drank vast quantities of beer and did our best to pick up women. Such culture as we permitted to invade our lives, other than through books and records, had to include conversation and drink in about equal measure. Song was also welcome. Chris introduced me to a pal of his, Paul Lamb, so handsome and perfectly formed that it depressed me just to look at him. One of Paul's mates was Dave Richardson, a genial cove who performed folk music in pubs, and he in turn introduced me to Don McNab, from Nottingham, who played the banjo and mandolin, just like my father, and specialised in sea shanties. For a while, Dave and Don and a couple of other students played together as The Black Pig (taken from the name of the ship in the TV cartoon series *Captain Pugwash*) and a couple of times, when I could get my head around the words, I sang with them, offering a smattering of Irish songs, including 'The Ould Orange Flute', as an addition to their North Country repertoire. Don was a highly gifted musician and one of the most affable blokes I met in Durham. But he was perhaps overly fond of the booze and did not, I think, make it as a professional performer. Dave, on the other hand, went on to found Boys of the Lough, which achieved minor celebrity in the 1970s and was still touring America as recently as 2005.

A pleasant life, all in all. But pointless. There had to be a reckoning, and when the end of the year came round a familiar problem arose. I had done well in English and religious studies, in which I took a passing interest, but gave the impression overall of working to a separate and private agenda. Most damaging to my prospects – more damaging than the fact I never did PE and still couldn't count above two in binary (could anyone?) – was the fact that I knew next to nothing about educational theory, an area of inquiry that I found achingly dull.

Teaching practice at the end of the second term was an eye-opener. It meant, for a start, that I had to open my eyes each morning, put on a clean shirt and catch a bus to school – which brought back painful memories. The primary school to which I was assigned was in Craghead, a town in the heart of the Durham coalfield, overlooked by lifting gear and slagheaps, where 90 per cent of the male population between the ages of 15 and 55 worked down the pit. The only reason there weren't any younger miners was that they were prohibited by an Act of Parliament, while older colliers were excluded chiefly by reason of chronic back problems and emphysema.

The children were very small and, frankly, infantile (they are in their 40s now), which took some getting used to. Their lives had hardly begun. Ahead of them, as they grew up, lay drink, drugs, war, the Sex Pistols, unplanned pregnancies, Mrs Thatcher and the Miner's Strike, climaxing in the thankful obliteration of their entire economy. But while I found it hard to relate to the children, or even understand what they were saying half the time, I still assumed that the whole thing would be a dawdle.

When they told me two weeks later that I had failed, I was shocked. I couldn't work out what I had done wrong. The headmaster, by contrast, knew exactly: I had the wrong attitude; I turned up late; I didn't prepare my lessons; I didn't seem to know what was expected of me or what I should expect from the eight year olds in my care.

'Did you even *look* at the books they gave you?' he asked.

'What books?'

Yet not all was lost. The visiting inspector, it transpired, was a man of kindly demeanour, or at least not a total curmudgeon. He had seen 'something' in my approach to teaching that impressed him and, after speaking with the head, decided to give me another chance.

Back at Bede, it was touch and go for a while whether I would get to stay on. My humiliation was total. The hearties were beside themselves with joy. 'Bloody Ellis, thinks he's fucking smart. Bloody thicko, more like.' I was naturally glad to be the cause of such joy.

The class teacher I worked with in my first fortnight in Craghead was nice but dim. He was going out with a local lass and expected to marry, have a couple of bairns and live in a two-up, two-down until retirement, which he would pass in the nearest working-man's club. For the moment, though, it was Sunderland Football Club that provided the bulk of his excitement. I found it difficult to take him seriously. For a start, English did not appear to be his first language. On day one, he handed me a series of cards that he said would help the children make sense of weights and measures. After each instruction, he had inscribed a large question mark. The first read, 'Weigh Yourself?' Next came 'Weigh Your Partner?'

What were the question marks for? I asked him.

He looked at me, pityingly. 'Oh, deah, Walta. You do 'ave a lot t'*lurrn*, doan't you? They're questions, y'see. Ah'm *askin'* them to do somethin'.'

The teacher in my second class was a distinct improvement – much more old school. He saw through me right away, but I didn't mind, as I'd decided the only way out of my dilemma was to be transparently honest. The inspector, he told me, would be back at the end of the week when he would 'invigilate' a lesson in story writing. In the meantime, I would have to teach the boys and girls sums, as well as something about the history of the Northeast. 'Other than that,' he said, 'just help out.'

Things went better than I thought. A lot better. Perhaps being on probation was what I needed. I made little cards, just like the ones that had been shown to me by the first teacher – but without the question marks – and the children and I had a fine old time with a set of scales and a measuring tape. I told them about St Cuthbert and the Venerable Bede and, if I remember rightly, something about the history of Ireland too. We even managed an art lesson, complete with aprons and jars of water and paint all over the floor. By the time the inspector called, I was back in everybody's good books, and my creative-writing lesson, conducted with the aid of a candle (they had to finish their story before it flickered and died) was judged to be a huge success.

The head wasn't fooled. 'You've got it, lad,' he told me before I left for the last time to catch the bus back to Durham. 'You could be a teacher and do some good in the world. Thing is, will you?'

The question, complete with its interrogation mark, hung in the air.

I didn't see much of Ronnie during the long summer break. He had gone to pick peas for Birds Eye Foods in Cambridgeshire. Alan and I tried to follow his example, but by the time we got there we were too late and missed out, which meant that we were stranded. What to do? Someone mentioned that Eastern Counties, the Norfolk-based bus company, was looking for conductors for the summer season. And since Norfolk was just across the way, we decided to give it a go. It worked. In King's Lynn, just south of The Wash, they were more than happy to see us. Less than a day after our arrival, having found beds in a hostel somewhere on the edge of town, we were temporarily enrolled in the Transport and General Workers' Union and ready to start collecting fares.

There was just one snag. Well, two snags actually. First, it was made clear to us that we were on no account to issue tickets in respect of all the fares we received, especially during the morning rush hour. Standard procedure, we were assured, was to pocket about a quarter of the money we took. If we failed to do this, we would be letting everybody else down and inviting an official investigation, and we didn't want that on our conscience, did we?

No, we said, we didn't want that.

'Just remember to give the driver his share.'

'Right.'

The other thing we needed to know presented an ethical dilemma of a different kind. 'We don't 'old with *'omos* round here,' the shop steward said. He had a patchy beard and rings round his eyes and looked as if he didn't hold with washing either. Everyone nodded in agreement. 'If the company asks you if you'd like to be an 'omo, you say no – understand? On no account are you to end up as 'omos because we won't stand for it. You got a problem with that?'

We looked at each other and at them. 'No problem,' we said.

'Good. Fuck off, then. Your drivers are waiting.'

We slung our ticket machines over our shoulders and broke open the tubes of change into our satchels. Then we headed out to the stand.

Alan waited until we were out of earshot. 'What the fuck was that about?' he asked me.

'No idea,' I said. 'But if anyone from management calls you in for a chat, watch your arse!'

Only later did we learn the true import of the Union's advice. 'Omos – OMOs – were one-man operators, a combination of driver and conductor. Eastern Counties was trying to break up two-man crews, which meant redundancies, and the T&G was not anti-gay, it was anti-unemployment.

While Neil Armstrong and Buzz Aldrin walked on the moon that summer, my routes took me all over Norfolk's lunar landscape:

Norwich, Hunstanton, Cromer, Swaffham and as far afield as Peterborough and Bury St Edmunds. In the early mornings, the local runs out to the food-processing plants and other factories on the outskirts of town were extremely busy, while the afternoon runs through the rural heart of the county allowed me to put my feet up on the top deck and watch the fields and villages go by. Back at the depot, lunch was a corned beef sandwich and a mug of strong tea, and when the shift was done action shifted to the Woolpack, in the Tuesday Market Place, where beer was 1s 3d a pint.

I met a local girl in the Woolpack, and the resulting relationship was for a while quite promising. She had blonde hair, blue eyes and legs that went all the way up to her arse. Dipaolo – notoriously hard to please – would have approved. Having been awarded a 2:1 in geography, she was due to begin researching a Ph.D. at University College London in September. But for the moment, she was back with her parents in King's Lynn and free as a bird. I liked her. She was bright and well informed, if a touch on the serious side, and I was impressed by her academic assiduity, which contrasted rather markedly with my own fecklessness. Needless to say, I wanted into her knickers. It had been a long time. But it was not to be. Even when we went away for a weekend to Betws-y-coed in North Wales, where the weather was so wet and windy that we had to spend nearly all of our time indoors, the action was distinctly one-sided. I got into her knickers all right. Each day, sometimes twice, she would draw my hand up her skirt and place it exactly where she wanted it. Then she would close her eyes and slowly shift her buttocks on the bed. Perhaps she was thinking of the geology of England, but she seemed to be soaring somewhat above. There was to be no payback. That was the terrible part of it. 'I'm not turning you on, man,' she announced, as I squirmed and pleaded in the blackness.

It was as if I hadn't lost my virginity after all, just mislaid it, and now it had been returned to me in near-pristine condition, marked 'One Careful Owner'. I was reminded that the B-side of the Stones' latest hit, 'Honky Tonk Women', was 'You Can't Always Get What You Want'. No wonder I was in a Leonard Cohen frame of mind.

The summer passed and by mid-September, with my relationship in King's Lynn still on the long finger, as it were, it was time to make my way back to Durham. A career in some unknown secondary school in Belfast, or Manchester, or London, had still to be secured. I may not have wanted to be a teacher, but what else was there?

To save money, I caught the ferry from Larne to Stranraer and hitch-hiked to Carlisle, from which hard-drinking town there was a rail connection to Newcastle. Somewhere on the A35, west of Dumfries, a middle-aged man stopped to give me a ride. At first, he seemed perfectly normal, but then he informed me that he was a schoolteacher and was particularly interested in the question of corporal punishment.

'Oh, yes,' I began, wondering where this was leading.

'Aye. No everyone agrees with it these days, but if you ask me it's bloody essential.'

'Er . . . quite so.'

'What aboot Northern Ireland? Do they go in for it there?'

'Well . . . you know . . .'

He turned toward me, a manic glint in his eye. 'We use the taws in Scotland.'

'Indeed.'

I recalled, from reading *The Broons* at my granny's, what the taws was – a leather strap, flanged at one end, with which schoolmasters thrashed errant pupils until their arses were hot enough to use as a toaster. Leader-writers at the old *Sunday Post* used to say it was only the taws that stood between order and anarchy in Scotland.

What was going on?

By way of an answer, my driver pulled the car off the road and got out. Then he opened the boot and, to my surprise, took out his taws. Removing his jacket and bending over the bonnet of the car, he handed them to me.

'I just wanted tae show you it – so that you'd know. But noo that we're here, the seat of my trousers seems to be particularly dusty. Must be all that chalk. Do you think you could help me to clean up?'

I stood on the roadside, fingering the taws.

'Go on,' he said. 'Lay into me. Go as hard as you like.'

I began in a tentative manner, barely flicking him with the strap. But as he urged me on – 'Harder! Harder!' – I soon got into it. I mean, it's not often such an opportunity arises and he was asking for it. What passing motorists, hurrying towards the M6, made of our little tableau I can only imagine. Thwack, thwack, thwack. After maybe a dozen strokes, with his backside singing 'Ave Maria', my benefactor-turned-masochist stood up and twisted round in my direction. His eyes were glazed and he stumbled over his words. Perhaps it would be best if we called it a day, he said. I agreed and fetched my bag from the back seat. Then I watched as he climbed gingerly back into his car and drove off. That evening, on the train to Newcastle, I found myself humming the old spiritual: 'If I can help somebody as I pass along, then my living will not be in vain.'

My mother would have been so proud.

In Durham, there was to be no return to Thorp House. Second-year students were not housed in college, we had to find our own accommodation. And this is where Jonathan came into his own.

During the long vacation, he had bought a house: 14 Magdalene Street, off Gilesgate, 500 yards or so up the road from Bede. It cost him, I think, £4,000, which he paid in full with a cheque. It was like running into the young Richard Branson. The house, at the end of a long terrace, dated from around 1880. It was small, with just two bedrooms and a tiny back garden. Jonto had a room to himself at the rear, which he shared with his violin. God knows what they did to each other. Chris and I shared at the front. It was wonderful. We didn't bother with a television: we weren't going to be the sorts who just sat in each evening and watched the box; we were going to have real lives. But we had our own washing machine and spin dryer, and our own fridge. We cooked for ourselves. We rediscovered toast and individual fruit pies. While Jonto played on his G-string, Chris set up the record player in the living room and played Bach and Dylan at full volume.

As the new term unfolded, another teaching practice came and went, this time without serious incident. Oddly (you might think), I remember nothing of the experience, save that the victims were teenagers rather than infants and the crime scene was in Chester-le-Street, where I later went with friends, all wearing cowboy hats, to see *A Fistful of Dollars*.

Intellectual life at Bede was distinctly low-key and depressing. It was as if teachers were to be trained to do everything except think. I put my studies on a strict care-and-maintenance basis and looked around for something – or someone – else to do. The choice was limited. For a while, I hung around with some second-year girls from the neighbouring St Hild's College, who were active in any number of societies and liked experimenting with different sorts of tea. They had a house in the North Bailey, opposite the east end of the cathedral, and set up their own camomile lawn on the neighbouring Palace Green. They were an incredibly cosy trio and, I'd have to say, civilised – in the way that only a certain type of English girl can be. I liked my young ladies. Whether or not they had sex lives, I am in no position to say. I know *I* didn't.

But better times, thank God, were just around the corner. Alan Kirker, embarking on his third and final year at Van Mildert College, had begun going out with a girl he had met while we were still at school – the girl he would end up marrying. But he knew that I was having a bit of a lean time of it on the romantic front and wangled me an invitation one afternoon to a party at Trevelyan College, an all-female institution on the town's southern edge. That was where I met Jean.

Jean was a jolly girl. She was great fun and up for most things short of group sex. It was at Trevelyan College in the middle of our first, or possibly second, date that I fell full-length on her in her narrow bed, venting 18 months of frustration in a single, glorious outpouring of lust. Trumpets and bagpipes sounded together. After feats of endurance that would live in history, Mafeking and Lucknow were relieved together. It was as if a huge lump of congealed porridge had been surgically removed from my abdominal cavity. I was free and inspired. Even the fact that Jean's room-mate walked in in the middle of the second act of a repeat performance failed to distract me. Suddenly, the world was a brighter place. Colours were sharper; birds sang sweetly. No longer did I turn away, scowling, from my fellow human beings.

Inevitably, this mood of optimism soon wore off. For a time, Jean and I enjoyed a healthy relationship. We did a lot of things together – apart from the obvious. But my sense of impending doom, like a pantomime villain, continued to burst in on our reverie, mocking my hopes, reminding me that everything in my dystopic personal universe was sure to go horribly wrong. By the time Christmas came round, I realised that I was never going to be a teacher and was only wasting my time by staying on at Bede. It was good that I could admit this at last, but also a challenge. For if not teaching, then what?

Help came from an unexpected quarter. My mother – more aware of my distress than I ever realised or gave her credit for – sent me a cutting from the *Belfast Telegraph*. The city's College of Business Studies was seeking applicants for a new one-year course in practical journalism. The qualification it offered was minimal: the proficiency certificate of the National Council for the Training of

Journalists. But it promised yet another fresh start, free of all the crap that made my quasi-academic life at Bede such a pain in the arse. I decided to go for it. I sent off my application, then got down to some serious partying.

Christmas passed by like a siege. Belfast, at the end of 1969, was a very different place from the city I grew up in. Catholic insurrection was widespread. The Northern Ireland Civil Rights Association was by now a powerful source of agitation. But as its demands for One Man One Vote, fair employment and the proper allocation of public housing ran up against unionist intransigence, more violent, revolutionary elements started to emerge. Three days before the New Year crawled, mewling, over the corpse of the old, the Provisional IRA was born, repudiating the parliaments of London, Dublin and Belfast and reaffirming what the Irish Republican Army referred to as its 'basic military role'. I had no idea what lay ahead. Nobody had. But it didn't look good.

Back in Magdalene Street, it was all change. Chris had a new girlfriend, Sally. He had also grown a beard, though, as I pointed out, you could still see his chin. Jonto had at the same time taken up with a local woman called Beryl, about ten years his senior, who, to judge from the bags under his eyes, was giving him as much of a good time as he could safely handle. He looked like he was on drugs.

Jean and I broke up almost at once. In this, she was blameless. On the contrary, I had much to thank her for. The fact was, I wasn't going to be around much longer. The College of Business Studies in Belfast had accepted me for the journalism course beginning in September, and Bede was all at once an irrelevance. I suppose I must have told the council at some point that I was dropping out. At any rate, my grant stopped and I signed on the dole to make ends meet. Much of my time over the remaining few months in England was spent in the Britannia Inn, in Gilesgate, spending my dole money. The publican, Harry Defty, and his wife became so used to Chris, Roger, Jonathan and me during this time that they left us to pull our own pints. An unexpected bonus in this fag-end phase was Hazel, a lively girl, you'd have to say, who introduced me to pleasures I scarcely knew existed. Sometimes, after she left to go back to her own college, I was so sore I could hardly move. I regretted that I was leaving. But I knew that I couldn't carry on like this. One morning, towards the end of March, I packed my trunk, called a taxi and headed back to the station, where for the last time I drank in the view of the Durham acropolis.

To my enormous regret, that was the last time I saw Roger – though I spoke to him recently on the telephone. He's retired now after 28 years in teaching and lives back in his home town of Harrogate, a few doors up the road from the house in which he was born. Chris visited him about 20 years ago when he was teaching in Ludlow. Roger, it turned out, was about to appear before the local magistrate. While attempting to get into his car one night after an evening's entertainment, he had inadvertently released the handbrake, so that the vehicle lurched forward and somehow ran him down. The local constabulary chanced upon the scene as he was struggling to recover his dignity. I don't know how it all came out, but he clearly survived and lived to fight another day. I'm sure the boys he taught down the years learned a great deal from Rog and much enjoyed the experience. I know I did.

I spoke in the last chapter about Ireland and the Irish. My point was to identify with Protestant sensibilities (which are the sensibilities I was brought up with) while making it clear that I favoured Irish unity within the European Union. But what about the English? How do I feel about the people amongst whom I have lived, off and on, for more than twenty years? I will make three observations. They are a sharp and funny people who drink more than is good for them and always have. Their educated elite are deeply impressive, yet shallow, taking neither themselves nor anyone else seriously. And, of course, they are riven by class. Yet, in spite of all the exasperation I have known down the years, I remain deeply fond of England. Most of my best and oldest friends are English and I value my continuing links with them above most things. I also appreciate that England (not Britain) is in the middle of a radical reinvention of itself brought about by mass immigration and the struggle by the indigenous English both to adapt to and survive what is happening to them. The English are much maligned in the rest of the world for their alleged inability to get along with others and their innate sense of superiority. But in my experience, they have advanced faster and further in the race game than either France or the United States, and if they sometimes get above themselves, it is a function of their long history, during which they have generally punched far above their weight. I wish them well and hope they get their act together soon. They deserve it.

Back in Belfast, having left Durham, there was the small problem of money. Dad wouldn't hear of me signing on, so found me a job with an acquaintance of his, Alec Buchanan, a fellow Mason, who evidently owed him a favour. Buchanan, brother of the then newly installed Church of Ireland Archbishop of Dublin, owned a wholesale curtain-rail company up the Crumlin Road, on the way to the airport, which supplied shops all over the North.

My new boss was straight as a die but utterly humourless, with grimy fingernails and a brain like an adding machine. He was as dedicated to the minutiae of curtain suspension as his brother was to the salvation of souls. Wooden poles, steel poles, Nylonglyde, Sololyde: Buchanan never met a curtain rail he didn't like. My job was to assemble the various rails, hooks, screws and other bits and bobs ordered up by retailers and then deliver them in the company van. A lot of the runs I made were in and around Belfast, but I got to go to Derry and Enniskillen as well, giving me an opportunity to talk to people about the Troubles and what they thought was going to happen next. Slightly closer to home was the excursion twice a week to Downpatrick, where Ireland's patron saint is allegedly buried. I liked to walk round the cathedral – a modest construction by comparison to St Cuthbert's – and stand next to the grave itself, marked simply 'Pádraig' (almost certainly a fake). On the way back, if there was time, Mahee Island, in Strangford Lough, was a favourite stop. My dad used to play golf on the local course before he was elected to Clandeboye. But what I enjoyed was the tranquillity of nearby Nendrum Abbey, a Celtic foundation sacked several times by the Vikings and now protected by the National Trust. I liked to sit up on the stump of the abbey's Round Tower and eat my sandwiches. You could see all the way across to Portaferry, on the Ards Peninsula, and south as far as the Mountains of Mourne. Before leaving each time, I touched a hawthorn tree in the field next door for luck. It was said to have magical qualities and to be a home for faeries; I reckoned that if it could do me any good, I'd be a fool to pass up the chance.

One of Buchanan's biggest customers was the Spinning Mill in downtown Belfast, which had its own goods yard. Two or three times a week I would load up the van with curtain rails, some of them 15 or 16 feet long, and deliver them to the Spinning Mill. The young fellow who took delivery from me and signed my dockets, and who nodded and grunted at me but didn't otherwise speak, was called David McKittrick. A few months later, when I started the journalism course, I found him sitting next to me. He, too, was a university drop-out. As Ireland correspondent for *The Independent* – a position which I secured for him in 1986, having turned it down myself – he would go on to win practically every award British and Irish journalism had to offer and write an acclaimed series of books on the course and future direction of the Irish Troubles.

While I anticipated my future, Northern Ireland became as unstable as a drunk on a unicycle. The Provisional IRA wasn't content, like the great majority of Irish nationalists, to play 'Patriot Game' on the gramophone. Not since Pádraig Pearse wrote of the need to warm Ireland's earth with the red wine of the battlefield was there such bloody certainty. On the Unionist side, the administration at Stormont, led by the well intentioned but ludicrous figure of Terence O'Neill, was almost wholly discredited. O'Neill, to his own surprise but no one else's, was the one who finally played the Orange card as the two rather than the ace of trumps. Power from this point on would shift from the Big Houses of the Ascendancy and their Orange acolytes to a new generation of loyalist hardliners for whom scorched earth was the answer to the blood-dimmed tide. Certainty was the new Protestant discourse. Loyalists had no idea what to do but were determined to do it anyway. It was around this time that the British Home Secretary, Reginald Maudling, paid his first visit to Belfast. He couldn't believe the chaos and bitterness that he encountered. As he boarded his flight home to London, he remarked to an aide: 'For God's sake, bring me a large Scotch. What a bloody awful country!'

Reaching ever deeper into the disequilibrium of our relationship, Ronnie Bunting remained a brooding presence. The difference now was that he was more Caliban than McCavity. Chris Dipaolo came over to see me for a couple of days over the Easter break – an emotional time for republicans, when they remember the dead of 1916. I wasn't surprised when he told me he wanted to visit the infamous Falls Road. I called Ronnie and arranged that we would meet him in the Old House, the shebeen in Leeson Street where he and I passed many a hard night while I was still at Queen's.

We turned up around eight in the evening. Alan and his girlfriend, Fiona, were with us. The Old House, in those days, was a couple of upstairs rooms reached by way of a narrow set of stairs leading up from a side door. Ronnie was seated at a table surrounded by cronies. There was no mistaking him. He wore a PVC jacket, black shirt and high-waisted loon pants. He seemed pleased enough to see us but, chillingly, acted more like a leader among his subordinates than the anarchist of old. He still drank lager, I noted, and still pecked at it like a bird. But he had acquired a darker purpose that I felt sure he was not about to share with me. The aura of barely contained violence about him was overwhelming.

The Old House, as ever, was a riot. Everyone wore small adhesive badges on their lapels or dress fronts bearing the emblem of an Easter Lily. It was for this reason that the Officials were known as 'Stickies'. Provisionals, being traditionalists, wore old-style badges that you stuck on with a pin. Noise swelled up repeatedly as if the customers were a collective organ with all the stops pulled out. There was music everywhere – guitars and penny whistles, an accordion and fiddle, probably uillean pipes over in the corner – and any number of singers. All this was against the general background roar: punters shouting their orders across the counter; barmen hollering back, announcing the delivery of a round; new arrivals calling out greetings to their friends; and endless, raucous laughter. I may have offered a song, I don't recall. If I did, it was most likely 'Ashtown Road', 'Four Green Fields' or 'The Butcher Boy' – though an Orange song (provided it was sung ironically) would have served just as well. At some point there would have been a spirited rendition of 'The Man From the *Daily Mail*', a strangely popular ballad satirising British journalists:

> *Oh, Ireland is a very funny place, sir, it's a strange and troubled*
> *   land,*
> *And the Irish are a very funny race, sir, every girl's in the Cumann*
> *   na mBan.*
> *Every doggy has a tricoloured ribbon tied firmly to its tail,*
> *And it wouldn't be surprising if there'd be another rising,*
> *Said the man from the* Daily Mail.

Chris, though understandably nervous to be an Englishman in such a setting, was enjoying himself. Ronnie's heavy sideburns, Clark

Gable moustache and unceasing surveillance made him look like a bandit leader. He certainly had the celluloid swagger of an early cinema hero. Like many Irish gatherings, the evening was a heady mix of fun, laughter and malevolence – a pressure cooker that could blow at any moment. As a Bollinger Bolshevik (more properly a Lanson liberal), Chris revelled in the pain and exhilaration of the oppressed. What happened next put paid to his complacency.

A harsh voice echoed across the bar from the doorway. 'Hey, Bunting, you Proddie bastard! Where are you? Why don't you show your face, you fucker?'

Three of the heavies sitting at Ronnie's table rose immediately and went over to the source of the trouble: a large muscled man in his 40s, with broad shoulders and a paunch.

'It's OK, lads,' Ronnie said, 'let him through.' Then he excused himself and stood up from his chair. Everyone in the bar was still. The atmosphere was thick with menace. The stranger could feel the hostility and the anticipation, but he stood his ground. Big men knew the odds. After a moment, he made up his mind and moved forward. One of Ronnie's 'minders' stepped in front of him but was pushed aside as the new arrival advanced like a bulldozer. With his first punch, he caught Ronnie on the side of the head, sending him reeling into a table laden with drinks. Everyone at the table jumped up in alarm. The assailant roared his way past the debris, but before he could land a second blow he froze in pain and astonishment. Ronnie's boot had swung up from nowhere and caught him full in the crotch. He began to fold. As he swayed, Ronnie reached to his left, picked up a whiskey bottle that served as a candlestick and brought it down full force on the man's temple. The glass shattered and suddenly there was blood everywhere. The stranger was paralysed with shock. He couldn't speak, but somewhere inside he was screaming.

'Time to go, I think,' Chris said, as if suggesting an early departure from a failing musical. Then he paused and glanced around. He was a big fan of *The Lord of the Rings* and suddenly detected in the rising tide of threat and counter-threat the mindless menace of the Orcs. He looked at me, his eyes pleading. 'For fuck's sake, let's get out of here!' Alan and I didn't need any further prompting. Fiona already had her coat on.

Outside, as the intruder was bundled, bleeding, into the street, a crowd gathered. Evidently, the man, whoever he was, had his supporters too. Someone shouted something. A man on our side threw a glass. Ronnie stood at the front of his people, jeering and gesticulating.

'Goodnight, Ronnie,' I said to him. 'We have to go. But thanks for a wonderful evening.' I doubt he even noticed.

Chris didn't hang around in Belfast after that. 'I was shitting my pants,' he told me recently. He caught the train to Lisburn, where he failed to make contact with a cousin in the forces, and then hitch-hiked south. Two days later, somewhere beyond Thurles, County Tipperary, he was picked up by a priest driving a Morris Minor. The priest, who was young, was going all the way to Cork and they soon fell into conversation.

'You'd be English, I'd say.'

'My mother's English, my father's Italian.'

'So you're a Catholic, then?'

'I wouldn't say that, exactly. But I was baptised, if that's what you mean.'

A pause.

'I expect you've been out with women and all that sort of thing.'

'Yes.'

'I mean, you know, *sex*.'

'I've had sex, yes.'

'I see. I see. That's very interesting.'

Another pause.

'Do you mind if I ask you something?'

'Go ahead.'

'It's just that I was wondering. When you had, er, *intercourse* – with a woman, I mean – how *long* were you in there?'

Chris, now a respected prison governor, was understandably disturbed by the priest's line of questioning but even more put out when the fellow's left hand moved surreptitiously off the gear knob and towards another neighbouring knob – *his*. The shock he felt was profound. He couldn't get out of the car quick enough. If only he'd had a decent leather strap!

Back in Belfast, Ronnie Bunting was confronted with an altogether different kind of moral dilemma. He was a Marxist, entirely without religious conviction, and the naked sectarianism of the new breed of republicans, whom he dismissed as the Rosary Beads Brigade, made it impossible for him to throw his lot in with the Provisionals. At some point, certainly by the time Chris met up with him in the Old House, he had instead joined the avowedly secular Official Republican Movement, with its principal powerbase in the Lower Falls and Markets districts of Belfast. Whether he was militarily active at the time, I don't know. What I *do* know is that he was in close contact with the most senior and dangerous elements of the Official IRA.

In the early summer of 1971, he called my mother at home and asked her if she could do him a big favour. A friend of his, he said, had had a terrible argument with his wife, who had thrown him out of the house. The friend, called Joe, was very upset by what had happened, he told her. If Mum could just put him up for a couple of days, he was sure they'd sort things out and get back together. My mother was puzzled. Why hadn't he asked me instead of coming directly to her? Because it was her house, he said, and he didn't want her to feel under any kind of obligation. That clinched it. She'd known Ronnie since he was 12 years old, and she and his dad were cousins. Sure what harm could it do? And after him asking so nicely. Joe turned up just hours later, before I even got home, and introduced himself. He was good-looking, charming, with impeccable manners. Mum took to him instantly. Dad was more circumspect. He approved of the fact that he got on well with our dog, a Tibetan terrier called Kwang, but he couldn't help wondering what he had done to make his wife so cross. I remember sitting down to dinner with the three of them (four, if you count Kwang). Dad asked Joe where he was from.

'The Lower Falls,' he said, 'but we were moved up to the Highfield estate, must have been 1959–60. Do you know it?'

'Know it?' my dad said. 'Sure I've a couple of shops there.'

'You're kiddin'?'

'The grocer's and the hardware.'

'Down by the Green? Small world.'

'Aye. But of course you wouldn't be there now.'

'Hardly.'

'Hardly. What happened?'

'What d'you think?'

There was a brief silence. Highfield had once been a mixed estate. By 1970, it was 100 per cent Protestant. 'So, where did you end up? Ballymurphy?'

'Close enough.'

Dad's eyes narrowed. After his tea, he would normally have lit up a cigarette, only he'd had to give them up: his heart couldn't take the strain. 'And what about now?'

'After we got married, the wife and me found ourselves a wee place in the Markets.'

That was better. Dad knew the Markets well. Madrid Street was just the other side of the river. 'And what do you do for a living, Joe? Not on the dole, I hope.'

'I'm a brickie.'

'Aye, well, there's always work in that. Make a fortune, some of youse.' He looked at me. 'Not like this one here. So, what's the problem? At home, I mean.'

Joe offered a sheepish smile. 'It's not what you think. Fact of the matter is, I had a skinful last night and we got into a bit of a shoutin' match. You know what the women are like.'

My father's face betrayed no obvious emotion. The *Belfast Telegraph* was lying on the table in front of him, full of the latest news about shootings, civil-rights protests and unrest in Derry. 'Terrible times we live in, son. Whole place gone mad. What about you, though? Things the way they are, you must have been tempted.'

Joe made a face. 'You mean the IRA? Jesus, no, Mr Ellis. I don't hold with none of that nonsense. All I want's a quiet life.'

'Good man yourself. Molly – give this young fella here a scoot of tea. Sure his cup's empty.'

Who did I think he was? I don't know. All I did know was that he had been invited into our home by Ronnie, and Ronnie subscribed to the view that no good deed should ever go unpunished. I didn't ask questions. I wasn't going to tempt fate. Like the old adage goes: whatever you say, say nothing.

Joe only stayed two days in the end. On the Monday morning, he announced that it was time for him to head back and face the music. Dad gave him a lift to the Markets on his way to work. We shook hands and he gave my mother a hug and told her he was terribly grateful to her for her hospitality. She thought that was nice of him. Like her own mother, she appreciated a show of good manners.

He wasn't Joe the brickie, of course. Or at least hadn't been for several years. He was Joe McCann, soon to be the Most Wanted man in Ireland. A day or two before going into hiding at my mum's, he had shot and killed a British soldier in Cromac Square and was on the run. He never stayed more than a night or two in the same place. In the months ahead, he would be responsible for scores of attacks on soldiers and members of the RUC. He also took the time to shoot John Taylor, the Home Affairs Minister at Stormont, who survived, miraculously, despite taking five bullets in his chest and jaw.

McCann's most famous exploit came when he and his men took over the Inglis bakery (my mother's favourite), next to an Army post, and set it ablaze, holding off almost an entire regiment of British troops. A photograph showing a silhouette of Joe down on one knee, with his M1 Carbine in his hand and the Starry Plough fluttering above, ran on the cover of *Life* magazine and a hundred other publications round the world. It was the most romantic image to come out of the Troubles. But the man was doomed. Charmed lives depend on luck, and luck always runs out. When soldiers of the Parachute Regiment gunned down McCann, unarmed, in April 1972, the result was the biggest republican funeral Belfast had ever seen. The cortège was said to be a mile long. Ronnie was inconsolable and adapted 'The Ballad of Joe Hill' – one of his favourite anthems – to suit the enormity of the moment.

I don't think my mum ever mentioned the McCann incident. I didn't tell her Joe's true identity and if she suspected something was amiss, she didn't say. My mum would have been good at being Jewish. She was a great one for absorbing everything that happened to her and accepting it as God's will. It wasn't that she didn't get angry sometimes (witness the rattling of the saucepans and the swish of the kitchen knives), but she internalised most things, covering over her disappointments like an oyster wrapping grit in pearl. She didn't complain; she 'tholed'. Whatever suffering was visited on us in this life, she reckoned, was all weighed up in the balance of the Last Judgement.

For her sake, I hope she was right.

But I'm getting ahead of myself. After his graduation from Queen's, Ronnie and Suzanne moved from their flat in the Stranmillis area to a council house in the Clarawood estate, not far from Orangefield. They had got married the previous year in an impromptu yet oddly formal civil ceremony (to which I was not invited), and Suzanne's somewhat forlorn hope was that they could settle down and raise a family. Clarawood, in the loyalist heartland, was a less-than-inspired choice for a renegade and, with ethnic cleansing on the increase, their stay was brief. Several short-term moves followed before they ended up in what would be their final home, in Downfine Gardens, Turf Lodge, an enclave of Official sympathies next to strongly Provisional Ballymurphy. Political agitation was one thing, but there were still practical matters to be considered. Ronnie – who would never have found work in a Catholic school (and wouldn't have wanted it in any case) – started teaching history in the Protestant Ballygomartin area, where presumably he did not advertise his politics. But this was odd, too – an indication of his curious naivety. There is nothing worse in the loyalist lexicon than a turncoat (a 'Lundy' in the local vernacular, after the Governor of Derry who wanted to surrender his city to King James in 1688) and once it was realised in the staffroom that Major Bunting's son did not exactly share his father's politics, the writing was on the blackboard. He got the hell out before they lynched him.

It wasn't only among 'his own' that Ronnie faced enemies. Irish revolutionary politics are lethal. It used to be said that whenever any group was formed, the first item on the agenda was the 'split'. Coexistence with former comrades was regarded as soft. People got shot in the back mainly because they were forever walking out on their opponents. In Belfast, the turf war between Officials and Provisionals was about to get ugly, ending in regular re-enactments of the Saint Valentine's Day Massacre. But during the summer of 1970, as republicans in particular and communities in general adjusted to what was happening around them, there was an uneasy peace.

I, you will not be surprised to learn, had no part to play in any of this. While Ulster moved into meltdown, my primary concern was to obtain my proficiency certificate and start earning a living – which meant sticking the pace at the College of Business Studies and then finding someone who was prepared to offer me a job.

The college, built of institutional concrete and glass, occupied a corner of Brunswick Street and Amelia Street (once celebrated for its prostitutes) close to the City Hall. It was approached by way of the ornate Crown Liquor Saloon and a betting shop known as the Beaten Docket. To my surprise, several of our lecturers turned out to be first-rate. Andrew Boyd was a caustic, quick-witted political commentator from a Labour background, who, in his biography of Brian Faulkner, Ulster's latest Prime Minister, observed of his subject's record in the Second World War: 'There was no conscription in Ulster. Service was voluntary. Faulkner did not volunteer.' Jonathan Bardon, a soft-spoken Dubliner who went on to write the definitive *A History of Ulster*, gave us a valuable southern perspective on events. Miss Martin (I'm not sure she had a first name, unless it was 'Miss') taught us shorthand and typing as if our lives – and not just our pensions – depended on it. And presiding over everyone and everything was Joan Fitzpatrick, a flame-haired temptress and one-time diva at the *News Letter*, who honestly believed that sound reporting, free of cant, was not only desirable but also a realistic and achievable goal. Her twin mantras – 'Say it, say that you've said it, then say it again' and 'Always cut from the bottom' – stood each of us, I feel sure, in good stead when times were tough and we didn't know what to do next.

My fellow students were an oddly distinguished crew. There was David McKittrick, of course, my graduate of the Spinning Mill, still unravelling 'spin' after all these years at *The Independent*; Malachi O'Doherty, elf-like and bearded, later to be a learned columnist on the *Belfast Telegraph* and editor of the magazine *Fortnight*; Charlie Mallon, from Roslea on the Fermanagh border, steeped in down-home republicanism, destined to be a top foot-in-the-door man for the *Irish Independent*; Gillian Chambers, the Prom Queen, who flirted with all of us then ran off to a new life in Hong Kong; Deirdre Mooney, sultry but unyielding, destined, to her own surprise, to feed celebrity stories to the tabloids from the south of France; Elizabeth Rice, another Dubliner, hard-working and anxious and a valued producer with the BBC; Laurence White and Robin Morton, one Catholic, one Protestant, colleagues on the *Belfast Telegraph* for 30 years; and Austin Hunter, who, after almost two decades with BBC NI, became chief press officer for the RUC, then, without missing a beat, editor of the *News Letter*.

Like they say in Belfast, they done good.

There isn't much to report about our year in Amelia Street, save to say that, throughout, everyone thought that my name was Seamus – which is not surprising given that this is what I told them, hoping thereby to appear more Irish than the Irish themselves. My mild deception caused me some embarrassment later on – most obviously when McKittrick turned up my birth certificate – but is echoed to this day in my insistence that my middle name, James, be rendered in its Irish form. (What the hell! Seán Mac Stiofáin, chief-of-staff of the Provisional IRA in the 1970s, was in reality John Stephenson from Leytonstone; Antóin Mac Unfraidh, one of Ireland's leading diplomats, later to work with me in Brussels, was born plain Tony Humphreys.)

One niggle relating to my training year is that I have no recollection of ever being awarded my promised proficiency certificate – or even of the subject coming up. Perhaps you had to apply for it in shorthand. If so, I didn't bother. What I did instead, on a whim, was write a letter to the editor of the *Cork Examiner*, the most distant of the southern dailies, offering my services overtly as a Protestant. The *Belfast Telegraph* had turned me down. So had the *Kilkenny People*. Well, what did *they* know? But the *Examiner* was all for me.

Its then chief executive, Donal Crosbie (known as Mr Donal, to distinguish him from his brothers, Mr Ted and Mr George), thought it was an excellent idea that the journal of Rebel Cork should have an 'Orange' reporter from the Black North on its staff. I was hired more or less by return of post, on a salary (net) of £15.63 a week and told to report for duty as soon as possible.

I set off from Belfast in a five-year-old Ford Anglia – the one with the inverted rear window, as featured in Harry Potter – on the morning of Sunday, 1 August. My journey south took me through the Irish midlands, into the Bog of Allen, and it was there, while taking what I thought to be a shortcut, that I blundered, at 60 miles an hour, into a sudden dip in the road caused by subsidence. The impact sent all four of my shock absorbers shooting through their mountings into the car's boot and engine sections. By the time I skidded to a halt, the floor of the vehicle (or *vay-hickle*, as they say in Cork) couldn't have been more than three inches off the ground. Given that I had no money, knew nobody for a hundred miles and, anyway, it was Sunday, I crawled the remaining hundred miles or so to Cork at 20 mph, arriving when it was already dark.

I parked in Oliver Plunkett Street, in the heart of the city, leaving my trunk in the boot of the car while I scouted round for a hotel. The *Examiner* had agreed to pay my bed and board for a week to give me time to find a flat, but I'd expected to arrive hours earlier and hadn't bothered to make a reservation. As luck would have it, there was a B&B about 50 yards down the street from where I left the car. It would do. I wasn't choosy. I checked in, called home to say that I had made it – just – and went out to find a restaurant. One Chicken Maryland later and I was done for the night. It had been a long drive. As I lay in my tiny single bed, reading the *Sunday Times* colour magazine (featuring a double-page spread of a young Germaine Greer wearing a golden bikini), I had a sudden feeling that I had, at last, left my old life behind and moved on to something new.

Germaine agreed. She helped me make it through the night.

Next morning, having taken my car to a local repair shop, I

reported (as it were) to the news desk of the *Examiner* in Academy Street, just off Patrick Street, where everybody made a fuss of me for several minutes before forgetting about me completely. Mr Donal was really pleased to meet me, he said, and he was sure I'd fit right in. I'd come a long way and made a big jump, and it was up to the staff to prove to me that I was welcome. This was nice to hear, but the truth of the matter was that I hardly knew which way was up. My typing was poor, my shorthand rudimentary and I didn't have a clue how Cork was run, or by whom, or why. I couldn't even find my way to the City Hall. There was so much to learn. First, though, I needed somewhere to live. Could anyone suggest anything?

Two young reporters immediately stepped forward. One was Dixie Brazil, aged about 24, just a couple of years older than me. He had a neat goatee beard and a slightly adenoidal voice. His mother, it turned out, ran the *Examiner* office in Limerick. The other was Denis Reading, from Southampton, who looked like Davy Jones of The Monkees. They had just taken a new flat, they said, at the top of Patrick's Hill. There was a spare bedroom, if I was interested. I was, I said, and the deal was struck.

Patrick's Hill starts at the western end of MacCurtain Street (named after the same Lord Mayor of Cork who my father had seen gunned down in Lisburn in 1920). It is one of the steepest streets in Ireland, rising from the valley floor of the River Lee to a height of around 500 feet in a matter of a few hundred yards. Our house was at the summit of the hill, and our flat was at the top of the building. The view was superb, including not only the city centre but also the nearby tower of Shandon Church, the bells of which are held to be world-famous and rang out several times a week. An obvious disadvantage was that it was no place to be staggering back to while drunk, which I anticipated would happen with some frequency in the months ahead. I was not wrong.

Dixie was an excellent fellow, as was Denis. Although young, they had both been reporters since leaving school and were thus already veterans. They seemed to know everyone who was anyone, including the 'cute hoors' of all parties who ran the city. Neither, I'd have to say, chose to spend much time in the kitchen other than to fetch beer. When they found me hoovering the fridge early on, in order to be rid of a network of radial fungi that had spread out from a dead chicken, they decided that their prejudices about northern Prods as both paranoid and puritan were obviously bang on.

The work I was handed in the early days was more tricky than taxing. I attended really small and unimportant meetings of various town bodies, such as the Junior Chamber of Commerce, reporting on who had said what about some or other aspect of the Cork economy. The arrival of the annual Cork Film Festival meant free tickets from the organisers in return for published snippets on who said what and what they were wearing. When the new Cunard liner *Queen Elizabeth 2* turned up in the harbour at Cobh, I was the one despatched by tender to interview celebrities (there were none, just rich retirees). A public lecture by some visiting vulcanologist on the pollution caused by lava flows produced my first byline – an exciting moment. I stressed the expert's view that nature was entirely neutral about the state of the environment and was at least as capable as humanity of mindless destruction. Volcanoes, he told us, were large-scale polluters. They also gave rise to tsunamis. The article was probably read by about half a dozen people.

A while later, my name appeared over a story in which the Irish President, Erskine Childers, met the Catholic Bishop of Cork, Cornelius Lucey, at the opening of a school extension in the city. It was a richly comical encounter. Lucey was a Catholic prelate of pre-Vatican II vintage, who almost certainly thought Protestants were diseased and bound for Hell. Childers was a meticulously turned out political grandee from the old Protestant Ascendancy class. His father, the original Erskine Childers (author of *The Riddle of the Sands*), had been a hero of the 1916 Rising, whose execution by the new Free State government in 1922 was one of the more poignant episodes of the civil war. The two old frauds approached each other warily. When they finally met, with the *Examiner's* photographer poised to strike, the Bishop held out his hand, knuckles up, so that Childers could kiss his ring, thus acknowledging the authority of Rome. Childers stared at him over the top of his glasses, clasped the extended hand, twisted it round . . . and shook it. Gasps all round. One up for the Prods!

As a general reporter, my speciality was anything and everything. It has remained so ever since. My first hurling match was a challenge. I could see that it was exciting end-to-end stuff, but I had no idea who any of the players were or how they were getting on. I couldn't even keep track of the score. At the end of the game, I asked an official to tell me what had happened, then reported his version almost word for word. No one seemed to mind.

I liked covering the local district court. Begging, prostitution and petty larceny were the regular stock in trade. Drunkenness and its impact on Cork's social order was another recurring theme. More than once, I was reminded of Flann O'Brien.

> The Justice: 'It was well gone closing, but when the Garda entered the premises there was still drinking going on. You were found hiding in a press? What was that about? Why were you there?'
> Defendant: 'For a joke.'

The job, as I always suspected, was perfectly straightforward. After a bit, I was allowed to report city corporation meetings, then sessions of Cork County Council. One of the stalwarts of the council was John L. O'Sullivan, a former member of the Irish Parliament. He was a courtly fellow, extremely polite, who had fought with Michael Collins against the British from 1916 to 1921. He was one of the last to speak with Collins before he was assassinated by a band of IRA diehards objecting to partition. Later, John L. joined the pro-Treaty party, Fine Gael. Though in his 70s by the time I met him, he still carried himself like a soldier. He told me over a cup of tea how he had once been ordered to shoot a British Tommy captured during the fighting. The fellow was very young, no more than 18, and O'Sullivan was loath to execute him. But he did what he had to, blindfolding his prisoner and giving him time to say his prayers before putting the gun to his head.

'How did you feel as you pulled the trigger?' I asked him.

'Well,' he said, in the peculiar sing-song accent of Cork, 'I couldn't help but notice as we took him out to the yard that he was wearing a fine pair of Army boots and that his feet looked to be about the same size as my own.'

'So you took his boots?' I said.

'God help me, but I did.'

And what did he think of the Provisionals up in the North.

'A load of bad *bestards*!' he said, lowering his voice to a whisper. 'If they want justice, they'll have to talk to the British sooner or later.'

'Just like you did?'

He smiled and patted my hand. 'Well, not everyone agreed with us then, either,' he said.

It's always unsettling to move from what you know to what you don't know. Cork was no more than 300 miles from Belfast, but it felt like a different world. The old certainties didn't apply here. I wasn't a Prod, I was from the 'North', which to them was a bizarre outpost of their past best forgotten. On Sunday mornings, I liked to walk along the Lee, which divided in two at one point, with an island in the middle, and imagine the events that had gone on here in the heroic days of the national struggle. The people of the city were like people everywhere: some nice, some not so nice. But what they had in common, so far as I was concerned, was an almost total ignorance of what was going on in Belfast and Derry, combined with a sublime indifference. This turned out to be a constant.

During the referendum on the Good Friday Agreement, held in the Republic in the late summer of 1998, I returned to the city for *The European* (then on its last legs) to sound out popular opinion. The referendum, required to ratify the abandonment by the Republic of its constitutional claim to the territory of Northern Ireland, was combined with a second plebiscite on the proposed enlargement of the European Union. Corkonians were of one mind, so far as I could tell. They didn't give a stuff about the people of the North, who could go jump in the ocean for all they cared, and they didn't want the EU to be expanded if that meant any cut in the scale of largesse coming out of Brussels for Ireland. It made me realise that people are selfish the world over but don't mean any harm by it. They just want to enjoy what's theirs and not be bothered by extraneous issues.

The *Examiner*'s offices in Patrick Street were next door to a fine Cork pub with the slightly exotic name of Le Chateau. It was in Le Chateau that I would chat at length to Val Dorgan, the chief reporter, invariably dressed in a black leather jacket, whose main advice to me was never get flustered, never pass up a drink and never trust anyone who hasn't earned it. Another regular in the *Examiner* 'snug' was Cahal Henry, the veteran editor of the *Cork Evening Echo*, our sister paper. Small and wiry, with sprigs of black hair that he combed over his bald head, Cahal was a stylist and a repository of ancient wisdom but most of all a smoker. He was not a believer in the first-person narrative. 'When the "I" creeps in, the "eye" starts to close,' he told me, dragging a lungful of smoke into the narrow confines of his chest. 'You must make up your mind, Walter. Are you a *journ*alist or a *news*paper man?'

I'm still working on the answer.

The annual Fleadh Cheoil na hÉireann, or national music festival, took place that August in Listowel, County Kerry. I wasn't going to miss that. I went there with fellow reporter Dick Hogan and his wife to enjoy the music and the *craic*. I had a great time. The music was amazing, the weather was fine and the drink just kept on coming. Unfortunately, a visiting ruffian took issue with me over something or other, long since forgotten, and after a brief but violent scuffle I ended up being arrested. Dick sorted it out, stressing that I was new to the area, a Protestant and a reporter with the *Examiner*. His view, which he shared with Dixie, that northerners were strange fellows altogether, was confirmed. I think his wife was more amused than anything.

It used to be said that when visitors arrived at Belfast airport they were advised to set their watches back 300 years. Something similar applied in Cork on the subject of sexuality. There was a lot of bawdy talk in Le Chateau but, so far as I could make out, there wasn't a lot of action going on. Divorce, contraception and abortion were illegal at the time, and the influence of the Catholic Church was so strong that only 'bad' girls ever consented to sleep with you (or, at any rate, with me). There was a girl called Anne, so elegant and poised that I could have spent an entire day just watching her pass up and down the street, swinging her hips. Unfortunately, unless I was willing to propose to her, this was about as much as she was prepared to allow. Sadly, she had to go. Then there was the sister of a colleague – a flamboyantly beautiful girl who could have stepped out of a canvas by Renoir. She, too, was mindful of her honour, and dubious of mine. Most frustrating of all was a honey blonde with a passionate nature who wouldn't allow herself to go 'all the way' for fear of what her father would say. 'Well,' I told her, 'I wasn't planning on telling him. Were you?'

She looked mortified. 'Oh, God! That's terrible, so. You mustn't say things like that. Sure how could I possibly tell him? What would I *say* to him?'

This was two years before Ireland joined the Common Market and began to come of age as a nation. The modern Republic is not only rich and successful – and arrogant with it – but freed of all theocratic trappings. Then, it was a very different story. No wonder emigration soared.

My time in Cork passed all too quickly. It turned out that the *Examiner* didn't so much want a Protestant in head office as not to have to send one of their own – inevitably a Catholic, with an accent you could cut with a knife, or a meat cleaver – to Belfast. The distance between the two cities was measured in a great deal more than miles; it was felt, at the time, to be an unbridgeable gulf. Mr Donal called me into his office and told me that he'd be awfully pleased if I would agree to represent the paper in the North, on an increased salary, of course, from January onwards. What did I think of that?

I was shocked. I was quite taken aback. Would I never get out of Belfast? Was I doomed to spend the rest of my life there? But, naturally, I said yes. It was a big story and a big opportunity. I was nervous, but I was also flattered.

Belfast, when I got back (again!) just before Christmas, was a society in arms. On 9 August, while I was starting the second week of my new employment in Cork, the Stormont Prime Minister Brian Faulkner – the same man who had not volunteered for war service in 1939 – decided to exercise his powers as effective commander-in-chief of the British Army in Ulster and detain known troublemakers without trial. It was an insane decision. Internment was a disaster. Most of the hundreds of men lifted by the Army were political activists, not terrorists, from the Official Republican movement, including Ronnie Bunting – one of only two Protestants seized. Hardly any gunmen and bombers from either wing of the IRA were arrested. The

RUC didn't know who they were and, as if instructed by Claude Rains's Vichy police chief in *Casablanca*, did no more than round up the usual suspects.

The effect of detention without trial in republican areas of the North was immediate and drastic. The sense of outrage ran deep and popular resistance began almost at once. Joe McCann, leading the assault on Inglis's bakery, wasn't the only gunman to take a stand. Within days, the Provisionals had raised their colours, to dizzying acclaim, in every Catholic street in every corner of the country. At the same time, angry loyalists formed a new paramilitary force of their own, the Ulster Defence Association, that within 50 days would have 50,000 members. The British government of Prime Minister Edward Heath, hamstrung by its constitutional obligation to support the civil power in Ulster (that is to say, the unionists), was powerless in the face of events.

Violence escalated at a frightening rate. On 4 December, McGurk's bar on North Queen Street (not somewhere I frequented) was bombed by the resurgent Ulster Volunteer Force, another loyalist group which traced its roots back to the Home Rule crisis of 1912. Fifteen people, including the owner's wife and daughter, were killed and another thirteen injured, several of them seriously. A week later, the Provisionals planted a bomb in a crowded shop in the Protestant Shankill Road, killing four people, one of them a seventeen-month-old boy. By the end of the year, with relations badly strained between Britain and the Republic, the body count had reached 180. More than 1,500 bombs had gone off over the 12 months, destroying or damaging property in every corner of the province. Mr Donal was right: Cork seemed a long way off.

Before I could begin to function properly, I needed accreditation to the Stormont and Westminster governments. There was also the small matter of getting to know MPs, officials, party hacks, revolutionaries and paramilitaries. On top of that, I had to find myself an office and somewhere to live. The trouble was, with stories coming in thick and fast, I never seemed to be anywhere long enough to do anything except find things out and report them down the telephone to Cork.

On the night of 17 January, while I was in the Black Bull pub in the Markets talking to Official Republicans about their worsening feud with the Provisionals, news came through of a daring escape by seven internees from the prison ship *Maidstone* moored in Belfast harbour. They had broken out of their 'cages', dived over the side and somehow managed to swim to shore. According to the television news, the seven had fled to the Markets district, which was now being surrounded by British troops.

The mood of the bar changed in an instant. Whatever had to be done to repel the Brits and give the lads a chance *would* be done. Minutes later, a group of armed men had been assembled. When I looked down, I found a revolver being pressed into my hand. I looked at it in horror. What in the name of Jesus was going on? And then a hard-faced man with blackened teeth said to me, 'Well, don't just stand there lookin' at it. Come on, the Brits'll be here any minute.'

The weapon felt heavy in my hands. It smelled of oil and grease. Nervously, I handed it back to him. 'Sorry,' I said, 'I'm a journalist. I don't shoot people.'

'Then you're a sorry fuckin' eejit,' he said, and turned away disgusted. 'Anyone else know how to use one of these?'

I don't know who took up the call but, for months afterwards, I wondered if the Army would find the gun and discover my prints on it.

Two weeks later, in the wake of Bloody Sunday, I was again asked by a republican why I wasn't prepared to take up arms to defend the Irish people. On this occasion, the man doing the asking was Martin McGuinness, second-in-command of the Provisional IRA in Derry. British troops had shot dead 13 unarmed protesters and wounded 17 more on the afternoon of 30 January. Those shot were attending a civil-rights demonstration that, predictably, had ended with rocks and bottles being thrown at the police and Army. I almost missed the entire business, which, to be fair, had not been advertised as a massacre but rather as a protest (if you were Irish) or an illegal march (if you were British). I heard the gunfire and the screams as I made my way past police and Army barriers, but by the time I reached the Bogside itself the killings had ended. The mood of the people was an incandescent blend of grief and anger. The Army has always maintained that its men, from 1st Battalion, the Parachute Regiment, were fired on first and were only acting in self-defence, but there is little evidence to back this up. Even if someone *had* taken a pot shot, the response was cruelly disproportionate. Bloody Sunday (which produced not one but *two* judicial inquiries, the second of which lasted seven years and cost £150 million) was the worst incident of its kind involving British soldiers since the days of the Black and Tans. McGuinness, still just 21, a former butcher boy, told me after I tracked him down to an upstairs room in the Creggan estate that if I, as a Protestant, truly supported Irish unity, then there was only one course of action open to me: the armed struggle. I begged to differ.

'You're a strange boy, Walter,' he said.

Thirty years later, while I was covering the terrorist attacks of 11 September in New York, McGuinness was Education Minister in the new Northern Ireland Executive, working alongside David Trimble, leader of the Ulster Unionist Party. He turned out to be a strange boy, too. Apparently it was 'odd' not to take up arms against your own people, but it was 'statesmanlike', after nearly 4,000 people had been killed and thousands more maimed, and bombs had destroyed an untold number of homes and businesses, for IRA leaders to rearrange the furniture at Stormont, then sit down with the 'oppressors' to discuss changes to the school curriculum.

Somehow, in the midst of these earth-shattering events, I managed to find an office. It was at the top of a narrow building in Lombard Street in the heart of the city centre – a building that also housed the *Irish Times*. I even hired a secretary, Fionnuala Cooke, later to become Lady Cooke when her husband, David, stepped down as Lord Mayor of Belfast. But though I was now settling in to the journalistic community and beginning to find my feet as a reporter, the tragicomedy of my past continued to drag me down.

Ronnie was released from internment in April 1972. I had heard nothing from him while he was inside; I was not on his Christmas card list. Alan and I tried to visit him in Belfast's Crumlin Road prison bearing the unlikely gift of a bottle of vodka and orange, but we were turned away. After his transfer to the newly constructed Long Kesh internment camp, ten miles west of the city, I didn't even try to make contact. I couldn't face it. I knew, though, that I couldn't hide forever. When he got out, I drove over to Turf Lodge to pay my respects. Just getting there meant running a gauntlet of police and soldiers, who had blocked off every entrance to the estate and let nobody through without searching them for weapons, then radioing their details through to the mainframe computer in Lisburn, known for some reason as Clarabelle. Turf Lodge, a red-brick estate thrown up in the 1960s, was an outpost of the Official IRA and felt like a town under siege. Everywhere you looked in Ronnie's living room, there was internment memorabilia: St Bridget's crosses made from straw, shillelaghs with 'Long Kesh Concentration Camp' written down the side, tiny prison diaries written on toilet paper. Neighbours kept dropping in, offering advice and a six-pack. Ronnie, as I knew he would be, was even more disdainful than usual. He had suffered for the people and he wore his suffering with insufferable pride. Suzanne, who had done all the waiting, rushed around making tea and sandwiches. She was obviously relieved that her husband was free. What she made of their worsening situation, I can only imagine.

For me, as much as for him, his release was a watershed. It was obvious that Ronnie and I were no longer, in any meaningful sense, friends. We were tied to each other by a grim, visceral bond, but we weren't pals.

Not that that put him off. Don't get that idea. Months later, in the middle of the summer, he called me in my office in Lombard Street and asked me to meet him in Robinson's Bar, opposite the Europa Hotel. I should have said no, but I was intrigued. When he turned up, we had a couple of drinks and chatted about the 'situation'. He seemed mellower than I remembered him. Then he indicated the suitcase sitting next to him.

'I want you to look after this for me, Smokey,' he said. 'I've been staying down South, so I have, but I have to head off again straight away and I don't want to be lugging this thing round. Sure it'll only be for a couple of days. A week, maybe.'

The case was padlocked. I looked doubtful. 'Yes, OK. What's in it, anyway?'

'Ach, just stuff. Clothes and books and that. I'd fetch them home myself, only I don't have the time.'

A week later, he called me and we met up again somewhere in west Belfast and I handed it back to him. He checked the lock. It wasn't until months later, when a pal of his was helping me with a story, that I learned the truth.

'Good of you to help us out that time.'

'What are you talking about?'

'The money.'

'What money?'

'From the robbery. Sure do you not remember?'

The case, as I might have guessed, hadn't contained 'stuff'. It was packed with somewhere in the region of a hundred thousand pounds in banknotes, the results of an armed robbery in the area north of Dublin. So long as they were outside the cause – beyond the pale – Ronnie didn't care who he hurt. He held to Stalin's dictum that friends from outside the movement were no more than useful idiots.

In December 1980, long after I left Belfast, the Dublin political magazine *Magill* ran a cover story about telephone surveillance in Ireland by the investigative journalist Frank Doherty, which contained the following, disturbing allegation:

> One of the most audacious interceptions was organised by the Official IRA and controlled by the late Liam MacMillan . . . the operational telegraph of the British Army in the North was tapped and its signals sent into the telex machine of the *Cork Examiner* newspaper's office, to which the Officials had a key.

According to Doherty, I arrived at my office in Lombard Street only at predictable times to telex my copy to Cork. At other times, apparently, the teleprinter 'spewed out' intelligence reports from British undercover 'Q cars', reports from the tactical headquarters of various British battalions and requests to the Army's command centre in Lisburn for permission to raid specified houses in search of named individuals.

'Also, at midday,' *Magill* continued, 'an intelligence précis of the previous 24 hours, which was broadcast to all British units, would be printed off by the telex machine.'

Doherty concluded: 'Ellis . . . had no connection with any Irish republican group and left Belfast to report for the *Irish Times* in Brussels without ever discovering the story behind his office telex.'

Was there truth in any of this? I don't know. The early 1970s were a frenetically busy period, dominated by bombings and shootings, and I was often away from my desk. But by the same token, I was liable to put in an appearance at almost any moment, from mid-morning right through to the early hours. There is also the small matter of my part-time secretary, Fionnuala – not best known for her republican sympathies – who was around for at least half of each working day and would presumably have noticed the arrival of men in trenchcoats attaching devices to her telex while humming 'The Ballad of James Connolly'. Yet even allowing for a measure of hyperbole on *Magill's* part, I cannot exclude the possibility that Ronnie did indeed secure a copy of my office key (as well, presumably, as one to the front door of the building) and somehow reconfigured my telex into the republican movement's Big Brother. Someone in British intelligence or the Official Republican movement clearly believed that I was duped and there is no doubt that Ronnie would have considered such a betrayal entirely justified.

But regardless of what was going on in my office, the self-inflicted wounds of Ulster were growing worse by the day. On 21 July 1972, on what would become known as Bloody Friday, the Provisionals set off more than 20 car bombs in and around Belfast city centre. Eleven people died, including two soldiers, and another one hundred and thirty people, many of them women and children, were injured, some of them horribly. The city went into shock. I spent much of the late afternoon walking around the different sites of the carnage. Some of the victims had been blown up so comprehensively that firemen and other emergency workers were shovelling their remains into plastic bags. Policemen and ambulance crews were weeping openly. Some of the men responsible for Bloody Friday later participated in the 'Peace Process', demanding 'equality of esteem' for all the citizens of Ireland. They might as well have signed the documents that made up the Good Friday accords in their victims' blood.

My own travails that year were not yet ended. In September 1972, having finally 'prorogued' the Northern Ireland Parliament and replaced it with direct rule from Westminster, the British government convened an all-party conference in Darlington (where else?) presided over by the new Ulster Secretary, William Whitelaw. The conference itself was a washout. It was boycotted by the main nationalist party, the SDLP, which was opposed to internment, and it refused even to address the demands of Sinn Fein or the various loyalist paramilitary groups. That was one thing. What marked it out for me was that on the second night, 26 September, I was arrested and held on suspicion of plotting to assassinate Whitelaw.

I had filed my story to the *Examiner* earlier in the evening. It was a dull piece. There wasn't much to say and the rest of the night was my own. Someone mentioned a nearby club and after the dreary events of the day, it sounded like fun. I decided to give it a go. Dominic Cunningham, a friend from the *Irish Independent*, said he'd come with me. An hour or so later, we stopped in at a filling station to buy petrol for the hire car I was driving. Just as we pulled away, we heard sirens wailing and brakes squealing. Before we knew it, we were surrounded by flashing blue lights. We could hear voices raised. 'Armed police! Don't move! Don't do anything! Just sit in the car.' Then uniformed men opened the doors on both sides and ordered us out. The filling station had just been robbed at gunpoint, we were told, and we were the chief suspects. I couldn't believe it. Dominic was speechless.

Back at the police station the true reason for our detention became apparent. I was taken to an interview room where two plain-clothes officers introduced themselves as members of Special Branch, the section of the police, with headquarters in London, that deals with issues of national security. My mouth went dry. They left me alone for several minutes and talked among themselves, occasionally turning round to see how I was getting on. Then they sat down opposite me, about six feet away. One of them had a file on his knee that he consulted before he spoke. The other just stared. I was in serious trouble, the one with the file told me. Oh, yes – they knew all about me. I regularly consorted with terrorists. My political sympathies were an open book. It was obvious, they said, that I was using my cover as a journalist to obtain information that would help expedite a terrorist attack. Other than being shot at, I don't think I've ever been so terrified. My dumbfounded denials were met with smirks and guffaws. 'Tell us another one, son. We've heard it all before.' Why didn't I just make it easy on myself? What was I planning? Who was I working with? Who was my intended target? Was it the Secretary of State? Was that it?

I asked about Dominic. They'd let him go, they said. It was me they were after. I felt the darkness and the cold close in on me. I was questioned in relays through the night, during which I was not allowed to sleep or given anything to eat or drink other than a cup of tea. The interrogation was relentless. Why had I joined the Communist Party? What was my relationship with Ronnie Bunting? Why had I visited his house the week after he was released from internment? Was it not true that he had sent me to Darlington to get him information he needed for a hit? Was I not, in fact, a member of the Official IRA?

Only as dawn broke did my situation suddenly improve. The two Branch men left the room and returned minutes later to announce, quite nonchalantly, that I was free to go.

I didn't understand. 'Free to go? But what about the armed robbery of the petrol station?'

They turned to each other and smiled. One of them said, 'Robbery? What robbery? There was no robbery. I don't know what you're talking about.'

'And the terrorist charges? You said I was plotting to assassinate Willie Whitelaw.'

'Did I? Well, we've looked into the matter and it's been decided you're not a threat, after all. You're lucky.'

'So, that's it?'

'That's it.'

By this time, I was furious and, in a welter of indignation, announced my intention to register a formal complaint, take up the matter with the National Union of Journalists and write up my story in the *Examiner*, if not the *Sunday Times*. I think I may even have said, 'You haven't heard the end of this, you bastards!'

Looking back, I was probably lucky they didn't shoot me in the head. The officers looked at each other. 'I see,' said one. 'Well, that's most unfortunate.' Then he whispered to one of his colleagues, who got up and left the room.

A minute or so later, a young constable came in. He walked purposefully towards me, holding out a breathalyser. 'Would you mind blowing into this, sir?' he asked.

'What do you mean? I wasn't drinking and, even if I was, I've been here for the last eight hours.'

'If you don't mind, sir.'

I did mind, but I blew into it anyway. The constable showed the breathalyser to his superior. 'Just as I thought,' the Branch man said. 'Driving while drunk. Book him, constable.'

A month later, I returned for trial with every intention of exposing the whole rotten process. To my surprise, my solicitor advised me most strenuously to make no mention of any 'wild charges' about abuse of police power. In fact, he said, if I chose to ignore his advice, I would have to find new representation. I gave up. On my behalf, he registered a plea of guilty to the reduced charge of drunk in charge. I was fined £500, plus costs, and banned from driving for a year.

It was, once again, the final straw. I re-resolved to have nothing further to do with Ronnie Bunting, the never-failing source of all my evils. Meanwhile, in the real world, the Troubles continued to worsen. The number of people who suffered violent deaths in Northern Ireland in 1972 was 496. There were 10,628 recorded shootings and 1,853 explosions.

V

On the Run

I DID NOTHING wrong, yet I felt I had been stitched up by Special Branch and let down by my solicitor. I'd also been warned by the local magistrate in Stockton as to my future behaviour. The result of this was that I returned to Belfast reinforced in my view that the British Establishment was a closed shop in which miscarriages of justice were routine and those responsible were protected by the old boys' network. Never again would I assume when I read about people protesting their innocence that the protesters – especially if they were Irish – were simply trying it on. But though I desperately wanted to reverse the injustice done to me, I could see no means of doing so. Instead, my best approach, I decided, was to steer well clear of Ronnie and concentrate full-time on my job as a journalist.

On 1 January 1973, Britain and Ireland joined the European Economic Community, a fact that, unknown to me at the time, would prove of great personal significance. Northern Ireland was from that day on a part of the European Project, and tied to the European economy, the European Court and European standards of behaviour. The effects of the change took years to make themselves felt. On the streets of Belfast, nothing altered. If there was a new sense of confraternity in London, Dublin and Brussels, it did not extend to the people of the Falls and Shankill roads, whose hands remained warmly at each others' throats.

Protestants were, by this stage, rioting in the same way as Catholics, though for the opposite reason. They felt that the British were prepared to sell them out (which they were), while Catholics were convinced, with considerable justification, that the RUC and British troops would never get off their backs. The two sides could no more 'understand' or 'empathise' with each other than they could mount a joint expedition to the moon. Bombs and shootings were a daily occurrence. Loyalist trade unionists began to flex their industrial muscle, organising political strikes and blackouts. Not to be upstaged, the Provisional IRA took its campaign of violence to the British mainland, planting bombs at the Old Bailey and the Ministry of Agriculture in London, killing one person and wounding hundreds more.

I was worked off my feet, filing not only for the *Examiner* but also for the *Evening Echo*, which went to press before midday and put out a second edition in the middle of the afternoon. In the circumstances, there was a chance – though I wouldn't have bet on it – that Cahal Henry, the *Echo*'s editor, was beginning to think of me as a *news*paper man. Yet writing for the Cork papers had its frustrations. Few in Belfast on either side of the religious divide cared a jot for the *Examiner*: most Protestants hadn't heard of it; Catholics, in general, were only interested in getting their opinions across in London and Dublin. My professional isolation was brought home to me one afternoon when I was talking on the telephone to Captain John Brooke, son of the former Stormont Prime Minister, Viscount Brookeborough, and himself a leading unionist politician, about the legal implications of an upcoming plebiscite on the border. Midway through our conversation, I happened to mention that I didn't think his views would go down well in Cork.

'Why on earth would you say that?' he wanted to know.

'Well, I do work for the *Cork Examiner*.'

'The what?'

'The *Examiner* . . . from Cork.'

'Good God!' Brooke exclaimed, as if he had just discovered shit on his shoes. 'I thought you said you were from the Court *Examiner*. Cork, you say? I'm afraid we have nothing further to say to each other, Mr Ellis. Goodbye.' And he put down the phone.

It was around this time that I began to be courted by Henry Kelly, the northern editor of the *Irish Times*. Henry was an extraordinary fellow. Destined to give up journalism to become a game-show host and disc jockey – and ultimately to go bankrupt – he was at that time one of Ireland's best-known and most respected journalists. He not only edited the *Irish Times'* Ulster coverage, he also found time to write *How Stormont Fell*, a rollicking account of the collapse of unionist domination in Northern Ireland. 'I was a great journalist, a great loss to the *Irish Times*,' he said once – and there is no doubt he meant it. He was blond and good-looking, if a touch louche: a bit like a minor character out of P.G. Wodehouse, only with a Dublin accent. Cricket was his game and Terry Wogan, or possibly Eamonn Andrews, his role model. When he ended up, years later, starring in pantomime as Wishee Washee or doing advertisements for Japanese Asahi beer (like a C-list premonition of Bill Murray in *Lost in Translation*), I couldn't help wondering which personality truly inhabited Henry's head. I recalled the day in 1981 when he telephoned me at home in London to invite me to meet him in the Sherlock Holmes pub in Northumberland Avenue. He was obviously excited, but then he always was. After he bought the drinks, he invited me to check out the clientele. 'Do you see anybody looking at me?' he asked. 'Staring at me, I mean.'

'No,' I said, wondering what the hell was going on. 'I don't.'

He smiled mischievously. 'Ah, but do you see, Walter, that's the point. They don't know who I am [he was at the time a reporter for *The World Tonight* on Radio 4]. But they will. Next time I come here, I won't be able to move. I'll be *mobbed*.'

I never managed to put this to the test, but he may well have been right, for just weeks later he bounded on to our television screens as one of the presenters of *Game for a Laugh*, a leading contender for Worst, Most Banal Show in the History of British Television. It was *The Generation Game* meets *Candid Camera*, a parody of popular entertainment in which ordinary people made fools of themselves unwittingly while the rest of us looked on, laughing. Henry looked like he loved it. He was in his element. Like Churchill, if in a somewhat less elevated context, he was a man whose whole life had been but a preparation for that moment.

But in 1973, Henry's golden future was not yet behind him. Still in his 20s, he swanked his way through the Belfast-based international news media, dining at lunchtime with key opinion-makers, opining every night on local television and RTÉ. He was not only a superb off-the-cuff commentator, he was also a genuine innovator who could mix facts with comment in a way that neither compromised the truth nor rendered the comment merely partisan. That he should have sought to recruit *me* to the *Irish Times* was a definite shot in the arm. Like a struggling contestant in *Going for Gold*, the pan-European quiz show that paid Henry's mortgage during the John Major years, I was playing catch-up and I was thrilled.

The problem was, what to do about the *Examiner*? Mr Donal, Mr Ted and Mr George had given me my big break. Was I going to sell them short for a job with more money on Ireland's premier paper? You bet I was! But I was embarrassed nonetheless. I didn't know how to explain my conduct in a way that allowed me, let alone them, to feel good about me. In the end, I did the only thing I could. I went to see them in Cork and stumbled my way through a shameful resignation, muttering about the 'chance of a lifetime' while assuring them of my eternal gratitude to the finest – indeed, *only* – group of professionals I had ever worked with. Mr Donal's stare bored right through me, reminding me of the headmaster who had so shrewdly assessed my first teaching practice. He did not flinch. He regretted my decision, he said, but he understood it. He also revealed that my mother had written a letter to him, thanking the *Examiner* for all the kindness it had shown me. It was a gesture, he said, that he much appreciated.

All that remained was for me to find my successor. I didn't have far to look. Roisin McAuley, later to write *Singing Bird*, an international bestseller about an opera diva who makes an odd discovery about her origins, was a BBC Northern Ireland newsreader at the time and increasingly frustrated by the limitations of her role. When I suggested to her that I put her up as my replacement, she jumped at the idea. A month later, Roisin moved from Broadcasting House to my little office at the top of the stairs in Lombard Street and I moved downstairs to the *Irish Times*. Not even the fact that, years later, she claimed in an interview to have been the *Examiner*'s pioneer correspondent in Belfast takes away from the fact that I had organised a sweet deal for all concerned.

The *Irish Times* has been an institution in Ireland ever since the days of the old Protestant Ascendancy. Formerly unionist in its politics, it had adapted to the new Irish State by simply transferring its conservatism to the new domestic arrangements. But under its then editor, Douglas Gageby, it was turned on its head. Gageby, a northern Presbyterian who had moved South and gone 'native', was a true 1960s liberal, and the paper he produced was one of the key agents of change in an Ireland that traditionally took its lead from the Catholic Church and the farming lobby. In one sense, my new editor was touchingly naive. He believed that the northern Troubles, which he found distasteful, would be sorted out by reasonable men and women sitting round a table and that old-style loyalists – represented then, as now, by the Reverend Ian Paisley –

would quickly take their place in the New Ireland. But though he was naive, he believed in getting to the heart of the matter and gave his journalists free range to dig and delve and to cover his features pages in 'fine' writing. I took to him straight away. He said he expected great things of me, and I was determined not to disappoint him.

Henry Kelly recruited me, yet no sooner had I joined the paper than he returned to Dublin to climb the executive ladder . . . until he found where it led: a dusty office on the second floor overlooking a courtyard stuffed with bins. It wasn't long afterwards that he began to look to London for his salvation. His replacement as northern editor was Renagh Holohan – a woman, by God! – who, while perfectly capable of analysing political and paramilitary trends, appeared to be less at home than her flamboyant predecessor in the pressure cooker conditions of 1970s Belfast and, crucially, less willing to delegate.

Renagh, if the truth be told, was a tough cookie – extremely hard working and capable. But she was anxious by nature and was forever upbraiding colleagues (mostly me) for turning up late or for writing 250 words on a story when she had specifically asked for 200. Her natural milieu was grand receptions, where there might be a glass of champagne, a titled Englishman and a tray of canapés. On such occasions, she was the life and soul of the party. She was understandably less thrilled by the prospect of counting the number of cigarette burns on the chest of a dumped corpse.

Murray Sayle, the grande dame of Australian journalists, spent a lot of time in Belfast in those days. A lugubrious fellow who plainly saw the world as his parish, he allegedly wandered into the *Irish Times* offices one night after midnight to find Renagh bent over the telex machine in tears. Some man, it turned out, had let her down and it was all too awful. She simply couldn't bear it. Murray nodded and lit up a cigarette.

I could picture the scene. 'But, you see, Murray, the thing is, I have to write this piece for the City edition and, Jesus, Mary and Joseph, the way things are, I'm finding it *really* hard to concentrate.'

'No worries, girl. Just budge over.' And, with that, Sayle sat down and wrote what turned out to be the front-page lead.

Next down in the Holohan hierarchy was Martin Cowley, a young Derry man with a pinched face, a hank of dark hair and a cheerful, no-nonsense approach to his job. 'Morning, cunthooks' was his invariable greeting. A true professional, Martin was a scribe whose shorthand actually moved at the same pace as the speech it was recording. He dressed well, preferring a sports jacket and slacks to a suit. Mrs Thatcher, when she came along some years later, took a bit of a fancy to him at a news conference. 'No, no, dear, not you,' she proclaimed dismissively of a well-known correspondent's attempts to catch her eye, 'the nice young man in the fetching brown jacket.'

Our photographer (or 'monkey') was Ciaron Donnelly, Lombard Street's Jack the lad, who had distinguished himself during the events of Bloody Sunday, shooting roll after roll of revealing and incriminating images as chaos and bloodshed broke out around him. Ciaron was a natural playboy for whom, as for so many others, the Troubles were both a godsend and a goldmine. Each day, he would send his first roll of pictures to the *Irish Times*. The rest he dispatched to the major European agencies and US magazines, including *Time-Life*, in return for fees that, to me at least, were beyond the dreams of avarice.

At the heart of the Belfast operation was Gill McKenna, the telex operator, always ready with a withering comment about the fascist or bourgeois slant of the copy she was forced to transmit. Gill looked like Rod Stewart in his later Caesars Palace days in Las Vegas. Or maybe, given the chronology, Stewart looked like her in her Lombard Street days. She smoked compulsively, and as the day progressed the detritus in her ashtray swelled to monstrous proportions. Without her, the whole machinery of the news operation would have ground to a halt. Her fingers glided over the keyboard of her telex for upwards of ten hours a day. It was only when the last full stop had been appended to the last sentence of the last report of the latest death that she would she pick up the phone and summon a taxi to take her home.

Renagh's remit at this time was the political process, centred on British proposals for a 78-seat Stormont Assembly and, as a sop to nationalists, an accompanying Council of Ireland. She worked really hard. Martin and I were left with violence, funerals and the non-stop bombast of the multifarious political and terrorist factions.

It was a harsh, unforgiving world. Several of the future big beasts of the media jungle were there. Simon Hoggart was cutting, and polishing, his teeth at *The Guardian*; Bob Fisk was the *Times'* man. They hunted in tandem: one upwind, the other downwind of their intended prey. Their shared assumption was that everyone on the unionist side was a fool or a liar and that the triumph of nationalism was not only a historical imperative but also intellectually and aesthetically attractive. They were not altogether wrong in this. Fisk has long since become an iconic figure in the Middle East, advancing his radical opinions without regard for Western – particularly American – sensibilities. Hoggart – the 'Third Man' in the sex scandal of 2004 that brought down David Blunkett, Tony Blair's trusted Home Secretary – chose a very different course and, though he continues to contribute political commentary, is probably best known as the chairman of Radio 4's *The News Quiz*.

Another of the rising stars in the early days of the Troubles was Kevin Myers. Brought up in Leicester, the son of Irish immigrants, Myers returned home as a student at the end of the 1960s and, alongside Henry Kelly and Vincent Browne – the latter destined to become one of the country's foremost investigative reporters – became a stalwart of the Literary and Historical Society (the L&H) at University College, Dublin – Ireland's equivalent of the Oxford Union. He is by nature a stylist and a controversialist – the writer closest in spirit to the legendary Myles na Gopaleen that the *Irish Times* has produced in a generation. But occasionally, when he can't be bothered, or can't resist, he strays beyond accepted limits. He loves to celebrate the fact that large numbers of Irishmen fought for the British in both world wars. He feels physically ill when he sees 'Baby on Board' car stickers, and on one notorious occasion had to apologise to outraged readers after he described illegitimate children as 'bastards'. Given that his handsome property in Kildare, complete with gun emplacements, abuts the historic boundary of British rule in medieval times and that his study is west of the line, this is surely appropriate. For, in every worthwhile sense, Kevin is beyond the Pale. His 'An Irishman's Diary' column carries headlines like 'Wrong, totally and utterly wrong', 'Protestant engineering' and 'Parsnips'.

One of the most lethal British correspondents was Keith Kyle of the BBC, who once upbraided his employers for their unswerving detestation of 'terrorism'. He was more of an academic than a reporter and deadly serious about his work. He was also enormous, built like a second-row forward. If you got in his way, he would chop you down. Once, attending an impromptu press briefing outside Stormont, I raised my hand only to be steamrollered out of the way by Kyle. As he shouted out his question, his size-12 boot was actually planted on my outstretched fingers.

Not everyone shared this cerebral approach to journalism. I remember the *Sun* correspondent announcing in the middle of some horrific incident that he had spotted an Army sergeant with a huge moustache. This was good news, he said, because it was Moustache Week in *The Sun*. *Telegraph* journalists relied heavily on the press offices of the Army and RUC for their news. Ulster, to the then *Telegraph* proprietor, Lord Hartwell, an ex-Army major, represented the twilight of empire, and for his correspondents – some of them Labour supporters – that meant Sundowners at the bar. *Mail* and *Express* writers were no different. Trevor McDonald of ITN, as charming and even-handed then as he is today, liked to turn up with his golf clubs, hoping to get in 18 holes.

The spider at the centre of the British propaganda web was Colin Wallace, head of information for the Army at its Lisburn headquarters. Wallace's life was touched by both comedy and tragedy. He was fired in 1975 for passing on classified information to Bob Fisk of *The Times*. Fifteen years later, he received £30,000 in compensation for wrongful dismissal, but in the meantime the secret service establishment had locked him up and thrown away the key. After alleging 'dirty tricks' on the part of British Intelligence, as well as the official cover-up of a child-abuse scandal in east Belfast (both true), he was charged with an obscure murder in Sussex and served ten years for manslaughter. Paul Foot, the campaigning *Private Eye* journalist, took up his cause, and in the end his conviction was quashed. But the damage was done.

Wallace, when I knew him, was an affable fellow, a part-time soldier and professional fantasist who doled out news to correspondents in conformity with his perception of what use they could make of it. Being an Ulster Prod, like myself, he believed strongly in the righteousness of the Army's role; yet, as a libertarian, he couldn't help noticing that his masters were not always 100 per cent scrupulous in their presentation of the facts. I was not one of his more favoured hacks: he liked me well enough personally, but the *Irish Times* was, for him, ever so slightly out of bounds and most of what he fed me was nonsense. I recall one afternoon sitting in his office – a Portakabin buried deep inside Thiepval Barracks – as he thumbed through a file of possible stories. None of them interested me. The one he thought I would particularly like was, in fact, the one that I most derided. The IRA, he said, had developed drone aircraft that could spy on Protestant areas and even drop bombs on them. I looked at the drawings, done by an Army artist. I'd never seen such bollocks. 'No, thanks, Colin,' I said, 'let's just stick to the facts.' He smiled and returned the document to his files.

That evening in the bar of the Europa, I was busy regaling colleagues with my tale of the Provo Air Corps when in came a grizzled member of the British press corps. I won't mention his name, he has long since been purged, but he sounded just like 'Whispering' Bob Harris of *The Old Grey Whistle Test*. He was terribly excited because his 'source' in Army HQ had just provided him with exclusive details of a story that the rest of us would kill for. None of us said a thing and, sure enough, there it was next morning. The IRA, we were informed, had developed a new remote-controlled strike aircraft that could rain terror on the streets of Belfast.

Colin had a quirky sense of humour and an instinctive understanding of tabloid values. It was following an exclusive tip-off from Wallace that the *Sunday Mirror* ran a story under the headline 'Danger In Those Frilly Panties', in which it was suggested that female IRA bombers were being killed by premature explosions as a result of static electricity building up in the nylon of their underwear. It wasn't true. It was absurd. But what harm did it do?

My own predilections – other than for frilly panties – remained very much in evidence in the spring of 1973. The driving ban imposed on me in Stockton turned out not to apply in Northern Ireland, which was a separate jurisdiction. Accordingly, when Ciaron Donnelly announced that he was selling his car, a souped-up Simca 1100, I offered to buy it from him. It was a mean machine. But almost better than the car itself was the fact that it was equipped with a radio telephone – a hangover from Ciaron's fixation with glamour and need for immediate access to news. In fact, as it turned out, the connection was only to Pacemaker, a Belfast news agency, but part of the deal was that they took and passed on messages, so that for a while I was never out of contact, even when I was 100 miles out of town. As far as I was concerned, the Simca was my Aston Martin DB5 and the phone had been installed by Q.

Sadly, the joys of the Simca were not to be mine for long. Late one night in Belfast, driving fast down Grosvenor Road toward the city centre, I realised much too late that my path was blocked by an Army barrier. A metal bar strung between two concrete bollards stretched across the entire carriageway. I tried desperately to stop, but I was doing about 60 mph in wet conditions and there wasn't time. Screaming, I ducked my head down, waiting for the inevitable, crushing impact. The fear I felt was pure and primordial. I was a gonner and there wasn't anything I could do to prevent it. But the inevitable did not occur. Somehow, miraculously, the Simca made it through. It was a low car, streamlined for speed, and the barrier merely took off the roof, transforming my saloon model instantly into the cabriolet version. Blood streamed down my face as I emerged on the other side.

Improbable though it sounds, things then got worse. Soldiers on duty at the barrier ran out of a hut in which they were sheltering from the rain and began shooting at me. I decided that this was no time for explanations and accelerated hard. One round went through my already-shattered rear window; another whistled past my head. But, like the barrier, neither bullet had my name on it and I managed to get away. To this day, I don't know what saved me (twice) or why I wasn't pursued. Perhaps there just wasn't an RUC or Army vehicle in the vicinity at the time. Perhaps I was just lucky.

When I got home, keeping to the narrow backstreets, I drove the car up the driveway and lurched into the house. My father was still up. He had just got back from the golf club. 'What the hell happened to you?' he asked, his eyes registering the blood running down my forehead.

'A bit of bother, Dad,' I said. 'I ran into an Army barrier and took the roof off the car.'

'You did *what*?'

'It was an accident. I couldn't see it. Drove straight into it. Lucky to be alive.'

Dad looked at my head, then he looked at my hands, which were shaking. Then he took me into the kitchen to wipe the blood from my face.

I moved out not long afterwards – for the last time. Just about my father's last favour to me was to get the car repaired by one of his pals in Newtownards. The friend in question – another Masonic contact – even improved the look of it by giving the roof a vinyl finish. But Dad never trusted my driving after that.

At least I hadn't been drinking. The same could not be said of me in connection with another incident that followed soon afterwards. On this occasion, I had had a few in the top-floor bar of the Europa Hotel, listening to Pat Smylie, an *Irish Times* colleague up from Dublin, work his way through the Kris Kristofferson songbook, and decided to drive home. This was unwise, not to say unlawful. Speeding through the city's deserted streets, I realised that I desperately needed to have a pee and pulled in, as I thought, to the side of the road. It was only as I re-emerged from my impromptu urinal that I found I had left my lights on and the car was, in fact, some three feet out from the kerb. Worse than that, it was surrounded by British soldiers.

'This your car, mate?'

'What of it?'

'What's it doing here?'

'Had to take a pee.'

A private sniffed my breath. 'He's drunk, corp.'

'Drunk, are you? Right. That's an offence. We're taking you in.'

This judgement for some reason made me mad; it brought out the libertarian in me. 'What do you mean you're taking me in? You're not the civil power. You've no right to—'

At this point, the corporal ordered one of his squad to restrain me. As the man attempted to do so, I wheeled round and punched him. He fell over. This prompted the rest of the group to pounce on me, hitting and kicking me and nearly suffocating the life out of me. The police arrived five minutes later and took me to an RUC station. The following morning, after I had passed the night in the cells, a mean-looking sergeant came in and slowly took off his jacket, which he handed to a constable. Then he ordered two of his men to hold me while he set about my stomach and kidneys with his fists. As I collapsed on to the floor of the cell, he scowled at me, his face, as they say, a twisted mask of hate. 'You fuckin' wee shite,' he said. 'Look at me! I said look at me! Ever lay a hand on a soldier again and next time, by God, I'll do more than teach you fuckin' manners.' He bent down and stuck his face in mine, so that I could smell his breakfast. 'Do you understand me? Do you fuckin' *understand*?'

I got the picture. A month later, I lost my second licence and was thus unable to drive anywhere in Britain or Ireland. Once again, it was not thought appropriate in court to raise the circumstances of my arrest. But this time, I was not complaining. I have never driven drunk since.

Getting beaten up in the traditional Jimmy Cagney sense is not a pleasant experience. It happened to me again nearly 20 years later when I was covering the civil war in Sri Lanka. Like other journalists, I had been trying for days to get up to Jaffna, where a major siege was under way. The nearest I ever got was Elephant Pass, where I was turned back at gunpoint. Back in Colombo, the government eventually arranged a special flight to take Western reporters up to the scene of the action. I was just about to board when two soldiers barred my path. I wasn't going, a Sri Lankan colonel informed me. My seat had been given to a local pro-government journalist.

'But I've paid for my ticket,' I protested. 'I've been waiting all morning.'

This ingratitude plainly irritated the colonel. 'Where are your papers?' he demanded. 'Show me your passport.'

I produced my Irish passport.

'You British,' he sneered, riffling through the green document (this was before uniform Euro passports). 'You think you still run the empire. Well, let me tell you, you are not running this country any more.'

It was a provocative statement and I was provoked. 'Take a look at my passport,' I said. 'I'm not British, I'm *Irish*.'

A curl came over the colonel's lip. 'British . . . Irish . . . you are all the same to me. We don't want your sort here.'

'Well, in that case,' I said, 'you're an Indian.'

'*What?* What did you say?'

'Indian . . . Sri Lankan . . . you're all the same to me.'

This was the moment at which the two soldiers who had prevented me from boarding the aircraft grabbed my arms. The colonel then started punching me with extreme rapidity, like Agent Smith in *The Matrix*, until I slumped to my knees, retching. 'This is not finished between us,' he told me. 'Tonight, I shall come to your hotel and *kill* you. Now, take him away.'

The other Western journalists meanwhile continued to troop on board. None of them attempted to catch my eye.

In Belfast, where the distinction between British and Irish was well understood, the big event of the summer of 1973 was the election of the new Stormont Assembly, from which, we were told, a power-sharing executive would be drawn made up of unionists and nationalists. Predictably, it turned out to be a shambles. Voters refused to come down on one side or the other. The result was an Assembly turned against itself from day one, with pro-power-sharing and anti-power-sharing politicians slugging it out quite literally on the floor of the old parliamentary chamber until the police were called in to drag them apart.

It didn't get any easier. One of the more eccentric unionist politicians, Professor Kennedy Lindsay, donned an African native costume known, he later revealed, as an Ogwere and danced around on top of the dispatch box. Another unionist, John McQuade, an

ex-docker, boxer and Chindit, issued the solemn warning that the
'testicles of the republican *oc-topus* were spreading over Ulster'. At
one point, screaming renegades from his own side forced Brian
Faulkner, the designated chief executive, into a corner, from which
undignified position he was rescued by Paddy Devlin, a burly
former IRA man who had once startled my dad by opening the
door to him clutching a vast and ancient revolver.

It was clear that the planned Executive, though sustainable on
paper, was hopelessly unrealistic in practice. The IRA was opposed
to power-sharing because it was a compromise and because Sinn
Fein was excluded. Loyalists hated it because it was seen as a
halfway house to Irish unity. They were both right. Within days of
the first meeting, the guns were out and bombs were going off on
just about every street corner.

We at the *Irish Times* were not to be spared the people's wrath.
One afternoon, as Noreen, our sainted office manager, was making
us tea, a call came in from the RUC. A bomb had been planted in
a car outside our building and we were advised to make our way
calmly, yet swiftly, out the front door in the direction of a newly
established police cordon.

Gill went to pieces. Martin adjusted his tie. Renagh said she was
in the middle of a story and asked if I thought they were serious.
At this point, a police megaphone underlined the urgency of the
situation. We were to get out and we were to get out *now*!
Uncharacteristically, I led the way. At the bottom of the stairs, I held
the door open until everyone had got out. Then I joined them. I
don't know why I felt so calm. It just didn't seem to me (perhaps
after my Grosvenor Road experience) that the Reaper was in any
hurry to make my acquaintance.

No sooner had we reached the cordon next to British Home
Stores than the bomb exploded. I had heard bombs go off many
times before but not so obviously up front and personal. It was
sickeningly loud. In an instant, all the windows in the street blew

out, showering the street with glass. Smoke rose up, ceilings collapsed, doors splintered. Papers from all of the offices in the street began drifting through the infected air.

No one was hurt, but the street was a wreck. Damage was not, for the most part, structural, but the repairs would take months. In the meantime, we needed new premises from which to work.

Mr Gageby, our redoubtable editor, was in no doubt about what needed to be done. 'You're at risk,' he said, 'and I won't have my people exposed unnecessarily to risk.' We were told to rent a suite in the Europa Hotel and move in immediately. It was wonderful news – I can't pretend otherwise. As bespoke explosions go, this one fitted me like a glove.

Not that the Europa was necessarily the safest place in town. Over the years, it would become famous as the most bombed hotel in the world. I remember once being evacuated from the coffee shop only to watch the deputy manager – a man with a moustache that would have delighted *Sun* readers – running out with a device, which he then tossed into the car park. When it went off seconds later, it blew off his shoes. But though the Europa was like Baghdad's Green Zone, surrounded by razor wire, sentry posts and armed guards, it was also, when you got inside, an amazing home from home.

Twelve storeys high, it boasted the Whip and Saddle bar and coffee shop on the ground floor, a 'French' restaurant on the mezzanine, and a bar and restaurant on the top floor overlooking the magnificent, if rapidly diminishing, panorama of the Belfast skyline.

The *Irish Times* was allocated Suite 611. We had a large living room, with sofas and twin desks, and a bedroom to either side. We had no fewer than three minibars and full access to room service. You can imagine how tempting all this was to a young man not yet 24 – and you may be sure that I succumbed to the temptation.

Most journalists in those days stayed at the Europa, or else at the Wellington Park, a slightly more down-at-heel establishment further up the road beyond the University. We drank copiously and ate a steady diet of steaks, burgers and club sandwiches. Late at night, we adjourned to the Penthouse Club, where we were served expensive cocktails and foreign beers by the Penthouse Pets, complete with fluffy ears and tails, while trios with varying degrees of musical competence belted out jazz standards in Belfast accents.

It was in the Europa that I made my first sustained acquaintance with haute cuisine. Up to then, the only vegetables with which I had come into any sort of regular contact were cabbage, cauliflower, carrots, sprouts, peas and beans. Meat – so well done it might as well have been served up in an urn – arrived with any two of these, plus potatoes boiled to buggery. Now, I came face to face with a bewildering array of exotic products, such as veal, prawns, avocados and aubergines. It was Max Hastings, now *Sir* Max (my future editor at the *Telegraph* but then in town for the *Evening Standard*), who taught me how to eat an artichoke. He had made his mark in Belfast several years earlier when he witnessed the RUC opening up on a block of flats with a Browning machine gun, killing nine-year-old Patrick Rooney asleep in his bed. Then, as now, Max was a larger-than-life character, like a bizarre fusion of *Boy's Own* thriller writer Andy McNab and *Private Eye*'s Ian Hislop. He demonstrated to me how to pull the leaves off the artichoke and to suck or nibble at the succulent part. 'Now you try.' Next, he enquired what sort of guns I shot with.

'Guns?' I said.

'Yes,' he said. 'Mine are in for servicing just now. A couple of Purdeys [or they may have been Holland & Holland] given to me by my father.'

It surprised me that he should have thought I was a shooting man. Now, if he'd been lunching with Ronnie . . .

Hastings and I lived in two different worlds. I was reminded of the *Private Eye* cover featuring Alec Douglas Home out shooting on his estate while, in the ground beneath, colliers struggled to extract

coal from a narrow seam. 'I've lived among miners all my life,' says
Home. But, like all the best reporters, Hastings knew how to
engage people at every level.

The hideous realities of everyday life percolated the Green Zone
with ease. Not only was the Europa itself subject to regular assault
by terrorists, but from our windows we could see orange flashes in
the distance and listen to the regular crump of explosions. Gunfire
was a constant. Sometimes the criss-cross of tracer bullets arced in
the sky above the city. At other times, it was just single shots. Army
helicopters patrolled the skies, their regular takka-takka-takka
shaking the glass, the beams from their searchlights penetrating the
darkest corners.

Everyone was affected. For my dad, dark corners were practically
all that was left. As if it wasn't bad enough that the horrors of his
childhood had returned to haunt him, with policemen being
murdered by gunmen and Catholics driven from their homes, his
health was in remorseless decline. It didn't help that he was robbed
once at gunpoint outside his shop or that, on another occasion,
when he was in hospital recovering from a heart attack, the shelves
of his shop were systematically looted. After his second heart attack,
he sold what was left of the business and vowed to take life more
easily. The problem was he got bored. When someone told him that
a southern firm owned, it turned out, by the future Irish Prime
Minister Albert Reynolds was looking for a salesman for its range
of petfoods in the North, he jumped at the chance. Soon, he was
back on the road, and it was clear that his old skills had not deserted
him. But then he had to give it up. His heart couldn't take the
strain.

Years later, in conversation with Reynolds, I mentioned that my
dad used to work for one of his companies.

'Doing what?' he asked.

'Selling dog food.'

'Is that right? What name?'

'Walter Ellis,' I said. 'Same as mine.'

He nodded thoughtfully, as if going through his mental Rolodex. 'From the North, right?'

'Absolutely.'

'That's it. Well, you can tell him from me he was one hell of a salesman.'

A masterly response, you had to hand it to him. Sadly, Dad was dead by then, but he would have been delighted that someone as important as Reynolds should have remembered his name. He loved celebrities. He wrote to Jim Callaghan once, when Callaghan was Prime Minister, pointing out to him that they shared the same birth date: 27 March 1912. A letter came back on Downing Street notepaper in which an official informed Dad of the Prime Minister's 'pleasure' at the coincidence.

Belfast in the 1970s was an eerie place and, much as we might have wished otherwise, we couldn't cover it from the Europa. We had to go to where the action was. This meant turning up for demonstrations on the Falls Road, or Ballymurphy, or the Shankill; inspecting bodies by the roadside; talking in whispers to men in balaclavas; listening to the harangues of demagogues. Life in Northern Ireland was like an abandoned play in which the lines of the script were written alternately by Kafka, Pinter and Beckett, edited by Frank Carson: it had no end in sight, no point and no charm.

I have sometimes wondered about the character of the Ulster people, Catholic and Protestant. It has been remarked of them by outsiders that they are open, welcoming and hospitable. And this is true. They make the best of what they have. Even when they have very little, they will happily share it with strangers. Nor do they, by any means, all hate the 'other side' or wish them ill. They simply want their side to be on top and for this fact to be accepted without rancour. Protestants will often tell you that they have Catholic friends who are the salt of the earth and only want, like them, to live and let live. The same is true of Catholics. They'll happily meet Protestant pals in town and go with them for a drink. They don't expect them to change their spots overnight and become nationalists. All they expect from them, they will assure you, is a bit of good-natured understanding.

Yet the two communities have never been more apart and isolated from each other than they are now. True, there are places, mostly wealthy or deeply rural, where Catholics and Protestants live cheek by jowl. But, for the most part, the two sides still go to different bars, different clubs and different sports venues, as well as different churches. They read different newspapers and often listen to different radio stations. In the ghettoes, it's all or nothing. You either live in a Prod area or you live in a Taig area. The two sides spend time with each other in shops and offices. They may even talk about their 'mates' from the other 'persuasion'. But at the end of the day, they head home in opposite directions.

Elections bring this ambivalence into sharp focus. People are forever being quoted on television vox pops expressing their disgust at the politicians and the fact that they won't knuckle down and sort things out. Yet, when polling day dawns, it's the extremists from both sides who get voted in. How otherwise would Sinn Fein and Paisley's DUP be by far the two biggest factions, leaving the more moderate (but still segregationist) unionists and SDLP trailing far behind? People say one thing when the cameras are on them – but their default positions have not altered, save for the worse, in more than 30 years of conflict.

Women, it is said, are the ones most likely to break the mould. Evidence for this is drawn from the various peace initiatives led by women down the years. First, there were the 'Peace People', led by Mairead Corrigan-Maguire and Betty Williams (who won the 1976 Nobel Peace Prize). Then there was the Women's Coalition, a bi-partisan political grouping that promised much but achieved little. Most recently, we had the McCartney sisters, who forced an

IRA climbdown after their brother was murdered by republicans in a Belfast pub. Where are they now? Ulster women are supposed to be strong-willed and 'sensible', and are reckoned, deep down, to have no truck with extremism. But women have made up a majority of the electorate for as long as I have been alive. Can it really be true that women vote down the line for moderate candidates, while men − vile beasts that they are − endorse only hardline positions? I don't think so. The numbers prove otherwise. But the myth persists and has within it enough of a germ of truth to make it worth repeating.

Back in the 1970s, my speciality as a journalist, such as it was, was the Official republicans, or Stickies, who by this stage were losing ground heavily to the Provisionals. Not long after, the Officials would split again, with a violent minority, including my pal Ronnie Bunting, disappearing into the Irish Republican Socialist Party (IRSP) and its military wing, the Irish National Liberation Army (INLA). But in 1973, the Sticky rump was still active in the Lower Falls, as well as in the Markets and Short Strand. When things were quiet, or when some outrage or other had just occurred, I would make my way into the west of the city to see what was happening and try to speak to a few of the 'lads'.

The Falls Road, particularly the lower section close to the city centre, was a dangerous place. The Army were everywhere. So were the Stickies. One afternoon, while making my way towards Divis Flats, the unofficial battalion headquarters of the local IRA, I walked past a building belonging to St Comgall's Primary School, opposite Percy Street. To my immediate left was a stone wall. To my right, down Percy Street, were the Brits. Suddenly, a gun barrel projected from the wall to my left. A gunman in a black balaclava had decided to have a go at the Army base 200 yards away. The noise was deafening. The muzzle flare seared my flesh. Almost at once, the Brits opened up in reply. I was caught in the crossfire. I dropped to my knees, shouting out, 'For fuck's sake, I'm standing right here. Do you want to get me killed?' It was a moot point. British bullets from Army SLRs were crashing into the wall around me, sending granite chips flying. Were they trying to hit me or were they trying to avoid me? I had no way of knowing. Abruptly, the IRA man called out to me, 'Sorry, big lad, didn't see you there!', and was gone. Seconds later, the Brits stopped firing as well, and I began to run as fast as my legs would carry me in the direction of St Peter's Pro-Cathedral. Sanctuary! I needed sanctuary.

It's true what Churchill said. There is nothing more exhilarating than being shot at without result. I felt more alive than I had in ages. It was the same when, years later, a member of the Romanian Securitate took pot shots at me from a rooftop in Bucharest – I discovered afterwards that there were bullet holes in my jacket, but not in me. It was as if I had been given a miraculous reprieve. In both instances, the adrenalin was pumping so hard that I'm sure I lost months of my life.

Riots were obviously unpleasant. The trick here was to look as if it was nothing to do with you and you were merely a disinterested observer. So long as neither side felt you were the enemy, you generally emerged unscathed; though, of course, there was always the possibility of an accident. CS gas was the thing to watch out for. It didn't discriminate between participants and journalists, and after getting a lungful of gas you were no use for anything for an hour at least. Rubber bullets also operated at random. They were supposed to be targeted and directed at the legs of rioters, but as often as not they were loosed indiscriminately into the mob, resulting in serious injuries, or even death. I tried to avoid these, if possible.

Throughout this time, the violence was increasingly haphazard and deadly. 'Terrorism' had taken on a new meaning. Ordinary Catholics were being picked off the streets by loyalists and then murdered. Some were tortured and their bodies hung from meat hooks. Soldiers and policemen were dying at a rate of almost one a day, most of them victims of the Provisionals, while bombs seemed to go off every five minutes. It was a real community effort. I learned later that a young man from the Highfield estate, where my father had his shops, was a member of the so-called Shankill Butchers – a loyalist gang known for dismembering its victims with butchers' knives. I used to deliver groceries to his house on Saturdays, and sometimes, when he was maybe 15 or 16, the future Butcher would come down the path to take the box off me so that I wouldn't have to carry it all the way into the house. 'He was that sort of a wee fella,' my dad observed. 'Always said hello and thank you. You'd never have thought he'd get involved in a thing like that.'

With so many murderers about, trust was a rare commodity. All of us had to watch our step. I was walking down the busy Whiterock Road in the rain one afternoon when an Army patrol went by and a group of Provisionals positioned in the nearby cemetery opened up on them with M1 carbines. Everyone threw themselves to the ground. When I got up, I was covered with mud. But at least I got up. An English reporter I knew nearly jumped out of his skin one night when he was parking his car round the back of the Europa and a man came up behind him and stuck something hard in his back. It was only another hack with a biro having a laugh, but my friend came close to a heart attack.

Personally, life was starting to pick up. There hadn't been much on the girl front for months. My half-hearted attempts to seduce the Penthouse Pets had predictably come to nothing. My heart wasn't in it, though I'd have enjoyed it on the night. In any case, their sights were set on the more glamorous London-based hacks who, with luck, would get them the hell out of Belfast. There was a brief affair with a republican activist from the west of the city who felt I should give up journalism and commit myself to the People's Democracy, but this had resulted only in a virulent case of crabs. She and her mates played with a Ouija board one night and insisted that some spirit from the Other Side had come through with details of a

Provisional arms dump in Armagh. I don't know what they expected me to do about it. There was also a nurse with strikingly red hair. She let me touch her up under her cape outside the nurses' home but said it was against her religion to have sex before marriage. Then, at some point, I don't quite know how, I began dating one of the telephonists from the Europa, a girl called Rosemary. We connected straight away. She was bright and funny and grown up and shared my conviction that the Troubles, far from being a noble cause or a stalwart defence of old values, were nothing but a black comedy.

Everybody liked Rosemary. She came from the Limestone Road, in the north of the city. Her parents were devout Catholics. They kept an effigy of Christ's Bleeding Heart on their living-room wall, lit by a blood-red lamp, and on the sideboard there was a figurine of the Child of Prague (pronounced *Preyg*). Rosemary's oldest sister had left Belfast for Canada some years before, and Rosemary had followed her out, remaining in Toronto for two years before deciding to return home after a love affair had ended badly. She should have gone to university and launched herself into a proper career; instead, she had ended up as a switchboard girl at the Europa. But it all worked out fine. The fact that the *Irish Times* had bedrooms attached to its suite was not a disadvantage in the furtherance of our relationship. It was handy as well to have someone in the know when things got hot in the city and phone lines were at a premium.

It was around this time that I met David Blundy of the *Sunday Times*, one of that paper's fabled Insight Team, whose investigations into Bloody Sunday had set the tone for much of the subsequent press coverage of Ulster. Blundy, killed in El Savador in 1989, would soon become one of my closest friends – or at least the friend I most closely valued. He was a truly astonishing man, not least for his effect on the opposite sex. Women began to undress within minutes of meeting him. He only had to smile at them for them to start unfastening their skirts and peeling off their tights. And when he left them – usually the following morning – they invariably begged for more, which had not been my experience. He was extremely tall, broad-shouldered and lean. His face, a mutual friend once remarked, was really two faces welded together: the left side was sad and long-suffering, the right side dark and demonic. The combination was irresistible.

Blundy (never David) liked people to think he was a working-class boy done good. He could talk 'posh' when he needed to, but his everyday accent was upmarket apples and pears, as if he had just stepped off the Tube at Elephant and Castle. There were vague references to his dad as a rag-and-bone man (long-since retired to Bognor) and for years I assumed, without asking, that he had gone to his local comprehensive in south London. In fact, as Tony Holden discovered while researching his life for a collection of his journalism, *The Last Paragraph*, his father owned an extensive antique and quality furniture saleroom, occupying half an acre, while the son was a product of the City of London School, one of the country's most exclusive educational institutions, with fees (in 2005) of more than £10,000 a year. Blundy may not have been a toff, but he weren't no cockney *neever*.

Did this make him a sham? No more than the rest of us. Journalists are always reinventing themselves. But it does mean that he could never quite be taken at face, or *faces*, value? There were two people to whom he remained constant: his ex-wife, Ruth, whom he had met at Bristol University (but never lived with after the wedding), and Anna, his daughter, who now writes thrillers and is obsessed with his memory. The rest of us took what we were offered.

When I moved later to Brussels as the *Irish Times*' European correspondent, Blundy paid me several visits. Each time, the female population was in a swoon as his proximity set off premature explosions in their frilly panties. One of his conquests was a future CNN correspondent – very pretty and very accomplished. Another was a dazzlingly beautiful secretary to the spokesman of the European Commission. Months after, when he had long-since forgotten their names, they would ask me, with a glint in their eyes, whether there was any chance he might be coming back soon. Treat 'em mean and keep 'em keen was his motto and, by Christ, it was effective.

In 1977, he came to stay with me in Bonn, where I was working for *The Observer*, following the disastrous break-up of his latest relationship. I waited for him in a bar, in the company of a girl I was crazy about but who refused to let me sleep with her. Blundy's arrival was dramatic. The bar had Wild West-style swing doors and, suddenly, he was there, silhouetted against the evening sky. Evelyn (for it was she) drew in her breath. 'Is that *him*?' she asked me, squeezing my hand with unexpected urgency.

'Er, yes.'

They left together that night. A few months later, she abandoned her studies at Bonn University and went to live with him in New York.

I sometimes think he had a premonition of early death. He certainly did not expect to make old bones. Round the corner from where Evelyn lived in Bonn was a funeral parlour. In the front window was an ornate rosewood coffin with brass handles. 'I can feel it calling to me,' he confided in me, only half-joking. 'It's like it's saying, why waste any more time? Why not just come inside and get it over with? Come on, hop in. You know you want to.'

In Belfast, most of the Penthouse Pets made an immediate play for him (how successfully, I cannot be sure – well, I can really), but he worked hard while in Northern Ireland, always, as he liked to put it, looking to name the guilty man or identify the defective part.

Rosemary and I had by now moved into a flat in the south of the city, number 79 Marlborough Park South, owned by our neighbour, Mr Diljit Rana, who was destined to become one of

Ulster's richest men with a fortune in excess of £60 million. Mr Rana was a splendid landlord who left us to ourselves but was always on hand when things went wrong. For the first time in years, I found myself chatting to a neighbour over the garden fence.

We occupied the ground-floor flat and once a month at least we would be wakened by the window being thrown back and the sight of Blundy stepping into the room. ''Allo, Rosemary!' he would begin. 'Any chance of a cuppa tea?'

She loved him (though not, I think, in *that* way) and would do anything for him. Her frequent attempts to fix him up with one of her friends never came to anything. Instead, he would invite us all out to dinner, friend and all, and put it on expenses.

He had a curious work cycle, like a priest. During the week, he was relaxed. There would be much consumption of whiskey and endless meals with pals. From time to time, he would vanish to meet his 'contacts' – people who wanted to tell him things – but come the evening he was back on the phone. 'Fancy a bit of supper, Walt? Wot about Rosemary? Bring her along.' But then, come Friday night, he moved into purdah. His room at the Europa would by this stage be chock-a-block with old newspapers, magazines, food trays, notebooks, whiskey bottles and cigarette ends. He would clear a space on the nearest available worktop, set up his Olivetti, light a fag and work without pause for the next 12 hours. Not until he had dictated the last word over the phone to Gray's Inn Road would he relax and assume his normal persona.

He may have been in purdah, but that didn't mean everybody else was. One night, a drunken woman from the hotel bar attempted to get into his room while he was working, shouting out to him that he could do anything he liked to her and she'd *love* it. He wasn't having it. He wasn't listening. Eventually, security had to be called to take the distraught creature away, still seeking to persuade him that she was the answer to his prayers.

For a couple of years in the 1980s, Blundy and I actually worked on the same paper, the *Sunday Telegraph*, on which he was employed as chief US correspondent, and on two occasions I stayed with him at his apartment on P Street, Washington DC, which he shared with his girlfriend, Samyra, and their new daughter, Charlotte. But it wasn't the same. He seemed distant . . . remote. The truth was that, probably, like so many journalists, he chose his friends from among those who were most readily available – in this case Americans and Washington-based Brits.

In 1988, he resigned from the *Telegraph* to join the fledgling *Sunday Correspondent*, always looking for greater editorial freedom. Just before leaving for the trip to El Salvador from which he would not return, he heard from Patrick Cockburn (whose acquaintance I had first made in the Club Bar during my student days) that I was upset by the fact that he never called and never wrote. He telephoned me out of the blue (a thing he never did unless there was good reason) and we spoke for a good half-hour during which he sounded depressed and unsettled. He said he had always valued my friendship, but well, fuck, you know, it was difficult, what with 3,000 miles of ocean in between. I asked him how things were going. He said relations between him and Samyra weren't easy. They had a daughter to bring up for the next 20 years and that was no joke at his age. He was in his 45th year and was worried all of a sudden that he had made no provision for a pension. What should he do? I wasn't really the one to ask, but I advised him as best I could and he said he would do something about it when he got back from Central America. 'Come and visit,' he said. 'It'd be nice to see you.'

About ten days later, in one of the less salubrious barrios of San Salvador, he was talking to a group of young militiamen on a street corner when a shot rang out. The bullet entered his body through his right shoulder, passed through his lungs and embedded in his spine. 'Get me out of here,' he said to a photographer from *Newsweek*. Then he slipped into unconsciousness. Three hours later, he was dead.

I was in India at the time, covering the general election that brought V.P. Singh to power (ironically, I was now employed by the *Sunday Times*). When the news came through that Blundy was shot, a Simply Red video was playing on the television in my room. Mick Hucknall, with his red hair hanging lopsidedly down one side of his face, was singing 'Holding Back the Years', still a favourite of mine after all this time.

It seems so long ago now. In Belfast back in 1973, other changes were afoot. Renagh Holohan had had enough of Belfast life and returned to Dublin. She was replaced by a journalist I'd never heard of called Conor O'Clery, who, up to this point, had apparently worked as a sub-editor in head office. Conor was thirty-four, married with five children and from Castlewellan, County Down. He had worked in the Northern Ireland civil service for about five years before going to Queen's University as a mature student and taking up journalism. Mr Gageby must have rated him, but it was hard to see why at first.

I soon saw the reason. He was a born reporter, with an ego to match, and went on to have one of the most celebrated – and lucky – careers in Irish journalism. On 11 September 2001, I was living in Providence, Rhode Island, and missed the first reports of terrorist attacks in New York and Washington because I was out shopping. Conor, on the other hand, was staring out of his apartment window less than 200 yards from the Trade Towers when he saw the first plane go in. The backdraught nearly put out his windows and for the next week he had a grandstand view of history. In 35 years on the *Irish Times*, he never missed a trick, and after opening bureaux in Moscow, Beijing and Washington, as well as New York, he ended up writing the longest valediction in the paper's history.

Yeah, but who cares? More important, from my point of view, was the arrival on the scene of David McKittrick, my pal from the College of Business Studies. He was replacing Martin Cowley, who had transferred to London. David had put on a bit of weight since we last met but was his same irrepressible self. When I joined the *Cork Examiner*, he joined the *East Antrim Times*, based in Carrickfergus, where he reported the minutiae of small-town life. His office backed on to a pharmacy whose owner ran a lucrative sideline gassing stray cats and dogs for the municipality. The deed was done in an airtight container just yards from David's desk. 'As I typed,' he once told me, 'I could hear the dogs whimpering to death.'

Few, if any, reporters of the Troubles have acquired McKittrick's reputation for shrewd judgement, even-handedness and probity. I don't know how many awards he has won over the years, but if they were Oscars he would be the most acclaimed actor in Hollywood history. His was a hard wake to follow in. I was never a top-class reporter, merely a competent one. My real strength was writing. I was good at describing things – and I had a reputation for being funny. But then David turned out to be a good writer too! It'd make you spit.

Neither he nor I remember the exact sequence, but for a year or so, until he met his future wife, Pat, he lived in the top flat of 79 Marlborough Park South, which he shared with a reporter from RTÉ, while Rosemary and I were living in the garden flat. David liked his bed. He also liked gadgets. He would sleep in until ten-thirty – or lunchtime on days off – surrounded by radios, televisions, record players and calculators. Later, the calculators were joined by Pat. But once he was up and moving, you hardly saw him for dust. He would disappear up the Shankill Road or the Newtownards Road for hours at a time, talking to men whose favoured garb was leather jackets worn over tight T-shirts and set off by a bloodcurdling tattoo. In the office, he sat hunched over his phone, taking voluminous notes and muttering, 'Uh-huh, uh-huh . . . Really? . . . Is that right?'

At the *Irish Times*, it was all change. Suddenly, *I* was the veteran.

Conor liked the idea that we were in the Europa, which could hardly have been more central. But he was determined about two things: one, he was going to be a star, and, two, we were going to help him achieve that end. McKittrick was given the key loyalist portfolio. I was allowed to hang on to my Sticky remit, but I was also to attend more press conferences and keep in touch with general news. As a sop to my vanity, I was given a weekly column, 'Inside Belfast', which was to be my vehicle for 'fine writing'. Conor, meanwhile, would break major stories and lead the plain people of Ireland into a new appreciation of the momentous forces at work in the North.

I have to say, it worked fine. My little column attracted quite a following, including Maeve Binchy, still dreaming of her first novel, who came up to the city now and again from Dublin to enjoy the craic. She still keeps a couple of my pieces in a drawer somewhere in her backroom in Dalkey. More importantly, Conor began to bring in scoops. He had a knack of getting people to tell him things they shouldn't. Maybe they thought that appearing in the *Irish Times* was the next best thing to anonymity. Whatever the reason, they spilled their guts to the man from Castlewellan, who was soon on the television and radio almost as much as Henry – but without the accompanying guffaws.

All this said, the real revelation was McKittrick. Born in Dover Street, between the Falls and Shankill roads, he grew up just yards from the house (on the other side of the invisible sectarian divide) in which Cardinal William Conway made his first entrance into the world. He knew all about the Fenians. They started, after all, just a couple of yards down the road. But he was a Shankill man through and through. As a boy, he and the local Taigs threw stones at each other and he was fluent in the catcalls of his tribe.

Luckily for him and for Irish journalism, his parents moved in the 1960s to Belvoir Park, a 'model' housing estate in south-east Belfast, next to a golf course and the meandering River Lagan. Mrs

McKittrick, *née* Hegarty, was an excellent, good-hearted woman, who reminded me very much of Alan Kirker's mum. His sister, Joan, was a policewoman. 'What do my sister and her mates have for lunch?' he asked me once – well, several times, actually. The answer was 'truncheon meat'. From his new home base, surrounded by trees and fields, he won a place at Grosvenor High, the grammar school just up the road from Orangefield. Thus, even when we were teenagers, our lives moved in awkward parallel.

In due course, he went to Queen's to study economics, only to discover that academic life was not for him. Sums were not *his* strong suit either. He dropped out after a year and fled to London, where for several months he worked as a labourer in Holloway Women's Prison, seeing things that no man ought to see. He returned to Northern Ireland after reading that the *Belfast Telegraph* was looking for trainee reporters, and while waiting for the journalism course to begin took a summer job selling curtains – which, of course, is how we met: supply and demand in perfect harmony.

Late 1973 was a crucial time for loyalists. Protestant power was waning. The Big House Unionists had lost all conviction and were, in any case, no longer trusted by their working-class constituents. If unionism was to have any future, it needed to speak with a new voice, and this turned out to be the voice of paramilitary madness. It was as if the gentry had been supplanted by the more rabid supporters of Linfield Football Club – which, in fact, was not far off the truth.

McKittrick knew everything about the loonies who ate Catholics for breakfast – possibly because he had snacked on them himself as a boy. As they developed ever more grandiose schemes to turn Northern Ireland into an armed camp in which rebels would pay the ultimate price for their audacity, each twist and turn of the argument was reported in the pages of the *Irish Times*. It soon became clear that the more vile, vicious and uncompromising the extremists became, the more they wanted their aspirations set out, accurately and in full, in Ireland's foremost paper of record. David duly obliged.

The paper's northern coverage now entered its golden period, in which even I played my part. Conor was so pleased that he decided to have an affair. Less joyously, Dublin's response was to set us up with new offices nearby in Fanum House, where our landlords, mocking my carelessness, turned out to be the AA. We moved out of the Europa sometime in the late autumn of 1973. I can't be certain that we marked our departure with a final raid on room service and the minibars, but it would have been entirely out of character if we had not. Everyone was agreed on one thing: 1974 would be one heck of a year. It was shit-or-bust time, and you could get good odds on both.

Privately, I was thinking about getting out of Northern Ireland. I wasn't sure where I would go. There was Dublin, of course, where more civilised discourse held good and I would be free to explore my own Protestant identity, such as it was, within the Irish State; or there was England – Fleet Street – with its myriad of mass-circulation papers and its increasingly multicultural society. One of the drawbacks of growing up in a provincial backwater, even a volatile one like Northern Ireland, is that you lose touch with the larger undercurrents driving the world. Distant from the mainstream, you think that your problems are the only ones that matter. You have no appreciation of your relative insignificance. Against that, growing up in Belfast gave me the sort of appreciation of fractured societies that actually helps in the understanding of larger-scale divisions. The Middle East, South Africa, the Balkans: people from my kind of background readily appreciate the tragedies of each of these places. It is when we get beyond gunfire and into more sophisticated realms of understanding and social experiment that our insights start to fail. We like our enemies

clearly identified. We like to know what, and who, we're up against.
If Catholics were really green and Protestants were truly orange,
many in Northern Ireland would find it entirely appropriate.

Now that I am in my 50s, I'm not always sure that I made the
right decision by getting out. It's not that I regret the many
experiences I've had and the different places I've lived; it's more that
I am left balancing depth against breadth and wondering which
teaches most. Also, when you're older, you feel once more the tug
of your roots.

Déraciné, or perhaps just re-potted, Ronnie Bunting was having
identity problems of his own. Following the murder of Joe
McCann, Cathal Goulding, the IRA's chief-of-staff, had vowed to
carry on the struggle of the Irish people and 'break the heart of
empire'. In fact, in the wake of public revulsion following their
'execution' of an Irish-born British soldier on leave in Derry, the
Stickies had called a ceasefire in the summer of 1972.

Militants in the movement couldn't believe what they were
hearing. One of Goulding's leading lieutenants, Séamus Costello, a
former car salesman from Bray, County Wicklow, began taking
soundings and soon realised that, if it came to it, he could walk
away and take with him the hardest of the hardliners. For Costello,
as for Ronnie, the prospect of an unarmed struggle was short-
sighted and illogical – hardly worth getting out of bed for. The fight
against the British was all or nothing, just as McCann would have
wanted. Politics was what you imposed *after* you'd won, not a
substitute for victory.

It was to prove a long and agonising argument, and while the
Officials debated, the Provisionals struck. By 1973, they had utterly
eclipsed their rivals and were embarked on the bloody campaign
that, ultimately, and ironically, would see them enmeshed in the
greatest compromise of all: sitting down with the unionists at
Stormont. But no one knew this at the time. Post-Bloody Sunday,
post-internment, the assumption of the Provos was that nothing

would do save bloody mayhem, followed, as night follows day, by a 32-county Irish Republic.

The Officials now lived in a world of their own. Costello, a matinée idol with a deathwish, was first sidelined by Goulding, then, after a long period of quasi-legal internal process, expelled. Ronnie was among those who went with the Wicklow man. Though they did not know it at the time, they were in the process of forming the INLA.

On 1 January 1974, even as the new Stormont Executive, headed by Brian Faulkner and SDLP leader Gerry Fitt (for whom his dad, the Major, had once been election agent), assumed control of the administration of Northern Ireland, Ronnie was working to turn Costello's refuseniks into an effective fighting unit. What they were fighting *for*, it was difficult to say. Ronnie believed in Mao, Che Guevera, the Tupemaros, the Shining Path, Unita, Lightnin' Hopkins, Big Bill Broonzy et al. He was for permanent revolution, whatever the cost. The shark that stopped swimming and stopped hunting was for him the shark that drowned.

He wasn't alone in this. Fulvio Grimaldi, an Italian photo-journalist who flung down a pocketful of bullet casings onto a table during the original inquiry into Bloody Sunday ('*There's* your evidence!'), told me once that the revolution never could stop and never should stop. It was the end, not the means. That, he said, was why the movement he belonged to was called Lotta Continua – The Struggle Continues. It was a melancholy outlook. For madmen like Fulvio and Ronnie, and maybe Bernadette too, Easy Street was the Boulevard of Broken Dreams.

The old Unionist government was corrupt and sectarian, while smugly believing itself a bastion of purity. The early SDLP, set up to serve as a nationalist counterweight, was, with the exception of John Hume and Paddy Devlin, self-serving and conservative – the Green Establishment in waiting. Cleaving to the true flame, lit in Dublin's GPO in 1916, the Provisionals were cynical and heartless. They would kill you as soon as look at you. The loyalist paramilitary groups, the UDA and the UVF, were banal and evil, wading through blood to a future as gun-runners, drug barons and pimps. But the INLA took the biscuit. It was not only banal and evil, it was *insane*.

While I attended meetings of the new Assembly and obituarised the victims of the conflict, Ronnie was engaged in wholesale death and destruction. Like Pol Pot, he wanted the bodies of the unworthy piled up on the streets. But things didn't always go well for him. After a mail-train robbery – intended to provide funds for the purchase of arms – went wrong, he was left standing in a field. His comrades fled the scene empty-handed and forgot all about him. Not long after, shots were fired into his home in Turf Lodge by a punishment squad from the Officials, narrowly missing his wife and infant daughter. Goulding, who once lauded him as proof that it was still possible to be a Protestant and a republican, had come to see him as an obstacle to political progress. There may even have been a feeling that he was a 'black' Protestant after all, who ought never to have been trusted. The Provos, at the same time, wanted his head because they suspected him of involvement in the death of one of their top men, Jim Bryson, killed during a confused shoot-out in Ballymurphy.

Back in the real world – or what passed for the real world – it was party time in Fanum House. We now had fourth and fifth members of our team. Fionnuala O Connor, a diminutive, Irish-speaking feminist, had been sent back to her native Belfast from Dublin to bolster news production, but also to give a woman's view of events. Within a matter of weeks, it was as if she had been there for ever. Fionnuala's husband, David McVea, a Protestant schoolteacher, would also play his part in the story. At the tail end of the Troubles, he worked closely with McKittrick and others in the production of *Lost Lives*, a monumental tribute to the inglorious dead, published by Mainstream and lauded by no less than Bill Clinton and Tony Blair.

On the business side – an indication of Gageby's determination that Northern Ireland should not be treated as a pariah state – Ronnie Hoffman was appointed to write about business and finance. Ronnie was both Jewish and English, but he, too, fitted right in, reporting examples every day of entrepreneurship and initiative in the midst of chaos.

Meanwhile, the British Prime Minister Edward Heath was in a bind over his Ulster strategy. Three months earlier, at a conference in Sunningdale, Berkshire, agreement of a sort had been reached about the future form of government for the province. The plan was that the Stormont Executive, now confirmed in power, would send representatives to a new Council of Ireland based in Armagh at which there would also be delegates from the government in Dublin. The Council's role was intended to be purely practical, dealing with such matters as transport, agriculture and energy distribution, but loyalists naturally saw it as the thin end of the nationalist wedge. They were confirmed in their suspicions when Hugh Logue, a leading member of the moderate Catholic SDLP, described it as the vehicle that would 'trundle' unionists into a united Ireland.

Personally, I had no problems in this direction. After all, I needed *some* sort of vehicle to trundle me along. But the Council turned out to be easily the most controversial aspect of the reform programme and the rock on which the entire project foundered.

During the phoney war that followed, Rosemary and I lived the life of Riley, hosting small gatherings in our flat, visiting Dublin at weekends, trying to put money aside for the purchase of a house. Radio 4 had discovered not long before that I had a good radio voice, and I appeared on *The World at One* and *The World Tonight*, and other news programmes, sometimes three or four times a week. Conor kept RTÉ and BBC Northern Ireland to himself. He also chivvied the rest of us along, making sure I got my column in on time, encouraging Fionnuala to stand up for herself and practically begging McKittrick to reveal the source, or sources, that were bringing him in a constant rain of scoops.

As tempers flared in Stormont and violence and disorder spread into almost every corner of the land, my wisdom teeth came out in sympathy. I'm not even sure I knew that there were such things as wisdom teeth. They sounded like a Victorian invention. But when they began pushing through my gums, threatening to disrupt my other teeth and even alter the shape of my jaw, it was clear they would have to go. I was taken into the Ulster Hospital – the same underfunded institution in which my father and mother ended their days – and put under the surgeon's knife. I felt odd and vulnerable. The last time I was in hospital, other than as a visitor, was after Alan Kirker dropped a fire extinguisher on my big toe. (He had said he was going to do it, but I didn't believe him. He, for his part, didn't think I would be so stupid as to not move my foot. I still suffer from the effects.) The nurse looking after me in the Ulster was married to one of my main Unionist contacts, John Laird, an Assembly member for Belfast West – now Lord Laird of Artigarvan, Patron of the Ulster-Scots Society of America. How long, I asked the future Lady Carol, would it take for the anaesthetic to kick in? She smiled down at me. Before she could answer, I woke up with cheeks the size of footballs.

Maybe these things go in pairs, for a few weeks later, as I was walking towards a bus stop in east Belfast, I realised that I couldn't read a shop sign on the opposite side of the road. Irritated, I crossed over to see what I was missing. The sign read: 'Optician'. Thus it was that I discovered I was short-sighted. I picked up my first pair of glasses a few weeks later. People said I looked odd, which was hardly surprising. A while afterwards, I began a short-lived experiment with contact lenses. Unfortunately, when the pair of permeable lenses I was given turned milky from the proteins I was secreting, my answer was to hand them over to my brother-in-law, Lesley, the textile chemist, who assured me he would return them bright as new. He wasn't wrong either. They were spanking clean.

The only problem was that they were now the size of saucers. I have worn spectacles ever since and never found them an inconvenience.

Politically, things were coming to a head. The Phoney War was over; the blitzkrieg was about to begin. While the new Executive tried to impress itself on a dubious home audience, events in Britain conspired to destroy six months of hard work and steady behind-the-scenes negotiation. The trouble was that the Heath government, like an overripe Stilton, was crumbling. The Prime Minister, who with great fanfare had taken Britain into the Common Market, was faced with spiralling inflation at home and determined trade union opposition to his policy of wage and price controls. When a miners' strike forced electricity generators to limit output, the result was a three-day working week and, inevitably, a general election. Come polling day, Heath duly came a cropper and was replaced by his predecessor, the Labour leader Harold Wilson.

Now the fun started. Wilson, a magician without a rabbit in his hat, had not been part of the Sunningdale Agreement and had no vested interest in the survival of the Stormont Executive, still less the Council of Ireland. He wished everyone well but had other things on his mind. Sensing this, loyalists combined to step up pressure on Westminster and demand a better deal. Faulkner and Fitt (now dead and deified) dug in their heels. So did the loyalists. In the Assembly, fights broke out again and the ceremonial mace was wrestled from its cradle and passed from hand to hand. What followed, the Ulster Workers' Strike, was the first example in Europe in the post-war period of a legitimate government being subverted by mob rule.

For my dad, for whom ambivalence was his only real political conviction, it was a time to stand up and be counted – twice. As a member of the middle-of-the-road Alliance Party made up of Protestant and Catholic liberals, he was a firm supporter of the Executive and the principle of power-sharing. But as a part-time employee of Crazy Prices, an economy superstore in Belfast's western suburbs, he couldn't help sympathising with the views of his customers, most of whom were bitterly opposed to the idea of a Council of Ireland.

When the crunch came, he sided with his customers (maybe it was the salesman in him). He volunteered as a spokesman for the openly sectarian Ulster Workers' Council, who had organised a general strike that paralysed Northern Ireland and would bring the Executive to its knees.

David Blundy was over covering the crisis for the *Sunday Times* and telephoned UWC headquarters. My father answered. 'Crazy Prices!' he began.

'What?'

'Crazy Pri— I mean, Ulster Workers' Council.'

They soon got talking. Dad had met Blundy several times and found him extremely amusing. Talking to him now, he was clearly embarrassed by his own role in the strike. Blundy told him not to worry, it was all a laugh. Neither of them is alive now to recall the joke.

The strike, with or without the light relief of my father, was a deadly serious business. My beat, geographically speaking, was east Belfast, where I was born and raised, and as I made my way around the mean streets surrounding the shipyard and aircraft factory I was struck by the level of support for the action and the extent of the intimidation shown to those who stood up for the Executive.

But there were exceptions. Not far from the Europa was Sandy Row, traditionally one of the most hardline loyalist areas. I thought I would spend an hour or two there, finding out what people really thought. One of the first things the Strike Council had ordered was a total boycott of Irish goods, but while I was in one of the pubs, which was decked out in Ulster flags and emblems of the UVF, I noticed that the men were mostly drinking Guinness. 'How's that?' I asked them. They looked a bit sheepish, then one of them admitted that there'd been special dispensation given for a tanker up from the brewery in Dublin. Some things were beyond politics, and one of them was Liffey Water.

Because almost all power generation and the great bulk of manufacturing industry in Ulster was in Protestant areas, the strikers were bound to win. The only thing that could have turned the tide against them was resolute action by Wilson, and this was not forthcoming. If Wilson was firm on anything, it was that he would not be resolute. On 28 May, with gangs of loyalists armed with staves roaming the streets, electricity cut off and water in short supply, Faulkner and his Unionist colleagues resigned from the Executive, leaving the SDLP and Alliance members stranded. It was then announced from London that there would be no Council of Ireland and that direct rule had been assumed once more by Her Majesty's government.

It was an abject surrender to violence and I felt personally betrayed. Ulster really was a political slum and, as landlords, the British bore the primary responsibility. You didn't have to dig deep to come up with the appropriate cliché. The best lacked all conviction, the worst were full of passionate intensity – and Guinness.

Ronnie Bunting was thrilled. A whole-hog man, he had no time for the compromises reached in smoke-filled rooms. For a start, he hated smokers. What he sought was not the mere unease of consensus, but the creation of a 32-county terrorist Republic ruled by commissars like himself. He spoke admiringly of Stalin's purges. 'Kill the kulaks!' was one of the old Bolshevik slogans that he loved to repeat. As he watched the news that evening, filled with the glee of loyalists and the despair of peace-loving people cowering in their homes, he must have been licking his lips.

As watersheds go, the Ulster Worker's Strike and its aftermath were hard to beat. I thought I had seen it all now – and I may not have been wrong. Watching more recent attempts to cobble together a power-sharing executive and all-Ireland institutions, the sense of déjà vu is almost overwhelming. The fact that progress has been frustrated this time at the ballot box rather than in the streets is, I suppose, a good thing. But the same awful unwillingness of Protestants and Catholics to trust each other and work together is just as apparent today as it was then. I still hope that I will live to see stable arrangements put in place that allow the two traditions to live together as equals, respecting each other's cultures – but I'm not holding my breath.

In the *Irish Times* office, the summer couldn't come quickly enough. Conor and the rest of us were exhausted. But as Rosemary and I made our holiday plans (we were to go to Juan-les-Pins and see the Mediterranean for the first time), something altogether unexpected happened. Douglas Gageby announced that he was retiring as editor of the *Irish Times* and was pleased to announce as his successor Fergus Pyle, then the paper's European correspondent.

It was another of those serendipitous moments that changes everything.

I knew next to nothing about Fergus. Indeed, it is even possible that I didn't know he existed. But all of a sudden, there he was in the editor's chair. Those who knew the score apparently shook their heads, for it turned out that Fergus was a Protestant, just like every other editor in the paper's history. It was as if the board was letting us know that, whatever else may have changed, the *Irish Times* remained an Ascendancy fiefdom.

But, hey, why should I worry? Maybe I would do well out of it. And, strange to tell, a couple of weeks later I took an unexpected telephone call. It was Dennis Kennedy, one of the paper's most senior executives – another Prod, though this time from the North – who wrote foreign leaders and generally beat the drum in D'Olier Street for the European Economic Community. What did I think of the EEC?, Dennis wanted to know. What did I *think* of it? I didn't think *anything* of it. It just wasn't a subject that ever came up. I suppose I was pleased that Britain and Ireland were part of it. You know the argument: strength in numbers; the way of the future; if you're not in, you can't win – that sort of thing. But nothing more profound. Dennis listened to this without comment, then asked me if I would like to succeed Fergus in Brussels.

Wow!

'Good grief!' I expostulated. 'You're joking. You're having me on.'

'No,' he said, 'I'm serious. Fergus and I are both impressed by the work you've been doing for us in Belfast and we'd like to talk to you about Europe. We'd like you to come down to Dublin on Monday and have lunch with us at the Bailey.'

Even now, I can only guess at their thought processes. Dennis was one of the great apparatchiks, who ended up as Brussels' man in Belfast. An Ulster Unionist by conviction but a European by desire, he had migrated south in search of a good career and the chance to influence events. I had never met *him*, but he, it turned out, was a keen reader of my pieces. When I joked in print about travelling by train across the Irish border and watching out for beggars, he must have seen in my satire an intimation of the problems that would soon beset Europe as a whole.

Or something.

Fergus's role in the affair is even more obscure to me. I have absolutely no idea why the new editor – who had never met me – thought I would be just the chap to master the Common Agricultural Policy, which, as far as I understood it, was almost the sole reason for Ireland's membership of the Common Market.

It should be borne in mind that the Republic of Ireland we know today is a vastly different place from the grim, inward-looking and primitive petty state that re-proclaimed its nationhood in 1973. Most of Ireland's income in the 1970s came from farming and the bulk of its exports went to the UK. The only non-food export of any consequence was people: to England, America, Canada, Australia and anywhere else that would have them. The

Catholic Church set the stamp of its culture on both state and people, and Northern Ireland was regarded as 'unfinished business' that no one was in any hurry to confront.

It could be that neither Fergus nor Dennis realised how inexperienced I was. Every other Brussels correspondent before or since was prepared for the job by working a lengthy stint on the foreign desk in Dublin, reading themselves into the subject and talking it over in depth with Irish government officials and leading lobbyists. Not me. One minute it was the Ulster Workers' Strike, the next the ins and outs of the Green Pound and an ascent, without oxygen, of the Beef Mountain. They must have thought that because I had come on a treat in Belfast in a short time, I could do the same in Brussels. In fact, I had no idea what went on in Europe. Apart from my school trip to La Panne at the age of ten and a more recent two-day trip to Strasbourg for a session of the European Human Rights Commission (my main memory of which was the glass lift in my hotel), I had never set foot on the Continent. I couldn't even speak French.

Against that, I was desperate to get out. And how hard could it be? So, I took the train down to Dublin and made my way to the Bailey in Duke Street, one of the city's fanciest French restaurants, where Fergus and Dennis were waiting.

Fergus was an odd bugger, though not unkind, who would be sacked ignominiously three years later to allow for the return of Gageby to the editor's chair. He died prematurely in 1996 (bravely, it is said) and was seen off to Valhalla by Ireland's Great and Good. When we met, he was just 43 and had been based in Europe, first in Paris, then in Brussels, for the previous seven years, where his hard work and enthusiasm had unquestionably helped educate the Irish people in the possibilities of European union. All of this, I have to say, meant little to me. I was more interested in his personal background. Historically, Fergus was one of the last of his class – Ascendancy Protestants who sat at or near the top of the better-established Irish enterprises. But he was no placeman or fool. He had taken a first-class degree in French and German at Trinity College and risen up the ranks of the *Irish Times* on the basis not merely of his antecedents but his application to the task. Before going to Paris, he had worked in Belfast, where it was joked that his accounts of the proceedings of the old Stormont Parliament were longer than the version that appeared in Hansard. Now, having emerged as editor in the manner, prior to Heath, of leaders of the Conservative Party, he was determined to continue the modernisation of the paper pioneered by Gageby, with a particular emphasis on Europe.

And I was to be his Man in Brussels.

The picture of Fergus I have just painted leaves out several salient facts. He was, as they say in Ireland, a bit of an eejit. Perhaps 'Holy Fool' would capture him better. He had brains and insight but no sense. No one with a true perspective on events would have filed articles 2,000 words long from the old Stormont, a corrupt and ludicrous invention. Equally, there can't be many who would crash their cars driving up the wrong side of a Belgian motorway or many journalists who specialised in finding the cheapest hotels and the most unpleasant offices in which to work. Fergus came from money (or at least knew the smell of it) and had always been comfortably off. He couldn't understand that 'ordinary' people might also wish to live beyond their means – and needed the means to do so.

When I explained to him that I knew nothing about the EEC and had only the most rudimentary schoolboy French, he dismissed my confession as if it was of no account. All he did, in between selecting wines, was stress to me the importance of keeping well-in with the Irish delegation in Brussels and the farming lobby. Was this the Big Picture?, I wondered.

What about contacts? What help could he give me?

He pulled out a battered diary. Well, there were various big meetings coming up in the autumn. There was the Council of Ministers meeting in Luxembourg on the 14th and 15th of September. Oh, and there was a meeting of the Turkish Association Committee also on the 15th.

What else?

Well, finance ministers would discuss petrodollars (whatever they were) on the 21st, and both sugar and beef were likely to come up at an emergency meeting of farm ministers. I'd need to check on that, as well as on the upcoming session of the European Parliament.

Yes, but what did any of this mean? Who were these people and what was going on? What should I look out for?

Fergus selected a *digestif*. I think he found my appearance slightly alarming. He was naturally dishevelled, but I worked at it. My hair was a homage to the late Jimi Hendrix; I wore an open-neck shirt with collars that reached down almost to my nipples; and my low loon pants flapped gently in the draught from the restaurant door. There was a pause. The Brits, he said, were likely to start whingeing about the size of their budget contribution and it was likely that the agriculture commissioner, Pierre Lardinois (whom I had assumed was French but who turned out to be a Dutchman), would come under pressure to abandon farmers' interests in favour of those of the consumer.

I was baffled. He might as well have been talking . . . French. 'I see,' I said. 'Anything else?'

'Sure, sure.' I was to keep an eye on the Germans to make sure they didn't block anticipated Regional Fund grants to Ireland. And I shouldn't pay too much heed to the daily press briefing. Other than that, it was plain sailing. Sure I'd have a great time.

I sighed, feeling like a boy being sent on a man's errand. Who should I talk to?

Fergus adjusted his half-moon spectacles and consulted his contacts book. He then read out the telephone numbers of the press section of the Commission and Council, plus the names and telephone numbers of key figures at the Irish mission. As a bonus, he vouchsafed that a Herr Wortmann in the finance directorate of the Commission was good on monetary issues. I should talk to him . . . only he didn't seem to have his number. Anyway, I should take him out to lunch. Oh, and on no account was I to forget Joe Oslislok, an Irishman of Polish extraction who was a translator in the legal section in the Berlaymont.

Dennis could see that I was uncomfortable. To put my mind at rest, he reminded me that I would have to contribute a European Diary, placing all of the above in context, within 72 hours of my arrival in Brussels.

This was indeed excellent news. My mood darkened. What about practical considerations? There must be things I had to do. I mean, I couldn't just turn up in Brussels and start living there. Wouldn't I have to register or something?

Yes, indeed, said Fergus. I would have to register at the Maison Communal. But I'd need an address first and there wasn't a lot of time. Driving was another issue. Fortunately, I'd just got my driving licence back, otherwise I'd have been forced to take the test in Belgium.

The thing was, said Fergus, I had to remember to drive on the other side of the road and always give way to the right – the so-called *priorité à droite*. It already sounded like a nightmare, but now it got worse. The editor, it turned out, had left his car – i.e. *my* car – at a garage in Brussels to be repaired after his recent wrong-way collision outside Bruges. I'd have to pay for that. The tax and insurance had probably run out – he wasn't sure – and he'd lost his registration documents. But other than that, I'd be fine. Oh, yes. If I ran into any problems, there was some sort of *Bureau d'Accueil* at the Berlaymont. I could go and see them . . . except they'd be on their summer break and wouldn't be back at work until after I'd arrived.

Hmm. I had brought Rosemary with me to the lunch, which I

think Fergus and Dennis thought a touch presumptuous. She was utterly perplexed by what she was hearing but tried hard to look on the bright side. I told Fergus that she and I were together and I would expect her to come with me. 'Sure, sure,' he said. 'Dennis mentioned something about that. I've agreed that since you're not married, you can claim for her as excess baggage.'

And that was that.

Later, I found out that the paper was not prepared to put us up in a hotel in Brussels for more than two nights. Instead, we could stay for a couple of weeks in the spare room of the RTÉ correspondent John McAleese, whose wife, Geraldine, was off in Ireland having a baby. Life on the road was to be no bed of roses either. I was warned to stay only in cheap hotels, a list of which would be sent to me, and at all costs to avoid Michelin-star restaurants. Oh, dear. What would Max Hastings say? My final discovery, on the eve of our departure, was that, in addition to earning only about three-quarters the salary that Fergus had been paid, my exchange rate would be fixed at 59 Belgian francs to the pound, rather than the 90 enjoyed by Fergus. In effect, I was to do the same job for less than half the rewards. It was at this stage that I learned the difference between being a southern Protestant and a northern Protestant. Southern Prods may have been dying out, but they were going out in style. I, by contrast, was no more than an employee.

Still, it was a rare opportunity and one I was determined to seize with both my hired hands. Back in Belfast, everyone was amazed by my good fortune and wished me well. Conor gave a party at his home in my honour and, over the course of the next few weeks, I met up and got drunk with all my friends of recent years.

It was odd suddenly seeing Belfast as part of my past, not my future. Apart from my time in Durham, and the few months I spent in Cork, I had lived there all my life. But now I felt sure that I would never return as anything other than a visitor. It was as if the city had grown smaller overnight. I felt instantly grown up. From now on, there would be more to journalism than 'having a go' and heading down to the nearest bar. I would have to deal with stern-faced Germans and inscrutable French persons, to say nothing of exotic Italians. What would I make of them all and of the European *grand projet*? At least Fergus hadn't made it easy for me. I had to give him that.

I went to see my parents to let them know what was going on. My father was pleased for me but puzzled. What an odd thing to do, to go and live in Belgium. He'd never met anyone who'd ever done a thing like that. What language did they speak there anyway? What was the Common Market all about? He'd seen the nine linked hands on the new 50 pence piece but that was as much as he knew. And how long would I have to stay there before they let me come home?

My mum, as ever, was sanguine and more realistic. She regretted the fact that she wouldn't see so much of me in the years ahead, but with Dad's health in decline, her hands would be full enough anyway, and she knew it. My sister and her children were most important to Mum at this point. Until I settled down and had a family of my own, she felt I could be left to get by unassisted.

Mum and Dad both wanted me to marry Rosemary. They were fond of her and felt she was good for me. They would have been distressed had they known that our relationship would eventually end in tears.

Leaving Ireland for good was a turning point. I tried to work out what my life had meant up to that moment and what I had learned from my first 25 years. I didn't know anything about the *meaning* part. I still don't. People who are religious, like my parents, see human existence as part of something grand and inspiring, with an ultimate purpose. Life for them is a kind of test, which, if they pass, leads on to an eternity of veneration. I can't see it myself. My mother, at the age of 88, spoke to my sister about the likelihood that she would shortly re-encounter my father, who had died in 1977 when she was just 61. She wondered what he would look like and what she would look like and what they would find to talk about. It was as if the heavenly choir was just the 'contract' part of eternity, the rest of which would be spent at home as usual, doing the washing, going shopping and watching TV. What a prospect! Another chance to watch *One Foot in the Grave*, or Jeremy Paxman asking Michael Howard the same question for a hundred million years.

My sister is another believer and plans, I think, to take over from my mother as the voice of my religious conscience. Mum used to quote Saint Paul at me and looked forward keenly to my Damascene conversion. 'Saul, Saul,' she would say to me, quoting Acts 9:4–5, 'it is hard for thee to kick against the pricks'. Never mind the pricks; the thing is, I've *been* to Damascus. I even made a point of walking along 'the Street that is called Straight'. But the biggest thing that happened to me there was that I contracted dysentery and had to interview the foreign minister swathed in 20 yards of toilet paper. So Elaine, God bless her, has her work cut out. My wife, whose uncle was the leading Oxford Dominican, Herbert McCabe, and whose Aunt Kathleen has been a Carmelite nun for nearly 60 years, sneaks off to Mass from time to time. Sadly, I can't join her, not even in her doubts. More and more, I am convinced that life leads nowhere – though I also know that humanity, by its nature, will always seek to disprove – or at least question – this reality. Where the energy comes from to sustain the myth is frankly beyond me. We are all going the same way; neither good works nor genius make the slightest difference.

The way I see it, Raoul Wallenberg, who saved as many as a quarter of a million Jews, has no more hope of salvation than Adolf

Eichmann, the architect of the Holocaust. Most of those he saved are now dead anyway. Shakespeare, for all his genius, is no more alive today than was the man or woman who emptied his chamberpot. He has no idea he is 'immortal' for the simple reason that he is dead and gone and will never again draw breath, either here or in the (non-existent) next world – the bourn from which, as he so rightly pointed out, no traveller returns. We go on as we do, not because there is a destination other than the grave but because we enjoy the journey – and we don't, in any case, have much of an alternative. The Reaper always wins.

At the start of this memoir, I mentioned how difficult I found it to travel back and inhabit the child I once was. I can stare into the eyes of my infant self and see things there that are somehow familiar. But I can't quite work out what is going on or where it is all leading. This is less true of my more recent incarnations. The me at Queen's is still a little hazy, the recollection and the narrative held together with paperclips and glue. But jump forward a year or two, to Durham, say, or Cork, and I feel myself starting to fit more easily inside my present persona. Partly, I'm sure, this is because the distance I have to travel is less, but it is also because my adult sensibility was by the age of 21 almost wholly developed, so that what I felt then is pretty much what I feel now. Even so, it has been an odd experience. As I write these particular words, I am sitting in front of my computer in Brooklyn Heights, New York. It is early March and the rain this morning has given way to snow. Outside my window, if I twist round, I can see the grey bulk of the New York Federal Appeals Court, flanked by the brownstones of Pierrepont Street. The Brooklyn Promenade is three minutes' walk away, affording me a view of Lower Manhattan and the site once occupied by the World Trade Center. But for as long as I have been writing this book, the present has drifted by almost unobserved. Instead, I have felt the past tugging at me, forcing me to confront old fears and to live again with people, some of them now dead, who once occupied a big part of my life. I haven't told the whole story (who does?). I could have added another 10,000 words just by putting everything in order and giving equal weight to all. I could also have admitted to my deeper existential crimes. But what I have tried to do is to place my own life, stuttering and fault-filled though it has undoubtedly been, into the context of my times. Where it seems appropriate, I have jumped from one time segment to another, so that Bonn and Brussels and Sri Lanka, though separated by years of time, are all part of the same time – my time.

Most Westerners, growing up in stable societies, did not go through what I and other Ulster men and women experienced in the 1970s and beyond. Though *I* may not have been abused as a child, the entire society in which I grew up was abused, causing me, like everyone else, to see life through a jagged and peculiar prism. I am luckier than many. I am 56, and for me the '60s were much the same experience as they were for young people in London and Liverpool. I remember the bands, the loon pants and the long hair; and the sensation (almost wholly spurious) that my generation was unlike any other, that from here on in the world would be a different place.

In fact, from 1969 – the Summer of Love – my world *was* a different place. Only not in the way I expected: it didn't grow, it shrank. It shrank into itself. And as the darkness closed in and the killings started, we who lived there found it harder and harder to look beyond and see ourselves for what we truly were. The fact that I became a journalist helped me to hold on to some sort of perspective. I was able to talk to reporters from England, the Republic, Europe and America, and, even if only for moments at a time, to see ourselves as others saw us. Those who were most affected, especially those who lived in the ghettoes, did not have the luxury of putting their society under the microscope: they were the ones wriggling on the slide. But, bad though it was, it could have been a whole lot worse. I could have grown up in Beirut in the 1980s, or Bosnia in the 1990s. I could be a teenager today in the suburbs of Baghdad, wondering whether to embrace George Bush's tainted democracy or become a suicide bomber. Northern Ireland was never like that.

So far as my personal deficiencies are concerned, I leave these for others to judge. Enough has been said already. I am not always proud of what I did or the way I behaved. My excuse is that I was young at the time – and foolish. My regrets are many. Most obviously, I wish I had extricated myself from the hold exerted over me by Ronnie Bunting while I was still in a position to make good choices about my future. Ronnie had his own dark destiny to fulfil; he should have been no part of mine. That was my weakness and my mistake.

Rien de rien! It happened. What is important is that I lived through it and I survived to tell the tale. In the autumn of 1974, as I took flight from Dublin to Brussels, all I could think about was the road ahead and the trials I would face. I wanted to enjoy myself as a new European and to profit from the experience. It was enough. The future stretched before me like a bar room at opening time: full of possibilities. And, truth to tell, life has given me more than I ever deserved. Even today, with my wife, Louisa, beside me and my son, the guitar hero, touring the world with Battle, there is much to look forward to. Yet there is an ineffable sadness about looking back. You see not merely the missed opportunities and the things done that ought not to have been done, but the fact that, in the end, our lives wash away and vanish, like leaves in the gutter after rain.

My mother died on 11 April 2005. She was one month short of her 89th birthday and had been in the Ulster Hospital – a place that I cannot enter these days without wondering in which bed I will ultimately be confined – for the previous four weeks. It wasn't an easy death. She was in pain and discomfort much of the time and was generally confused and helpless. But her heart was strong and in the end, after an awful day, what took her was an injection of morphine into her stomach. My sister and her family bore the brunt of her suffering alongside her and were relieved when it was finally over.

Mum survived my father by nearly 28 years. Sometimes, I think, she forgot about him, as if he was no more than someone she used to know. At other times, it was as if he had never left her. When I flew over from New York to see her during her final illness, she talked of how she and my dad would shortly be together again and once more she wondered how they would get along, given the difference in their ages.

Her religious faith remained strong to the end. The minister of her church in Holywood, County Down, prayed with her several times in the ward, as did the Salvation Army chaplain from the Sir Samuel Kelly retirement home in which she passed her final years.

The doctors who attended to her weren't sure exactly what it was that hastened her end after so many years of stable old age, but it is probable that she had a stroke. Whatever it was, it robbed her of the articulate speech she prized so highly. Yet while her voice could hardly frame the words, there was no doubting the sentiment. 'Neither principalities nor powers,' she repeated over and over, 'can separate us from the love of God.'

But there were earthly considerations, too. A few years back, at a family gathering to mark her 80th birthday, she surprised many of us by the strength of her new-found political convictions. She supported the Northern Ireland peace process and believed that the best hope for an end to violence lay in Protestants and Catholics, unionists and nationalists, sitting down and sorting out their problems on a family basis. 'Brits out!' she announced at one stage, startling everyone around the table.

Although a convinced Presbyterian and monarchist, Mum believed in the underlying unity of Ireland. My sister and her husband, Bryan, once took her on holiday to Portugal. She didn't like it. She couldn't bear the hot sun and she hated the unfamiliar, oily food. But she loved the flight home because it gave her the chance to sit next to a couple of nuns, whose religious certainties mirrored her own.

Events in the wider world often passed her by. She observed once that the Soviet Union had come and gone in her lifetime as if it was a passing fad, like the Twist. She had little understanding of, or interest in, Europe or America and used to ask me what the point had been of my going there to live. But to the end, she knew right from wrong. She opposed the invasion of Iraq and denounced George Bush and Tony Blair as a pair of 'silly old coofs'. In her will (a small-scale affair), she left several hundred pounds to charities working in the developing world.

I'm glad she is free of her suffering and has gone (so she said) to a better place. I shall miss her.

One of my father's favourite songs was 'I'll Walk Beside You', a sentimental Irish melody that, when I was young, I thought excruciatingly over the top and mawkish but now see as a true expression of his feelings for my mother. He sang it to her every time we went out in the car together. Sometimes, she was embarrassed; sometimes not. I offer it as his epitaph, and hers. May they rest in peace.

I'll walk beside you through the world today
While dreams and songs and flowers bless your way,
I'll look into your eyes and hold your hand
I'll walk beside you through the golden land.

I'll walk beside you through the world tonight
Beneath the starry skies ablaze with light,
Within your soul love's tender words I'll hide.
I'll walk beside you through the eventide.

I'll walk beside you through the passing years
Through days of cloud and sunshine, joys and tears,
And when the great call comes, the sunset gleams
I'll walk beside you to the land of dreams.

Chronicle of a Death Foretold

THE YEARS SINCE I lost touch with him were for my old friend Ronnie Bunting a time of unrelieved violence and anxiety. The INLA, like the Baader-Meinhof gang and Italy's Red Brigades, was willing to have a go at almost any target for almost any reason, provided it advanced the profile of Irish republicanism and international socialism.

And mayhem.

It wasn't easy. During its early years, the INLA struggled just to survive. The Provos, the British Army, the RUC and the Irish government, along with various loyalist terror groups, predominantly its erstwhile comrades of the Official IRA, were determined to strangle the movement at birth. But try as they might, they couldn't do it. Instead, as the group defended itself with the ferocity of a mother grizzly defending her cubs, it slowly established itself as a player. Many IRA men of both persuasions died at the hands of INLA gunmen and bombers. Loyalists also suffered. So, increasingly, did Crown forces.

As a result of the slaughter, Ronnie was on just about everybody's hit list. But then again, almost everybody was on his, including, for all I knew, me. *Sorry, Smokey, but you just didn't measure up. No hard feelings.* On 5 March 1975, he was driving, with two INLA volunteers, from his home in Turf Lodge to an unknown destination. The car was probably not the green A35 I had sold him for £35 in 1970. This vehicle served him well for a year or more but developed a serious problem with its gears, which meant that for several weeks he drove round his local area in reverse. On this occasion, as he turned in more orthodox fashion onto the Monagh Road, a series of rifle shots rang out. One of the bullets hit him in the neck, narrowly missing his formidable jugular vein. With commendable calm, his neck and shoulders streaming with blood, he accelerated and drove himself to the Royal Victoria Hospital, where he was treated for his injuries while one of his fellow travellers, concealing a revolver inside his coat, gave a statement to the RUC.

The incident shook him. There had been two previous attempts on his life, and he knew he was living on borrowed time. Realising, as if for the first time, that he had a wife and two children, he decided to extend his overdraft. He called me at my apartment in Brussels.

'Walter! Ronnie here. How's it goin'?'

'Ronnie! What the—?'

'I've been shot.'

'You've been what?'

'Shot. Shot in the neck.'

'Jesus! What happened?'

'Long story. But look, here's the thing. I need your help. I need to get out for a few weeks, a month maybe. How are you fixed to put us up?'

Wow! My mind clicked into instant rebuff mode. I knew that if I didn't say no straight away, he would browbeat me into saying yes, or else make me feel so guilty that I'd be practically begging him to stay.

''Fraid not,' I said. 'Out of the question. It's a small flat, it's paid for by the *Irish Times* and I'm not having you and your family staying here while half the gunmen in Ireland are looking for you. I'm sorry, I really am. But that's it. You'll have to find someplace else.'

He didn't persist. That wasn't his style. But a day later, the phone rang again. This time it was his father, Major Bunting, whose voice I hadn't heard in years. He was in tears. I could hear the sobs in his voice.

'Ronnie tells me you're not willing to put him up.'

'That's right, Major. It's too dangerous for me − and my girlfriend. Anyway, too much has happened. Things I don't want to talk about. And I'm not prepared to play the patsy any longer.'

'But they'll kill him.'

'They could kill *me*.'

He didn't give up. He was pleading for his son's life. 'You're his friend. We're related. You've got to do *something*. In the name of God!'

I didn't relent. For the first time in my life, so far as Ronnie Bunting was concerned, I stood firm. But the anguish in his father's voice was disturbing. I knew how close he and his son were, despite their diametrically opposed political views. The Major muttered something and broke the connection.

I never spoke to either man again.

But the connection between Ronnie and me, in the Army's mind at least, was not yet broken. Travelling back to Belfast from Brussels, via London, for Christmas in 1975, I was taken off the Aer Lingus flight at Heathrow by officers from Special Branch. They seized my passport and called up my details on a computer. As I waited (in vain) for some indication of what they were looking for, one of the officers turned to me and asked me how I had enjoyed my time at Bede College.

'What's that got to do with anything?' I asked.

He smiled at me. 'Just answer the questions. What were you doing visiting Ronnie Bunting after he was released from internment? Are you still in contact with him? Have you spoken to him in Brussels? What were you doing in Darlington in 1972? Are you a militant republican, Mr Ellis? You wouldn't be the first east Belfast Protestant to go bad, would you?'

I stuttered through my answers and in the end they let me go with a warning. But was I paranoid to see in the Northern Ireland of those days the beginnings of a police state? Is this what Tony Blair has in mind for us in the UK?

I didn't know it at the time but after my refusal to provide him with a refuge Ronnie and his family moved to Wales instead, where he lay low while his wound healed. But all the while he was plotting his revenge.

He returned to Ireland three months later, not to Belfast but to Dublin, where it was hoped by the leadership of the INLA that the elements of some kind of grand strategy could be put together. Ronnie rented a small flat in Pembroke Lane, just off Baggot Street, one of the capital's most fashionable thoroughfares, using money from bank robberies. But no sooner had he and Suzanne and their children moved in than they were besieged by INLA squatters. Northern volunteers either on the run or looking for a bit of R&R took to staying for days, even weeks at a time, kipping down on mattresses or sleeping bags, straining the small flat's resources and setting each other's nerves on edge. Fights and drunkenness were everyday events – so much so that, according to *INLA: Deadly Divisions*, by the late Jack Holland and Henry McDonald (to whom I am indebted for much of this information), the landlords no longer even attempted to collect the rent. Seamus Costello called the resulting dosshouse 'Bash Street'. In a parody of the class war they were pledged to eradicate, he and his southern colleagues in the IRSP regarded the northerners as uncouth and vulgar.

Ronnie couldn't stand it. He wasn't a hotelkeeper, he was a freedom fighter. After a hurried conclave with Costello, he returned to Belfast in the late autumn of 1976. The rank he took with him was crucial to the development of the INLA for the next four years: OC Belfast. It was then that his organisational skills at last came into their own. Operating out of a house in Sevastopol Street in the heart of the Falls, and with a part-time job at the Royal Victoria Hospital, he organised a host of shootings and other outrages. A soldier was shot dead in Turf Lodge; a second trooper was killed in the Markets; and a third seriously wounded in the grounds of the RVH – all within weeks of Ronnie's takeover.

But then something happened that was entirely predictable and wholly unforeseen. On 5 October 1977, Costello was 'whacked' by an Official IRA hit man. It was an opportunistic hit. Jim Flynn, a close associate of Cathal Goulding's, is said to have tracked Costello's movements over several days and then blown him away as he sat in his car beneath the railway bridge at the corner of Northbrook Avenue and the North Circular Road. The Officials denied responsibility for the killing, but five years later, on 4 June 1982, an INLA assassin gunned down Flynn as he left a pub in Dublin's North Strand district. With the chilling irony that seems to recur so frequently in Ulster's grim history, he died just yards from where Costello's life had ended.

The loss of the founder and president of the IRSP – a key strategist of its military wing – sent shockwaves through the movement, putting everyone on the defensive and driving a wedge between the southern and northern commands. But it gave Ronnie much greater freedom of action. From now on, as acting chief-of-staff, he would not be satisfied with isolated shootings. His goal henceforth was to put the fear of God (or Mao) into the British Establishment. Links were forged with the Baader-Meinhof gang, then at the height of its infamy in West Germany – links which led to a failed kidnap attempt on the German Consul in Belfast and to assistance from the Germans in the planned assassination of the British Ambassador to Dublin, Sir Robert Haydon.

Haydon was very lucky that he and his wife were not killed as they attended a Remembrance Day service in St Patrick's Cathedral – the scene, a decade earlier, of Major Bunting's efforts to lay a wreath in memory of the British dead of 1916. Ronnie conceived a plan to set off an explosive charge beneath the prie-dieu, or prayer stool, of the ambassador's reserved pew. The only reason the charge didn't go off was because the cathedral's medieval stonework refused to admit the remote signal from a car cruising the streets outside. Afterwards, in spite of Ronnie's preference for letting the authorities know of the narrowness of the ambassador's escape, an INLA volunteer actually broke into the cathedral, removed the bomb and defused it for future use.

Another of Ronnie's grand stratagems, originally drafted by Costello, was a tie-up with the PLO and Libya's Colonel Gaddafi. This ploy actually bore fruit for the movement but not until after both INLA men were dead.

Throughout 1978 and into 1979, with Ronnie as *capo di tutti capi*, the INLA carried out a series of attacks against British security forces, as well as RUC and prison officers. Deaths were surprisingly few, but there were many injuries and a large number of explosions. Ronnie, claiming each action as 'Captain Green', wanted to concentrate on the armed struggle and lift the body count, but as a political animal he also had to be concerned with the issue of prisoners, especially those on the H-blocks at Long Kesh, whose 'blanket' protest, involving the refusal of inmates to wear prison uniform, had drawn widespread international sympathy. To keep the offensive side of the operation in the public eye, he arranged a 'photo-shoot' in which selected INLA gunmen, himself included, posed for pictures, one of which showed a volunteer about to throw a PLO-provided hand grenade.

But all the while, he was looking for the Big One – the act that would put the INLA centre stage. His opportunity came when the Labour Prime Minister James Callaghan, with the British economy in a state of incipient collapse, called a general election for 3 May 1979. The hot favourite to take Callaghan's place in Downing Street was Margaret Thatcher, the outspoken Conservative leader. With the Iron Lady, as her designated Ulster Secretary, came her close friend and adviser Airey Neave, the MP for Abingdon.

Neave was a decorated war hero, the first British officer to escape from Colditz, the Nazis' notorious high-security prison. He was also a barrister and served the indictments against many of the leading German war criminals at Nuremberg, including Goering and Hess. As Thatcher's choice to take over in Northern Ireland, he planned to make life miserable for terrorists of all persuasions, hunting them down like dogs and, if he could manage it, sending key offenders to the gallows.

Ronnie had previously planned to kill Roy Mason, Secretary of State for Northern Ireland in the outgoing Labour government, another tough opponent. But he was delighted to switch targets. The problem was, Neave was a careful and experienced operator and once he achieved office he would be guarded night and day not only by Special Branch but in all probability also by the SAS. If he was to strike, it had to be before the apparatus of the state moved in to protect his quarry.

He was in luck. An informer inside the Palace of Westminster discovered that security at the House of Commons did not, properly speaking, extend to its underground car park. Security guards were apparently few and far between and CCTV cameras were rarely monitored. Ronnie was no expert in these matters, but he assembled a team that produced a brilliant plan. Plastic explosives and a mercury tilt-switch mechanism would be combined in a small device that, in a matter of seconds, could be attached to the underside of Neave's car. The bomb, with a one-hour active life, was duly installed by two INLA volunteers posing as workmen. They had only one chance. The election was just three weeks away and Parliament was about to move into recess. But they made no mistakes, even improvising a last-minute timer from a wristwatch.

When Neave got into his car, a blue Vauxhall Cavalier, shortly before three o'clock in the afternoon on 30 March 1979, nothing unusual occurred for the first minute. He reversed out of his parking bay and turned the car around to face the exit. He was looking forward with relish to the campaign ahead. But as he ascended the incline that led out into Parliament Street, the bubble of mercury in the tilt switch moved downwards and completed the circuit. The bomb went off and Neave took the full force. His legs were severed and his face half blown away. Although he lived for several minutes, there was never any hope that he would survive.

In Belfast, where in his McCavity role he awaited news from the front, Ronnie was cock-a-hoop. 'We did it!' he crowed to a band of supporters in the IRSP's new headquarters on the Falls Road. Then he threw his arms round Seán Flynn, a former OC and stalwart of the movement. Drinks that day were on the house.

Britain was outraged. Neave was one of the most respected men in the country, a fighter for democracy all of his life. Ronnie may not fully have realised it, and analysts since have tended to forget, but the action he set in motion that day was a tremendous success. Only Neave could have carried through the draconian security measures he had announced as the strategy for a new Conservative government. Humphrey Atkins, his replacement as Ulster Secretary in the new Thatcher administration, was a much softer touch. Even so, one of Atkins's first acts was to rectify a strange anomaly in the law. From now on, the INLA was a banned organisation. That it was not so already was one of the more bizarre hangovers from Labour's years in power.

Even as Ronnie celebrated his triumph, he knew there would be a price to pay. Mrs Thatcher was filled with a cold fury against the organisation of madmen that had killed her friend. 'She'll want her pound of flesh,' Ronnie told his closest intimates. And so it proved.

It is likely we will never know who killed Ronnie Bunting in the early hours of 15 October 1980. The Ulster Defence Association and its extreme paramilitary wing, the Ulster Freedom Fighters, were generally credited with his murder, but it is reasonable to suppose, given the course of events and the vitriol that gathered around Ronnie's name, that, at the very least, the British Army stood back that night and allowed the UFF to do its work.

The Army and RUC – to say nothing of the Garda Síochána – had not let up on him since the Neave assassination. He was stopped and questioned almost every day, sometimes more than once. On 8 August, he was held for three days at the RUC interrogation centre at Castlereagh, just around the corner from our old school. He told the Association for Legal Justice afterwards that a policeman had said to him, 'Look at my face . . . this is the face you'll see before I kill you.' Remembering my own experience with an RUC officer, I believed him.

The stage was now set for the final act in the drama. Ronnie had gone to bed in his home in Downfine Gardens, in the heart of Turf Lodge. His wife was asleep next to him. In the other bedrooms were their children: Fiona (seven), Deirdre (three) and Ronan (eighteen months). Noel Lyttle, another INLA comrade (also, astonishingly, a Protestant), was staying the night, sleeping on the floor next to Ronan's cot.

At three-thirty, in the very dead of night, Ronnie and Suzanne were wakened by the sound of sledgehammers being used against their double-locked front door. Seconds later, they heard feet on the stairs.

Suzanne described what happened at an official inquest in February 1981. She was convinced the assailants were not loyalists but members of the SAS. 'The attack was too well planned and carried out by men who were cool and calm and knew what they were doing.' She said they wore green ribbed pullovers with suede patches on the shoulders and ski-type masks with holes for their eyes.

Noel Lyttle was the first to die. Ronnie and Suzanne heard the shots that killed him but had no means of defending themselves. Unaccountably, or perhaps because of the number of times he had been pulled in by the police and Army, Ronnie did not have a gun. All he and his wife could do was huddle together behind their bedroom door. The killers pushed against the lock, which quickly gave way. One of them fired shots through the gap, wounding Suzanne in the hand. She fell back onto the bed.

'Then the bedroom door opened and two men were standing in the doorway. I heard more gunfire and when I looked one man was continually shooting into Ronnie's body. His body was laying at the top of the stairs with his head back. I went berserk.'

One of the killers began backing carefully down the stairs, while his accomplice kept firing at Ronnie's prone body. Suzanne jumped onto the back of the one doing the firing and attempted to strangle him. Below, in the hall, the second gunman calmly raised his weapon and aimed two shots at the woman so determined to prevent their escape. One struck her under the shoulder, the other in her right arm, forcing her to let go her grip. According to an account she gave to the *Irish News*, she then slumped down next to her husband. 'I knew he was dead: his eyes were wide and staring.' It was at this point that the gunman with whom she had grappled paused on the stairs and shot her once more, through the mouth.

Suzanne survived, though her condition was critical for several days. She now lives many miles from Belfast. Bernadette McAliskey, another survivor of assassins' bullets, has become one of her closest friends. Her strange, heroic journey into the heart of darkness was almost over.

The double murder gave rise to all kinds of speculation.

Accusations flew that it was an SAS execution. No getaway car was recovered and no formal claim was ever made by the UDA/UFF. Mrs Thatcher, it was widely assumed, had had her pound of flesh.

When I heard about Ronnie's murder, I was in Strasbourg covering a session of the European Parliament for the *Financial Times*. It was my sister who rang to tell me what happened. I didn't feel the sense of loss I had experienced over the death of Blundy. Blundy was my friend; Ronnie was my 'familiar' – a demon who tormented me. Now, at last, he had been exorcised.

Suzanne was unable to attend the funeral. She was lucky to be alive. Major Bunting was the chief mourner. He refused to allow Ronnie to be buried alongside other INLA volunteers in the republican plot at Belfast's Milltown Cemetery. In death, he decided, his son would be reclaimed by his own. He is buried in a churchyard in Donaghadee, looking across the Irish Sea to Scotland, not far from the lighthouse once tended by his grandfather. Among his companions, as it happens, are a group of at least seven local men who fought in the 1798 Rebellion, one of whom, William Morrison, was executed by the British. So already there is the possibility of a split, following by a re-grouping.

The Major died of a heart attack four years later. He never recovered from the death of his son. There is a photograph of him as he stands at the graveside, bowed and humble, wiping the tears from his eyes. Like his son after Burntollet, he was shattered. Ronnie would have expected no less.